NATIONAL PORTRAIT GALLERY

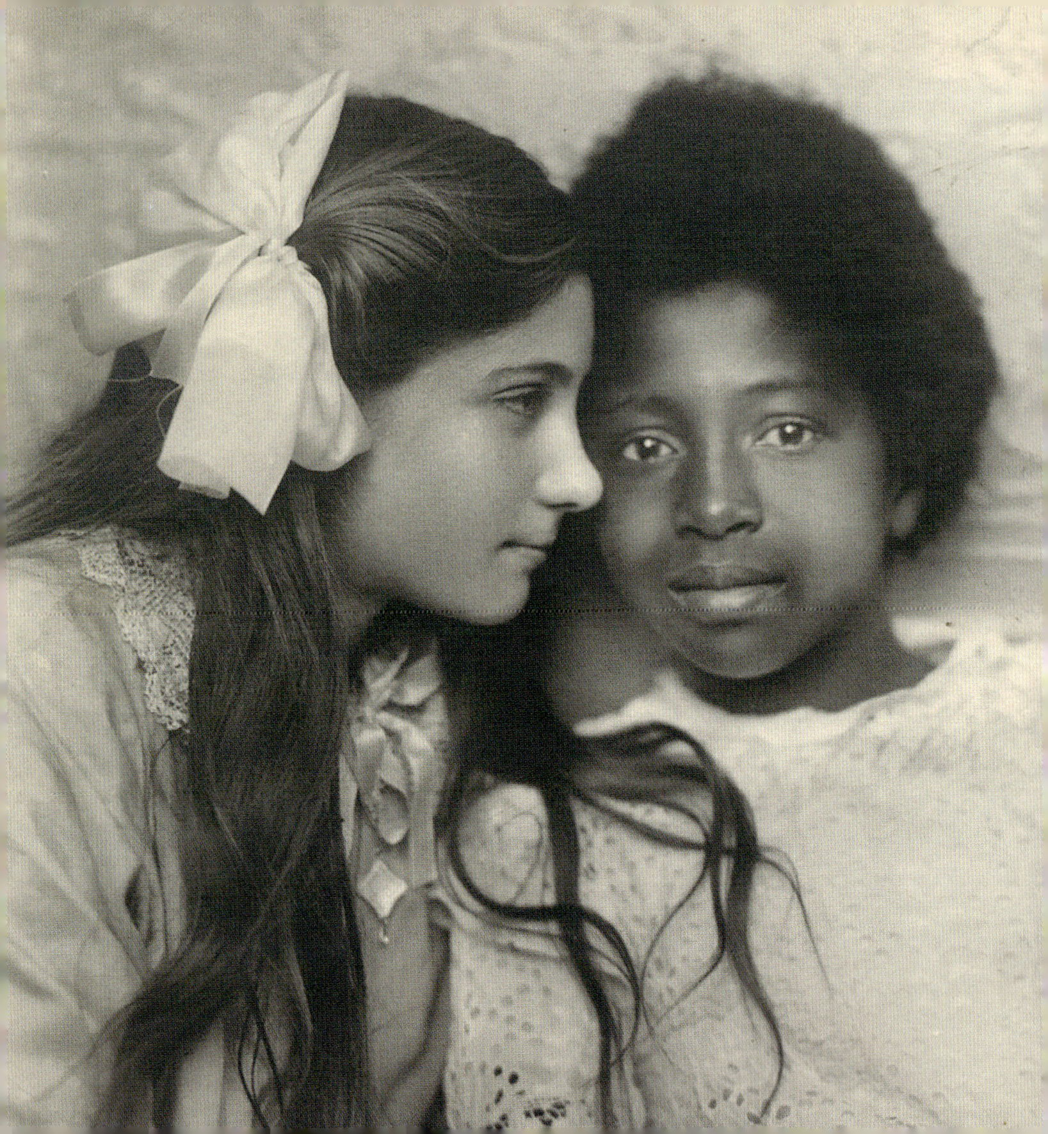

NATIONAL PORTRAIT GALLERY

100 PHOTOGRAPHS

CONTENTS

PAGE 2

UNKNOWN CHILDREN

Marcus Adams, mid-1910s

OPPOSITE

VIVIEN LEIGH (1913–67)

Madame Yevonde, 1936

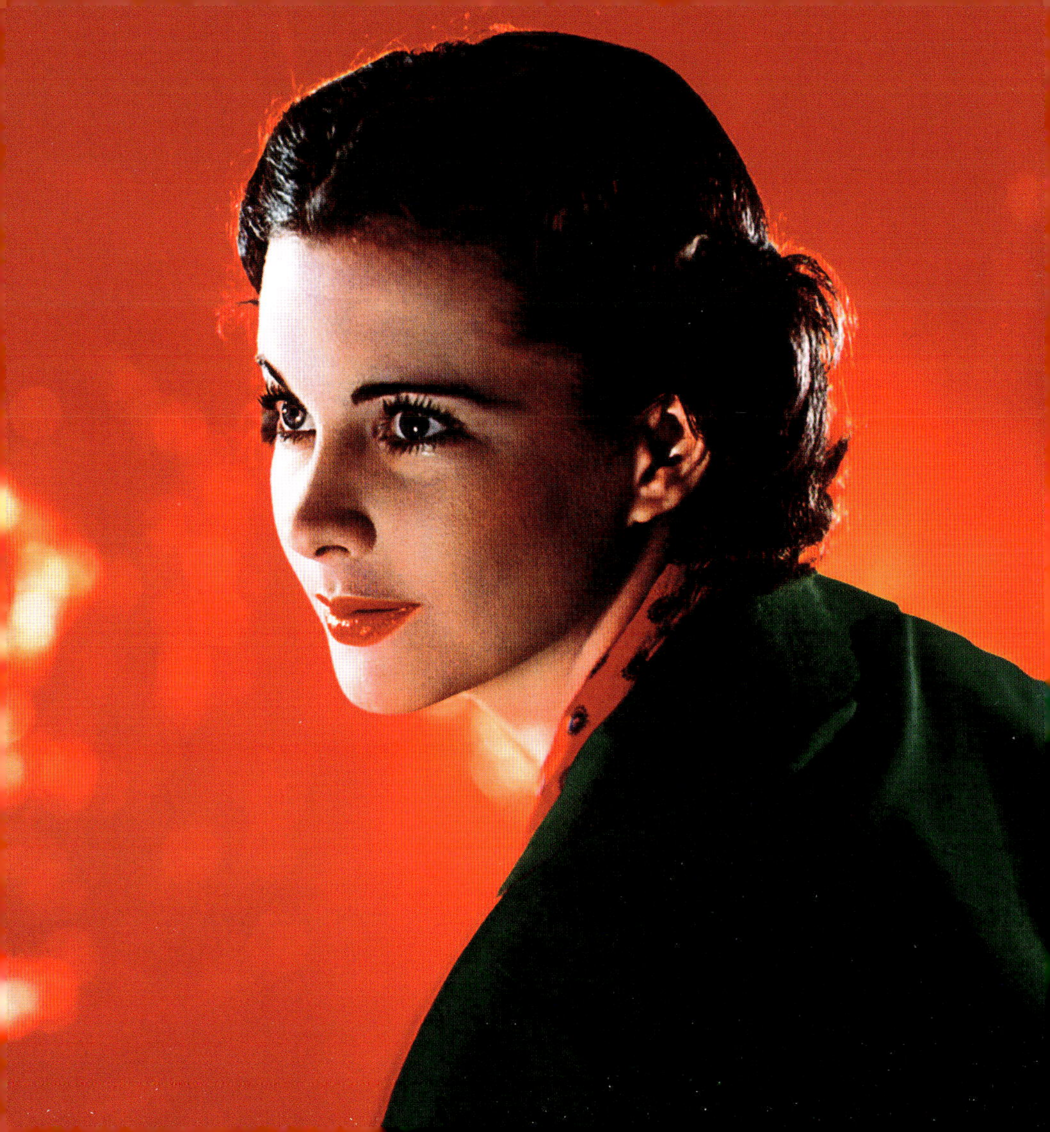

INTRODUCTION
PHILLIP PRODGER

When the founders of the National Portrait Gallery began their grand project to collect and display the best of British portraiture in 1856, they started by laying down a few simple rules. Foremost among these was the principle that the Collection should contain portraits of people who are making, or who have made, significant contributions to British society and culture. They wished to make society more open by setting positive examples to inspire visitors, irrespective of their circumstances or birthright. No more would representations of the great heroes of British history be confined to palaces and manor houses where only the rich could see them, and no longer would elite social circles be self-perpetuating and incestuous. Now, a place would exist where anyone could go, regardless of wealth, education or social status, to find encouragement. For this plan to work, the pictures would have to convey the key qualities of the people they represented. They would have to capture the imagination of visitors, motivate and bestow understanding. In other words, they would convey not just the subjects' life stories or accomplishments, but something deeper – what made them tick. What they sought was much more than a mere record of sitters' features. It was their identity.

The question of identity is puzzling, elusive and indefinable. It's also one of the things that makes portraiture so magically engrossing. Looking at the people represented in this book, we see glimpses of who they are, and how they present themselves to the world. But who were they really? Are they the same people now as they were ten years ago? Were they ever what they appear to be in their portrait? Where do image and identity meet? Identity is shifting and fluid – we are different people now than we were when we were babies, and different yesterday than we are today. Yet there are certain elements of ourselves, unfathomable strands of thought and feeling, that define us. A great photographer can find those things and bring them to our attention. A successful portrait is a dance, a negotiation between photographer and sitter that reveals something mysterious and honest. The viewer is part of that dance, too – looking, projecting and interpreting.

There are currently over 250,000 photographs in the collections of the National Portrait Gallery, including many of the most important ever made in Britain and abroad, and encapsulating all the major movements and techniques of the last two centuries. It is designated the National

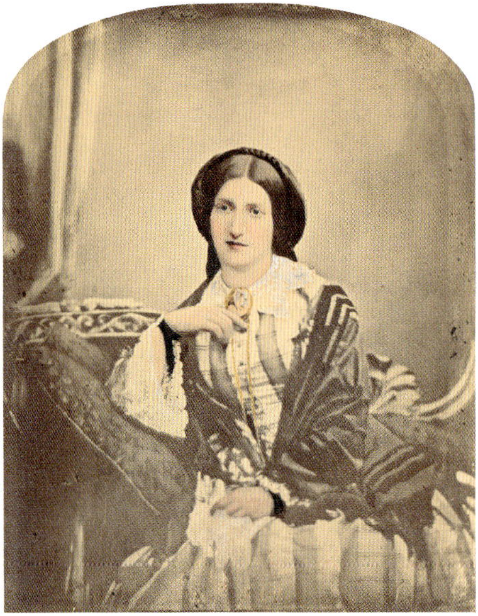

ISABELLA BEETON (1836–65)
Maull & Polyblank, 1857

Collection of Photographic Portraiture, recognised worldwide for its unparalleled holdings from the earliest days of photography to the present. Within it is, arguably, one of the finest collections of photographs by women, reflecting the distinguished history of female photographers in the United Kingdom and the practice of portraiture in the country. This book contains only a small fraction of the Gallery's photographic holdings – 100, or roughly 0.05 per cent of the entire Collection. It is not intended as a 'greatest hits' or a balanced survey. It is a subjective choice based on that early promise of the Gallery and its founders – to inspire, motivate and convey understanding.

The photographic collections, as they are now, began in earnest under the directorship of Sir Roy Strong, who assumed his position in 1967. At that time, a handful of photographs were already owned by the Gallery, but mainly as the by-product of related archives. Some, including the dramatic picture of Suffragettes on a government watch list (see pages 52–3), were discovered in official files. Prior to Sir Roy's directorship, photographs were also collected directly, but only under exceptional circumstances, as when, for example, former Director Henry Hake wished to add to the Collection a representation of Isabella Beeton, the author of *Mrs Beeton's Book of Household Management* (1861). Since writing cookery books was not a highly valued profession in Beeton's lifetime, and since she was a woman in a male-dominated society, Hake found to his chagrin that no painting of her existed. Consequently, the best way to represent her was through Maull

& Polyblank's somewhat faded, hand-tinted albumen print of 1857.

Early skepticism about the artistic value of photographs resulted in an oddity nearly unique among major museums – the creation of two separate but overlapping collections of photography. The first, long referred to as the 'Reference Collection', was begun as a repository for photographs of a purely documentary nature. An example of this is the National Photographic Record (NPR), initiated in 1917 under the stewardship of Walter Stoneman, the chief photographer for the photographic firm of Russell & Sons. From 1917 to 1970 the project continued, with some 10,000 sitters ultimately recorded. To ensure the scientific value of the proceedings, sitters were photographed against neutral backdrops, facing the camera, with their eyes level and with neutral expressions, according to a set protocol.

This extraordinary undertaking was of course anything but 'documentary', since it was governed by clear aesthetic principles and according to subjective standards. The routinised, machine-like grids of images produced under the auspices of the NPR are both its downfall and its charm, since the project was very much a product of its time, representing a desire to focus on particular

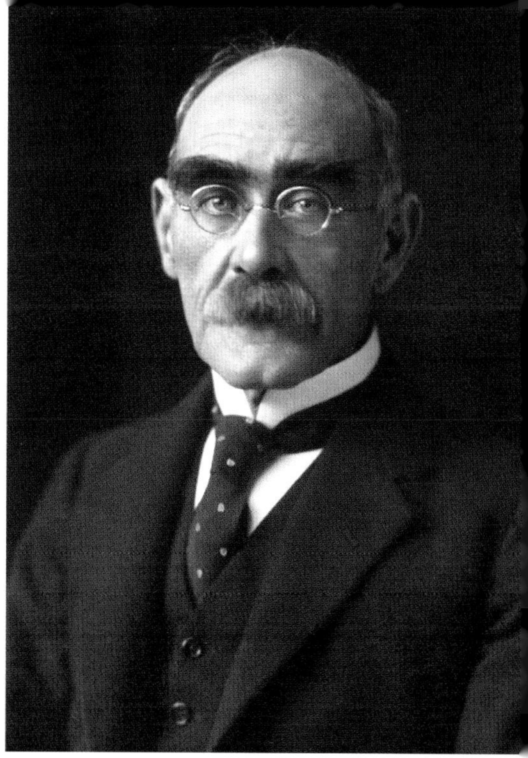

RUDYARD KIPLING (1865–1936)
Walter Stoneman, 1924

aspects of a person's physiognomy as revelatory of character. For example, sitters are invariably shown wearing jackets and ties, according to the fashions of the day, with hands and feet obscured. Such photographs tell us many things, and some of the best may even provide a window on the sitter's character. But the pictures that rise above the rest, that convey the founders' notion of 'identity', are very rare indeed. As a whole, the collection tells us that from 1917 to 1970, achievement in Britain was mainly the province of heterosexual white males of a certain age. But then, one hardly needed to make 10,000 photographs over the course of fifty-three years to know that.

The photographs collection expanded conceptually and materially in 1976, when photographs were admitted to the Primary Collection for the first time. The earliest accessions were internal transfers from the Reference Collection. The first of these, numbered P1 in the Gallery's cataloguing system, is a curious cornerstone – an exquisite, hand-tinted Daguerreotype of the theologian Frederick William Robertson by William Kilburn. (Maull & Polyblank's portrait of Isabella Beeton would become P3.) Currently, there are more than 2,000 photographs in the Primary Collection, complementing the core photographic holdings.

The Gallery takes very seriously its responsibility to include a broad range of sitters, regardless of ethnic origin, sexual orientation, disability or age. (In practice, it collects few pictures of children, since individual children rarely make substantial contributions to British culture, although there are exceptions.) Aristocratic titles are not, in themselves, sufficient to be included in the Collection. The Gallery

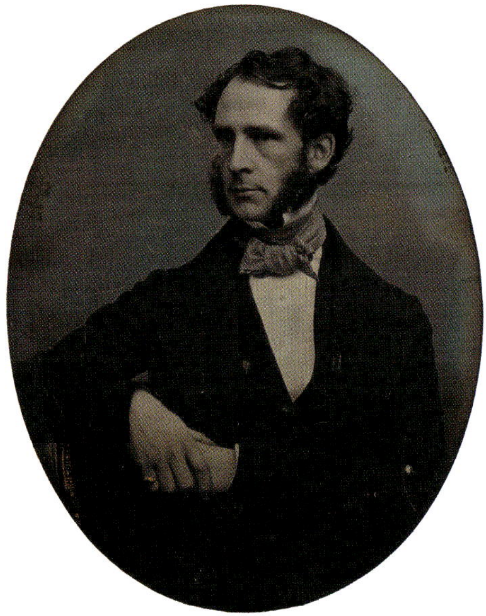

FREDERICK WILLIAM ROBERTSON (1816–53)
William Edward Kilburn, late 1840s

works hard to educate itself about achievement in all facets of British society, resisting the temptation to fall into narrow patterns of collecting, and frequently consulting with members of diverse communities to identify individuals whose contributions to British society and culture merit attention. Much work remains to be done, in the contemporary sphere and especially historically, where powerful examples are not always easy to find.

Under Sir Roy Strong, the photography department became known as the Department of Photography and Film, although the 'film' designation was later dropped, since very few were collected. In the twenty-first century, when many contemporary photographers move adroitly between still and motion photography in all its forms (what is sometimes described as 'time-based media'), the Gallery is beginning to look at the question of film afresh. In 2017, for example, it acquired a film portrait of David Hockney by Tacita Dean, and commissioned from Nigel Shafran a video portrait of the presenters of BBC Radio 4's daily current-affairs programme *Today*. These joined the handful of historical films already in the Collection, such as Peter Gidal's *Heads* (1969).

It may seem surprising that photography did not become a fully-fledged part of the Gallery's collections until the 1970s. However, when the institution was founded in the 1850s, photography's role and value was still an unsettled question. Those museums that did take the medium seriously, such as the South Kensington Museum (now the Victoria & Albert Museum), featured design and craft. When the great photographic pioneer and inventor William Henry Fox Talbot gave his estate to the nation, for example, it was directed to the Science Museum, as an example of technology, not the British Museum or the National Gallery, as an example of art or culture. Moreover, painting carried with it unquestionable cachet. To have a portrait made photographically was a fine thing, but if you were *really* important, you were painted in oils. Much of this prejudice has since drained away, although vestiges can still be seen, particularly in the commercial world, where paintings continue to be valued much more highly than photographs.

Among the rules the founders laid out in pursuit of pictures that conveyed the genuine identity of the sitter, and not just their physical features, was the requirement that, in order to qualify for inclusion in the

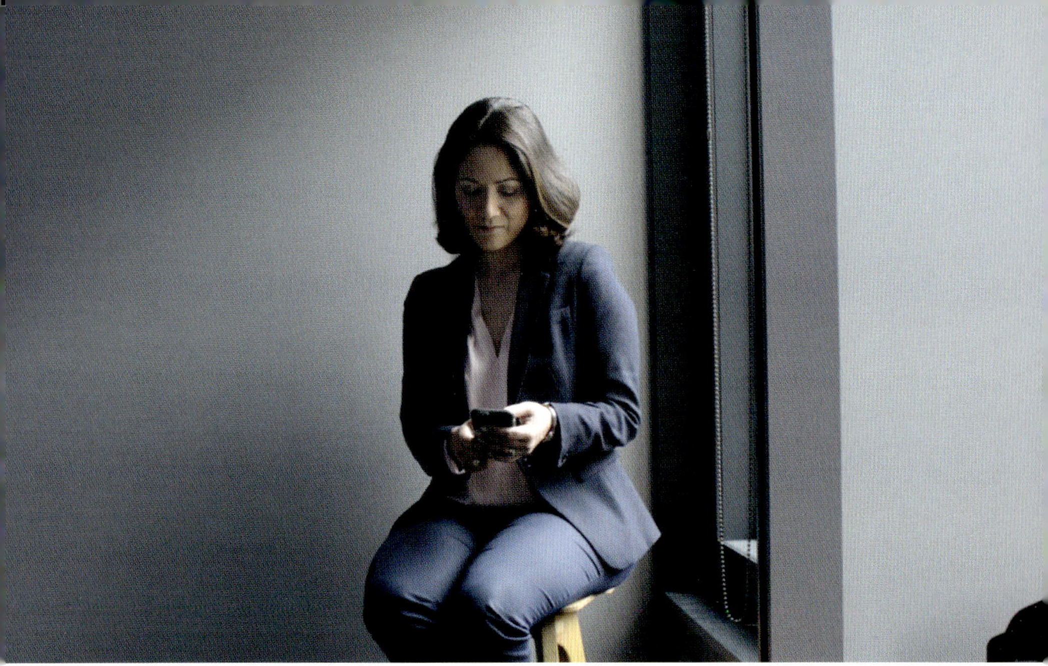

MISHAL HUSAIN (b.1973)
A still from the film *Today Everyday*
Nigel Shafran, 2017

Collection, portraits had to be made 'from life'. No posthumous pictures or images derived from secondary sources (such as books and magazines) were allowed. Embedded within this stipulation was the essentialist notion that somehow, whether in painting, drawing or photography, to be in the presence of a great portrait is to be in the company of the depicted person themselves; that is, a viewer might encounter people, even people they have never met, in a meaningful way, through pictures. On the face of it, this would seem to have necessitated photography's inclusion from the start. How better to capture a person as they were 'in life' than with a camera? What could be more true and direct? But photography is not so simple, and its relationship to identity anything but straightforward.

Photography has two special characteristics that separate it from other arts: the ability to freeze motion in time, and the capacity to render things effortlessly, with lifelike realism. Realism, or more precisely verisimilitude, is a complex and important issue on its own. This is the capacity for photographs to be so convincing that the viewer almost feels as if they are looking at a slice of real life. The belief that the photograph is a 'mirror with a memory' is long ingrained in the public consciousness, and undoubtedly the amount of detail a photographer can render in a picture, down to the minutest detail, is all but impossible for a painter to match.

At the same time, given enough time and skill, a painter may well paint with 'photographic' precision; conversely, photographs can be blurry and indistinct, or manipulated to no longer resemble reality. This is one reason why, despite a number of stunning exceptions, the National Portrait Gallery's Collection has comparatively few so-called Pictorial photographs. The Pictorialists, who thrived around the turn of the twentieth century, aimed to make pictures that conveyed mood and atmosphere (see those on pages 38–49) – pictures that were correct in terms of sentiment, if not physiological accuracy. Likeness, though, is a balancing act. It is less about whether the picture is objectively accurate than it is about being recognisable. The measure is not mechanical verisimilitude, but the subjective, unquantifiable and very human measures of recognition and truth.

More than anything else, it is the question of time that makes photography such an improbable vehicle for portraiture. What we measure in lifetimes, the camera reduces to split seconds. How, then, can it possibly succeed? The camera is a machine: lifeless, unknowing and cruel. When it comes to identity, it is the ultimate blunt instrument. Yet somehow the best portraitists manage to condense a lifetime of personality into a brief flicker of time; to find within the camera a window on character – of the sitter and sometimes even the photographer. It should not work, but it does. These pictures prove it.

PHILLIP PRODGER
Head of Photographs,
National Portrait Gallery, London

100 PHOTOGRAPHS

JENNY LIND (1820–87)
AND MARIETTA ALBONI,
COUNTESS PEPOLI (1823–94)
William Edward Kilburn, 1848

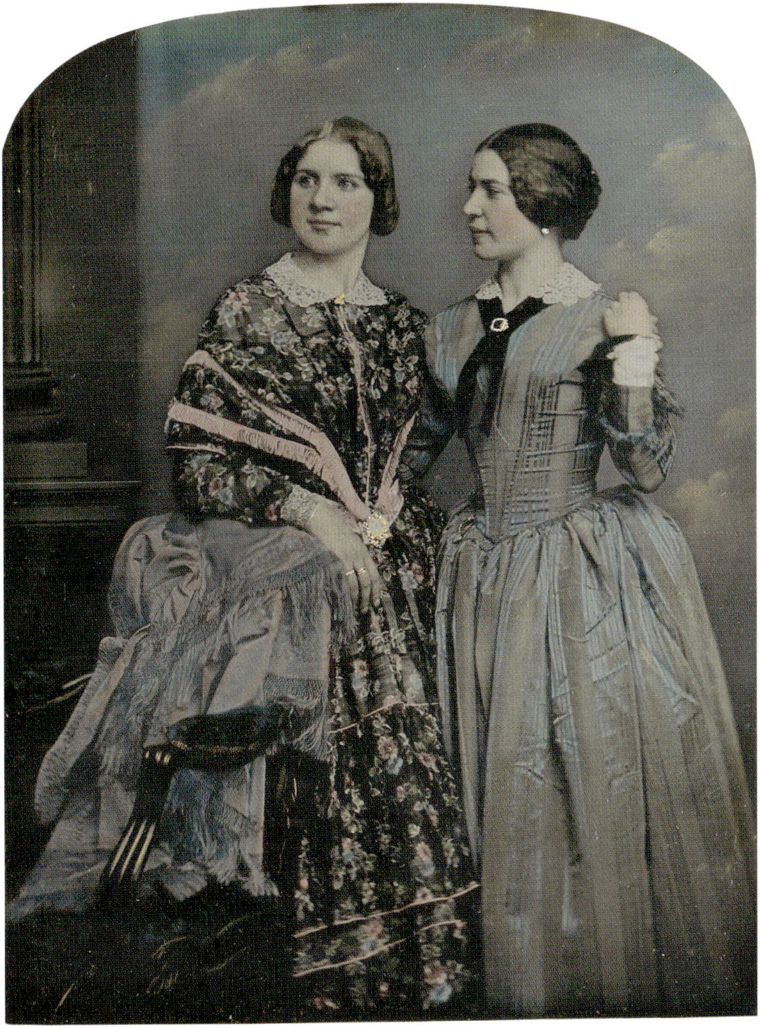

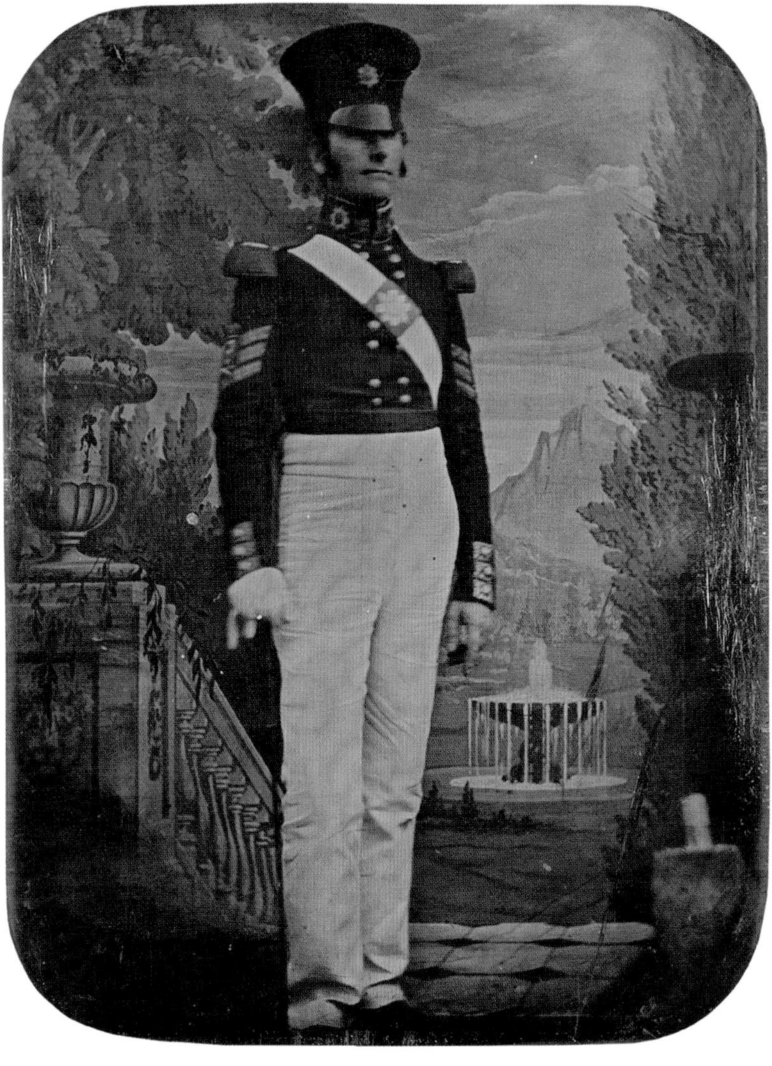

OPPOSITE

SOLDIER

Antoine Claudet, 1842–4

RIGHT

THE MISSES GRIERSON

David Octavius Hill and

Robert Adamson, c.1845

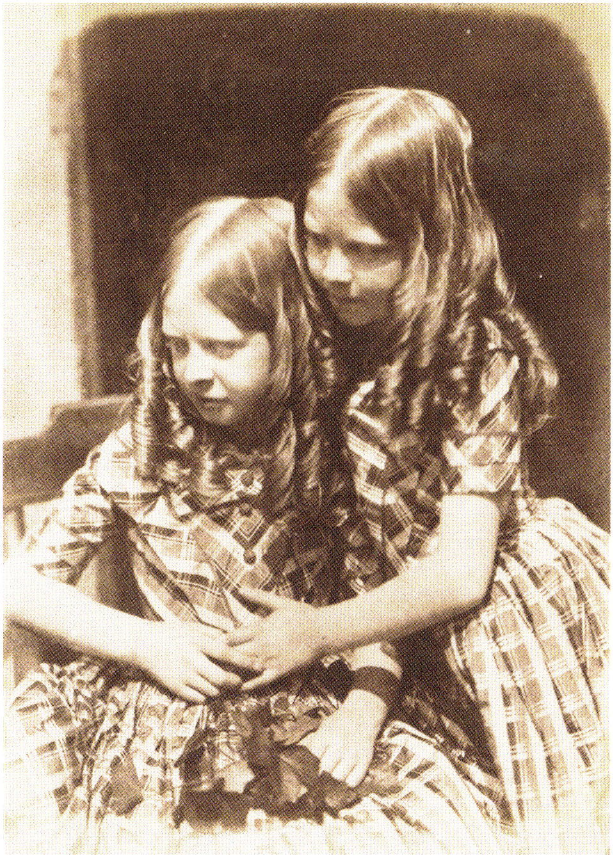

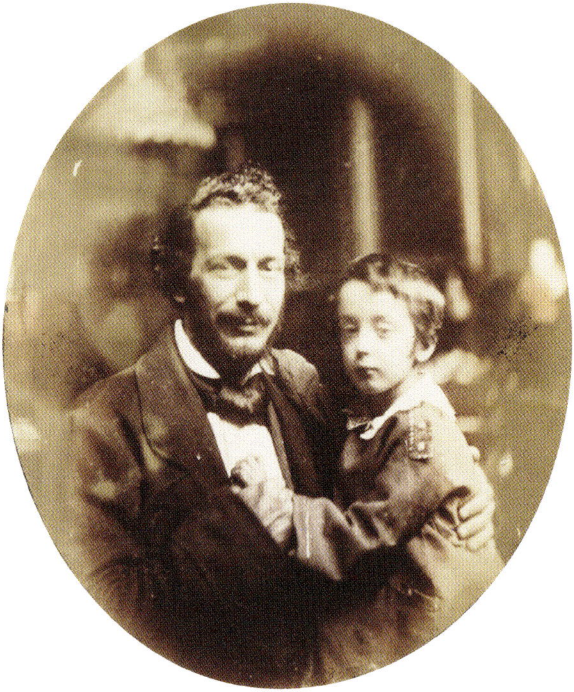

LEFT

SPIRIDIONE GAMBARDELLA (*c*.1815–86) WITH HIS SON, DION GAMBARDELLA (1849–86)

OPPOSITE

SPIRIDIONE GAMBARDELLA

Both photographs attributed to Sir Anthony Coningham Sterling, c.*1852*

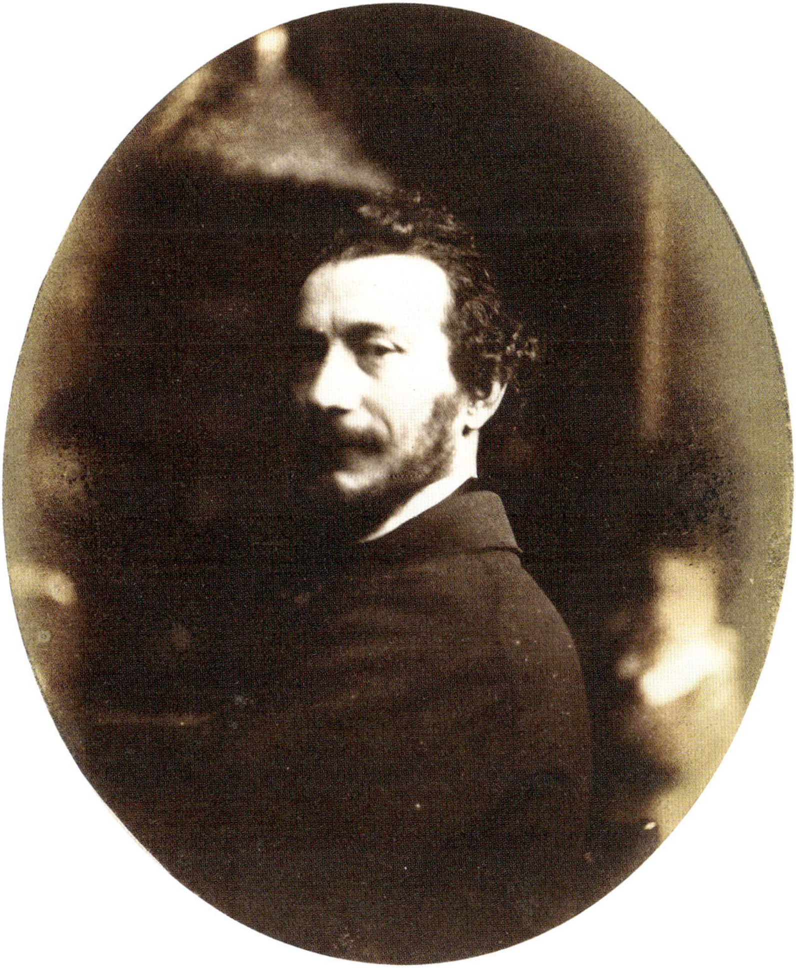

BELOW

SIR RICHARD ENGLAND

(1793–1883)

Roger Fenton, 1855

OPPOSITE

THE OLD GARDENER SIMPSON AND HIS WIFE

George Washington Wilson, 1854

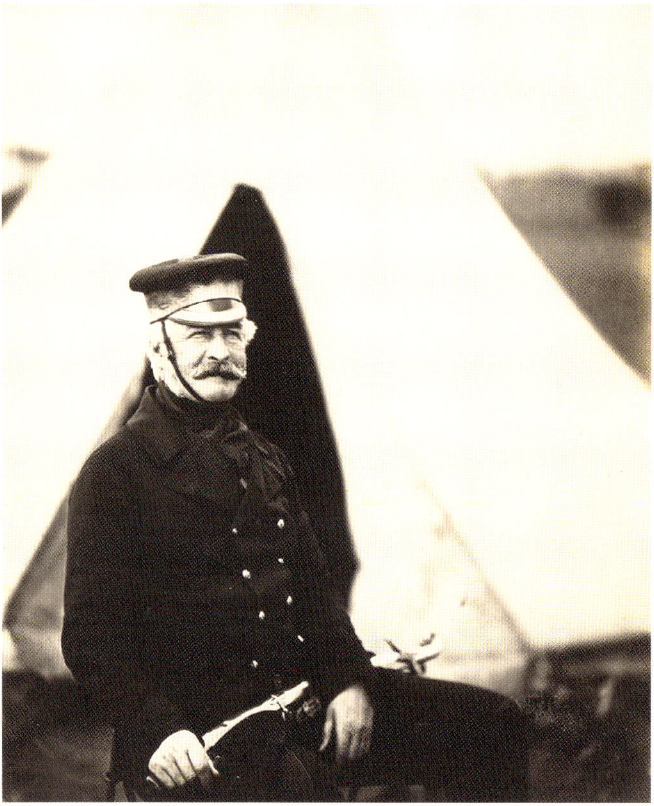

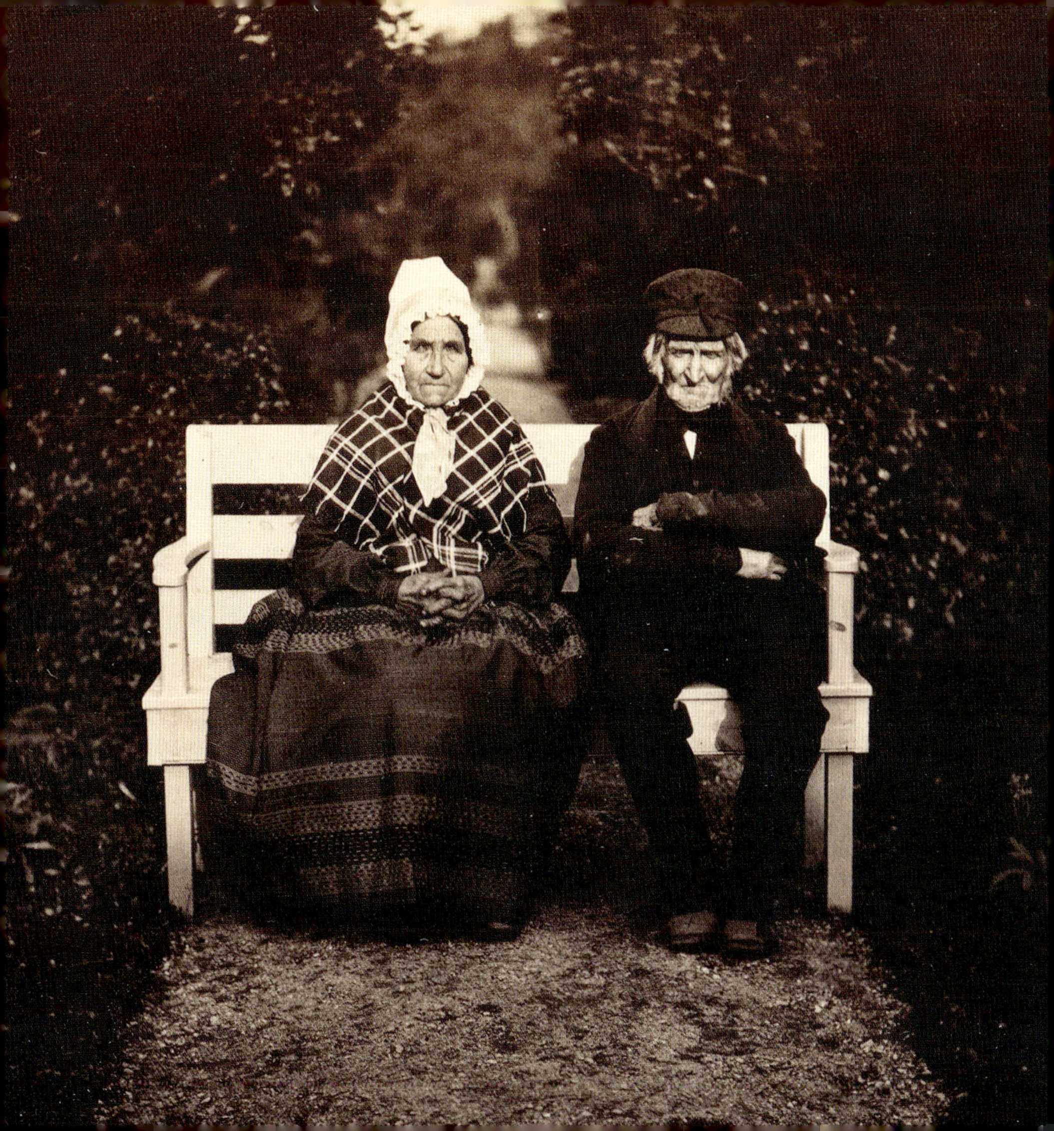

OPPOSITE AND BELOW

ISAMBARD KINGDOM BRUNEL

(1806–59)

Robert Howlett, 1857

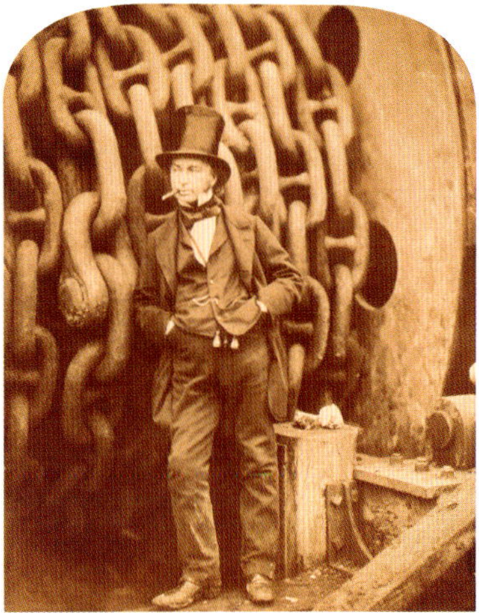

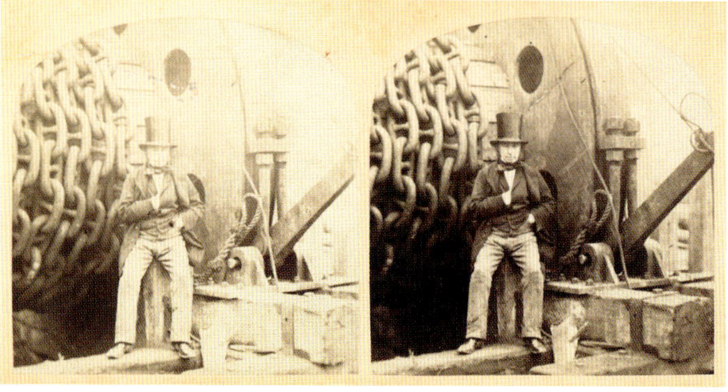

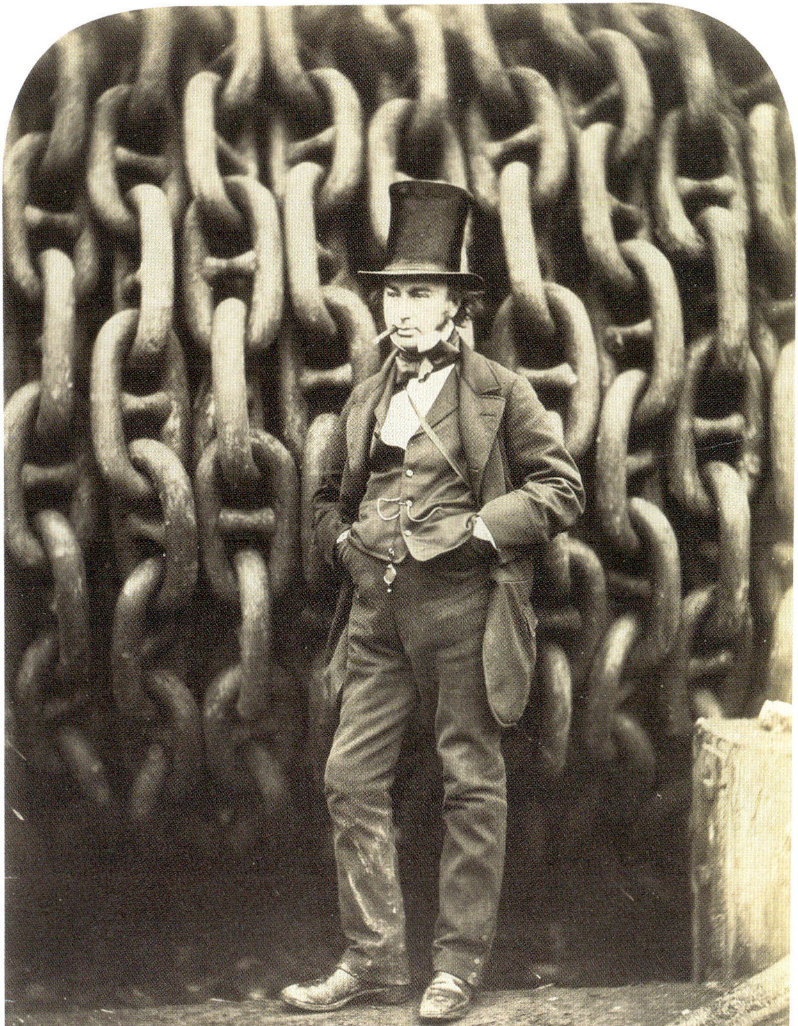

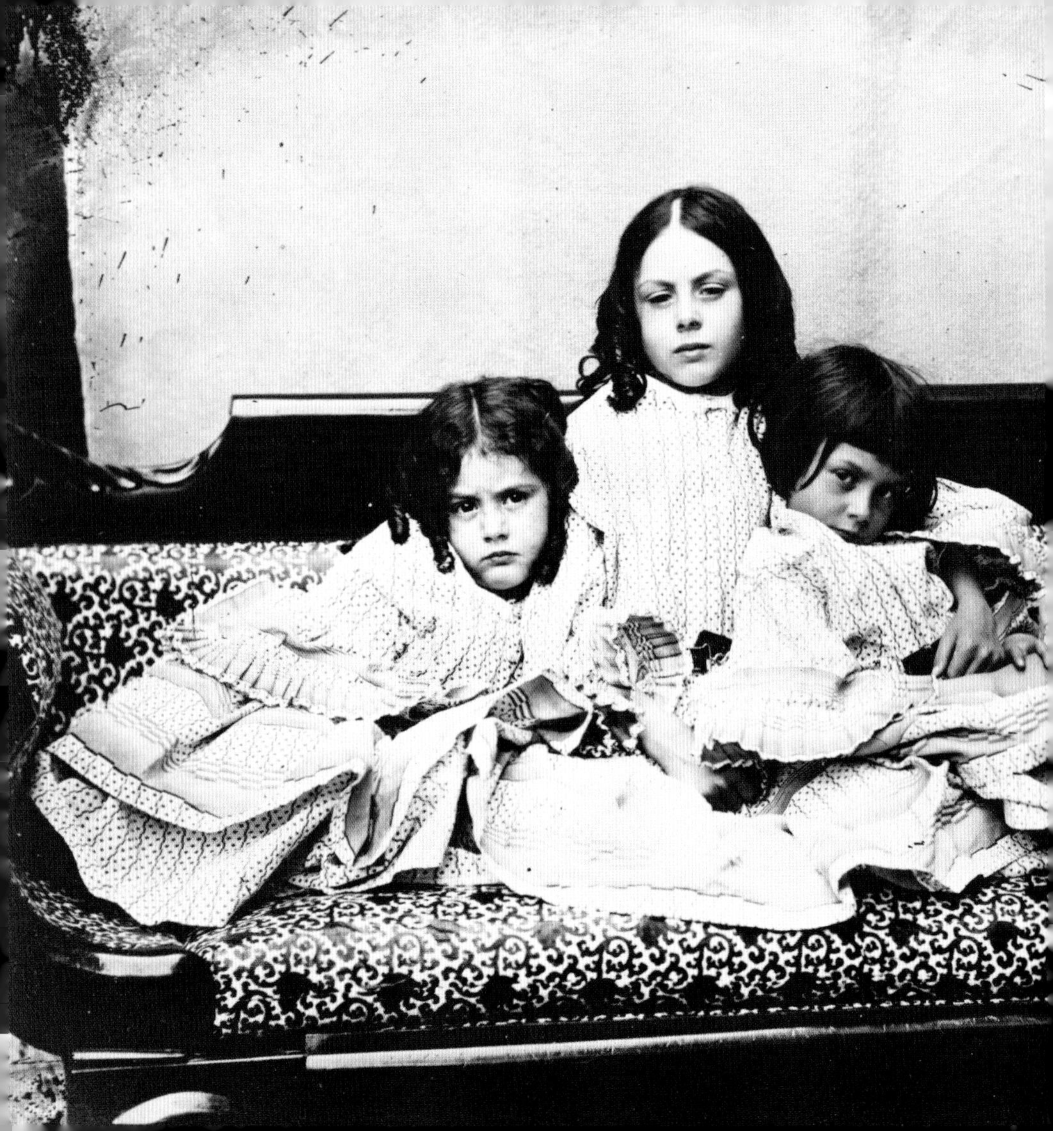

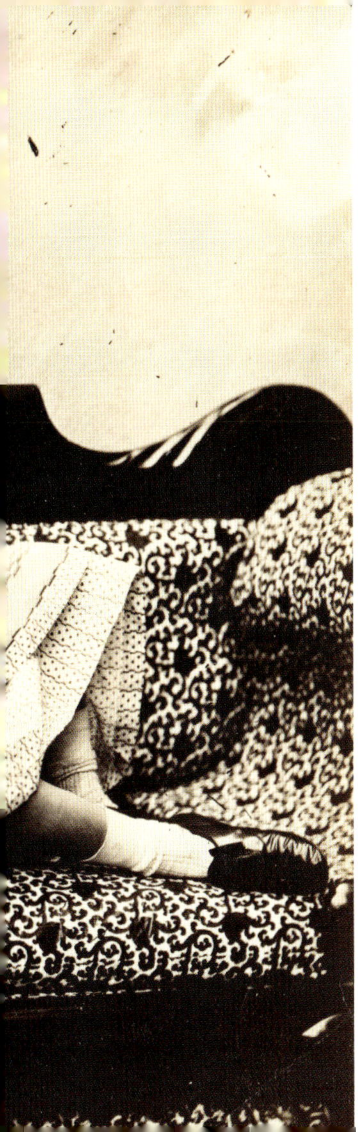

EDITH (1854–76), INA (1849–1930) AND ALICE (1852–1934) LIDDELL
Lewis Carroll (Charles Lutwidge Dodgson), 1858

UNKNOWN YOUNG WOMAN

Oscar Gustaf Rejlander, 1863–6

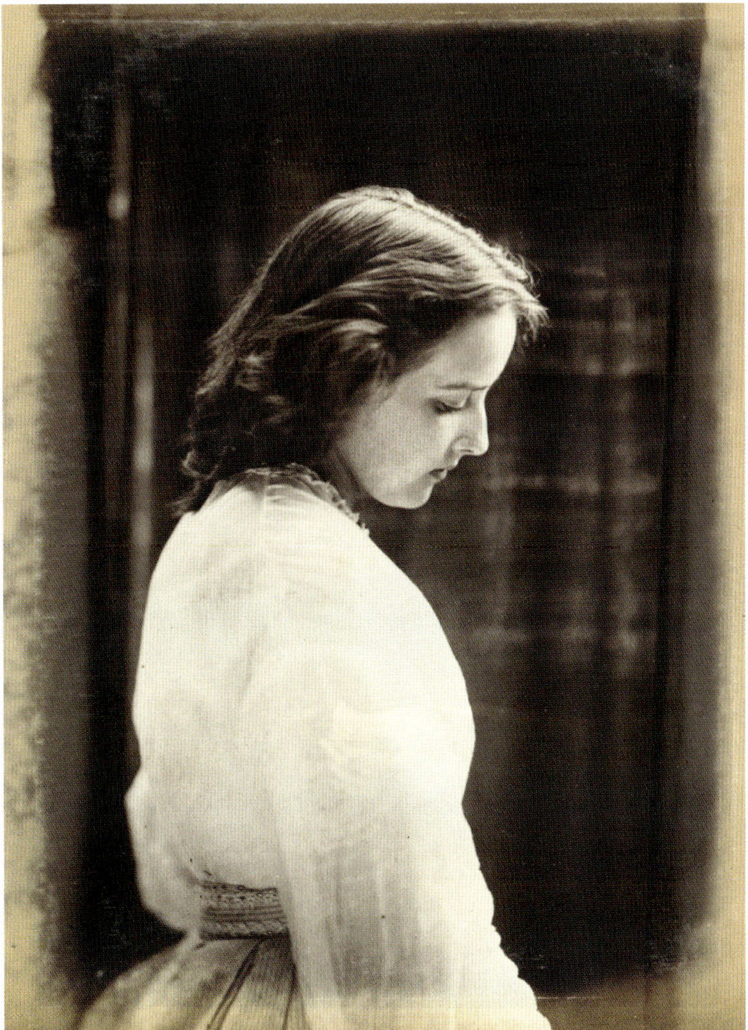

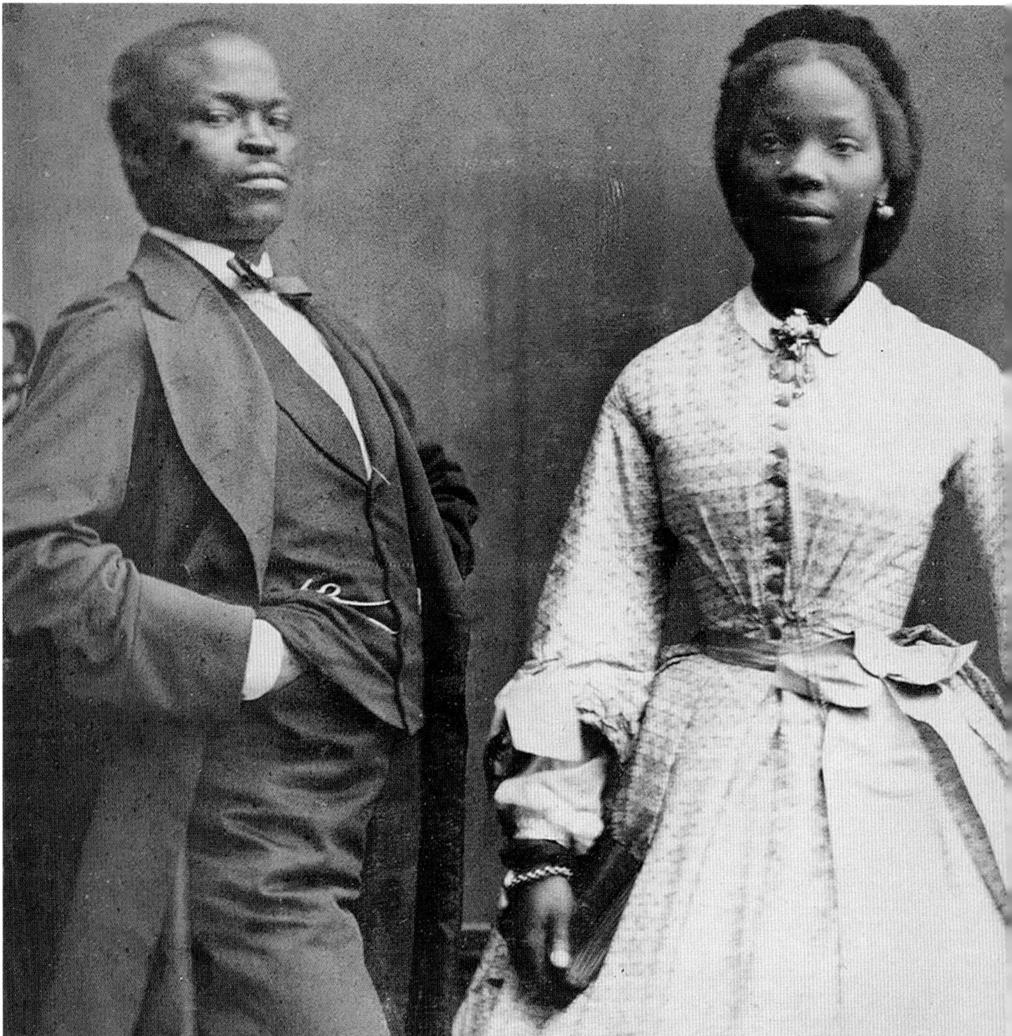

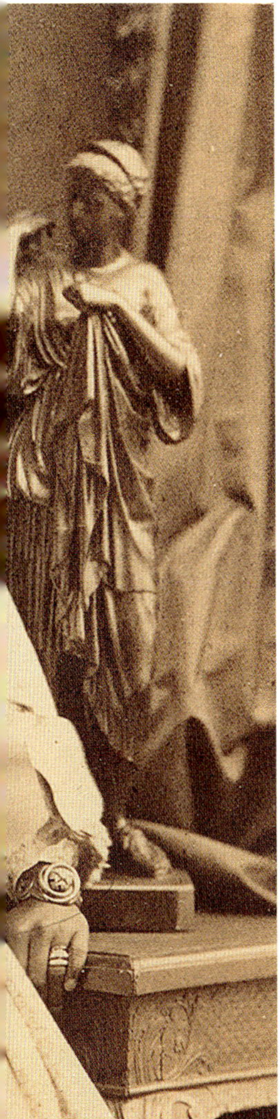

JAMES PINSON LABULO DAVIES (1828–1906) AND SARAH FORBES BONETTA (1843–80)

Camille Silvy, 1862

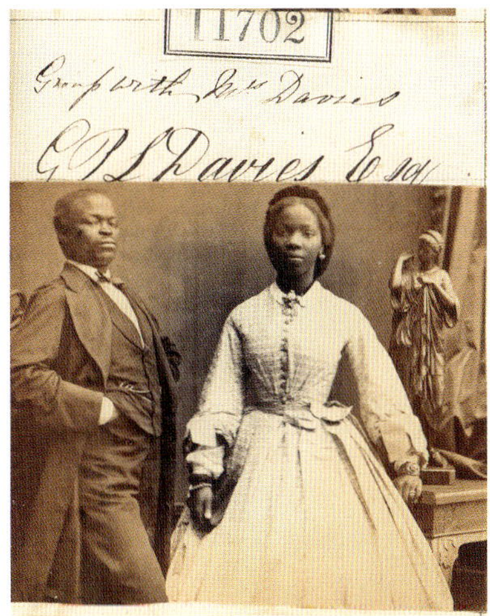

CHARLES DICKENS

(1812–70)

John & Charles Watkins, 1863

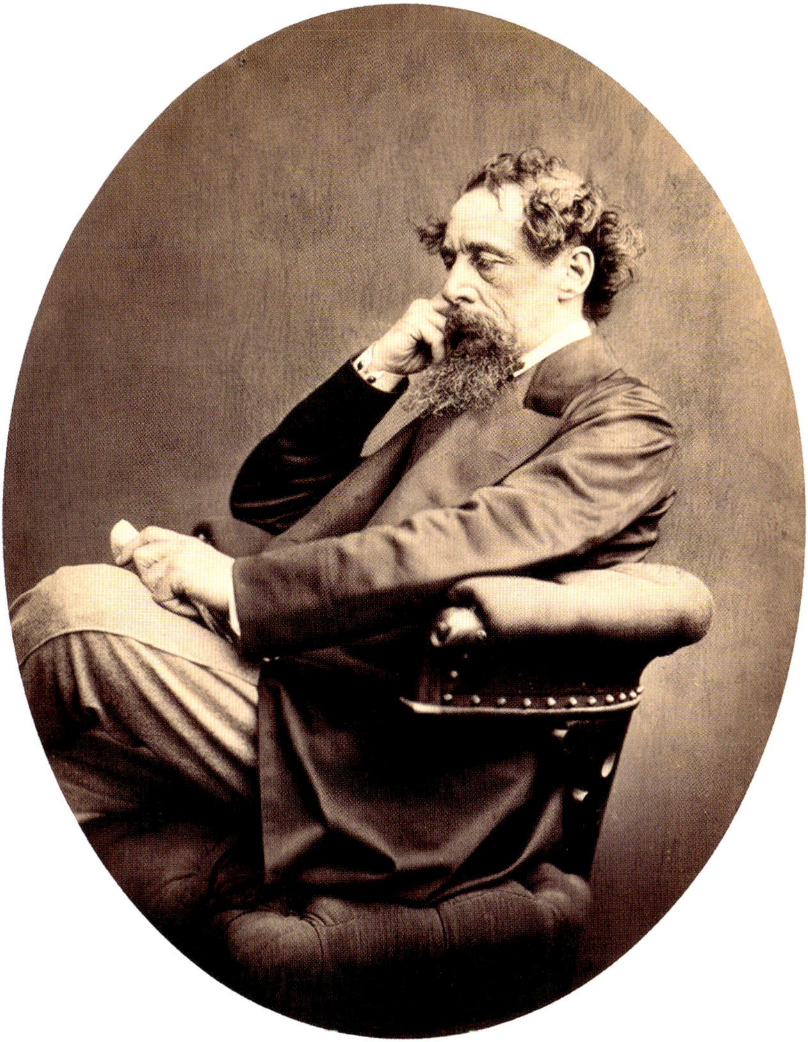

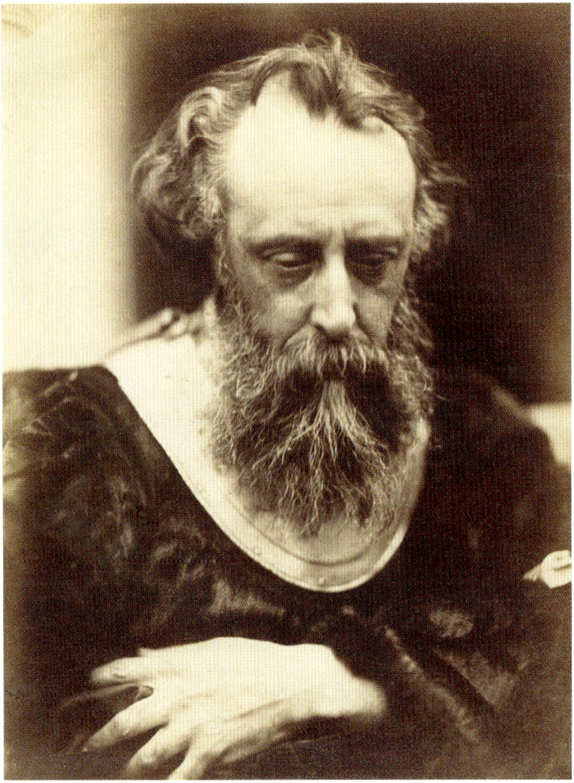

LEFT

G.F. WATTS

(1817–1904)

David Wilkie Wynfield, 1863

OPPOSITE

CHARLES DARWIN

(1809–82)

Julia Margaret Cameron, 1868

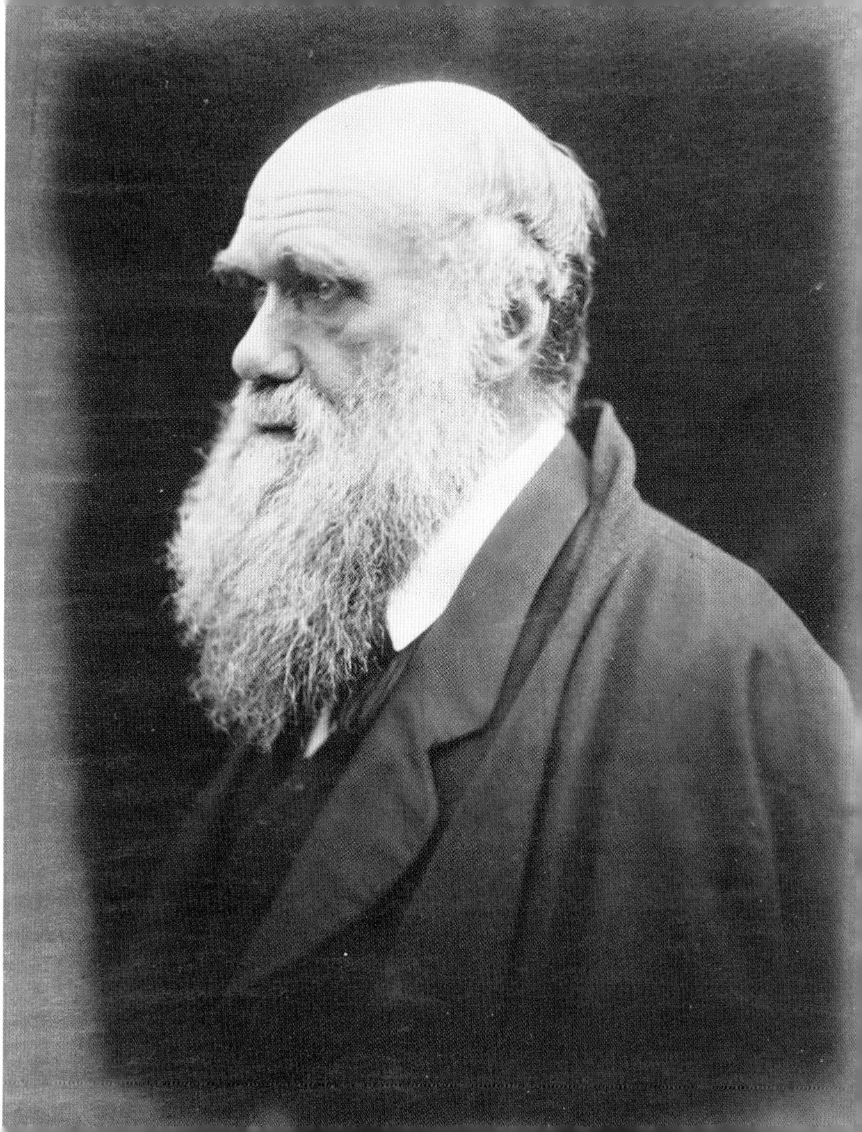

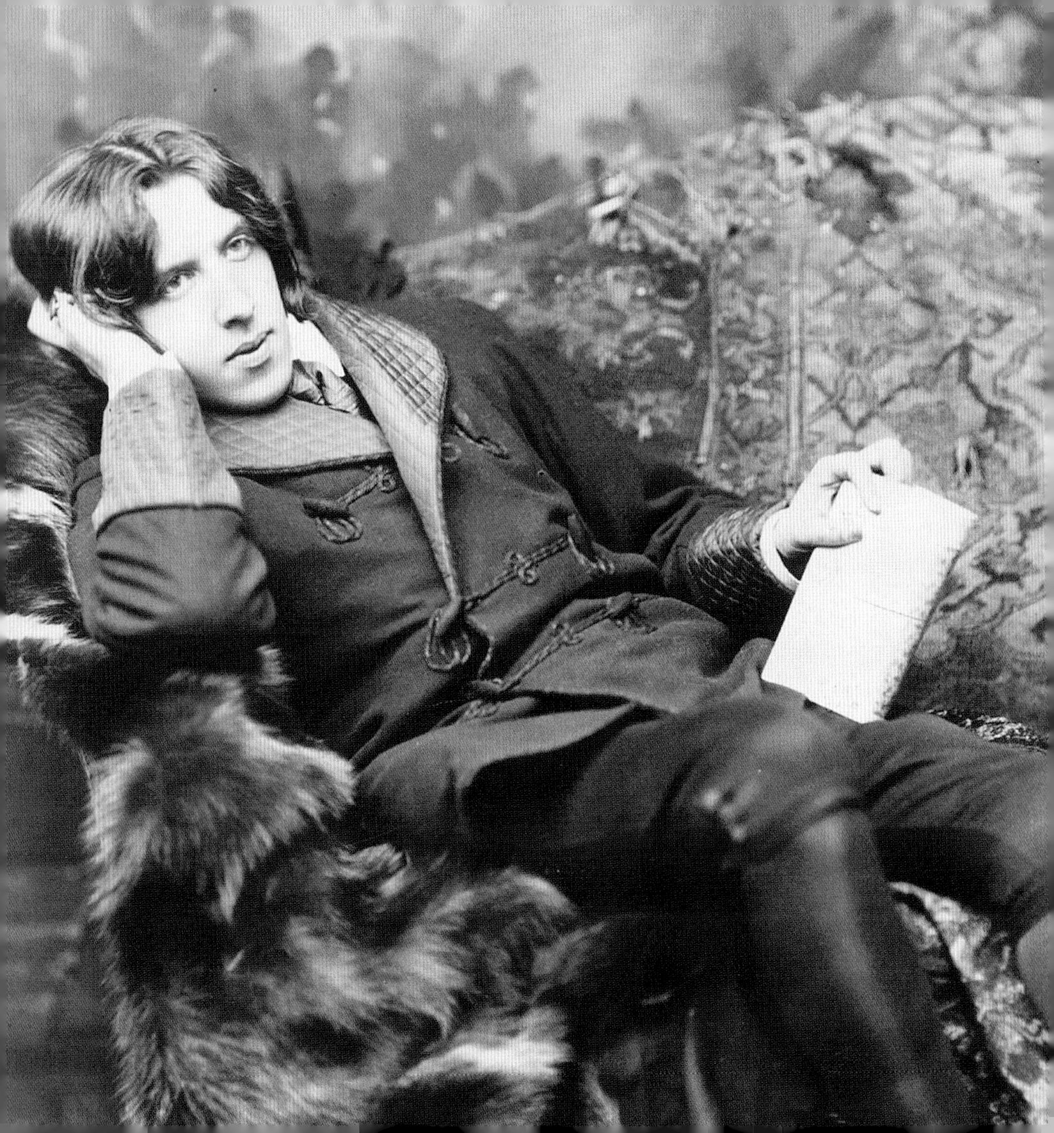

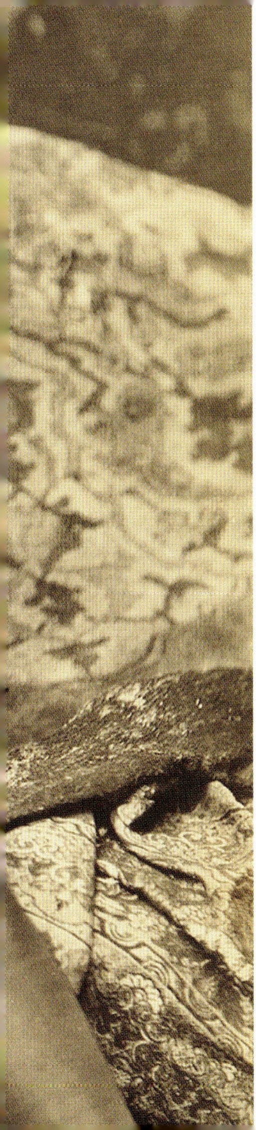

OSCAR WILDE

(1854–1900)

Napoleon Sarony, 1882

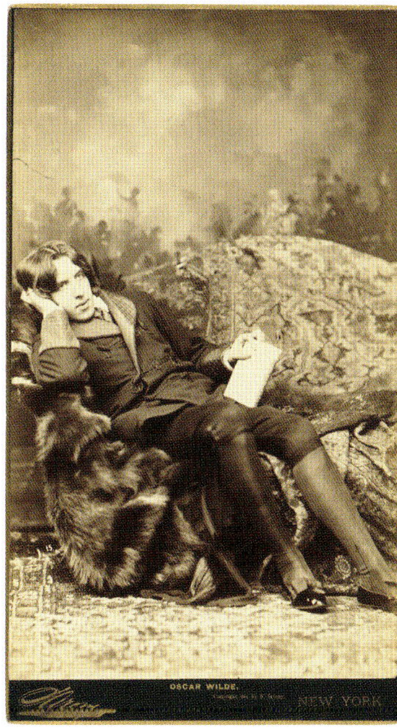

ADELAIDE PASSINGHAM

(1867–1954)

Eveleen Myers, early 1890s

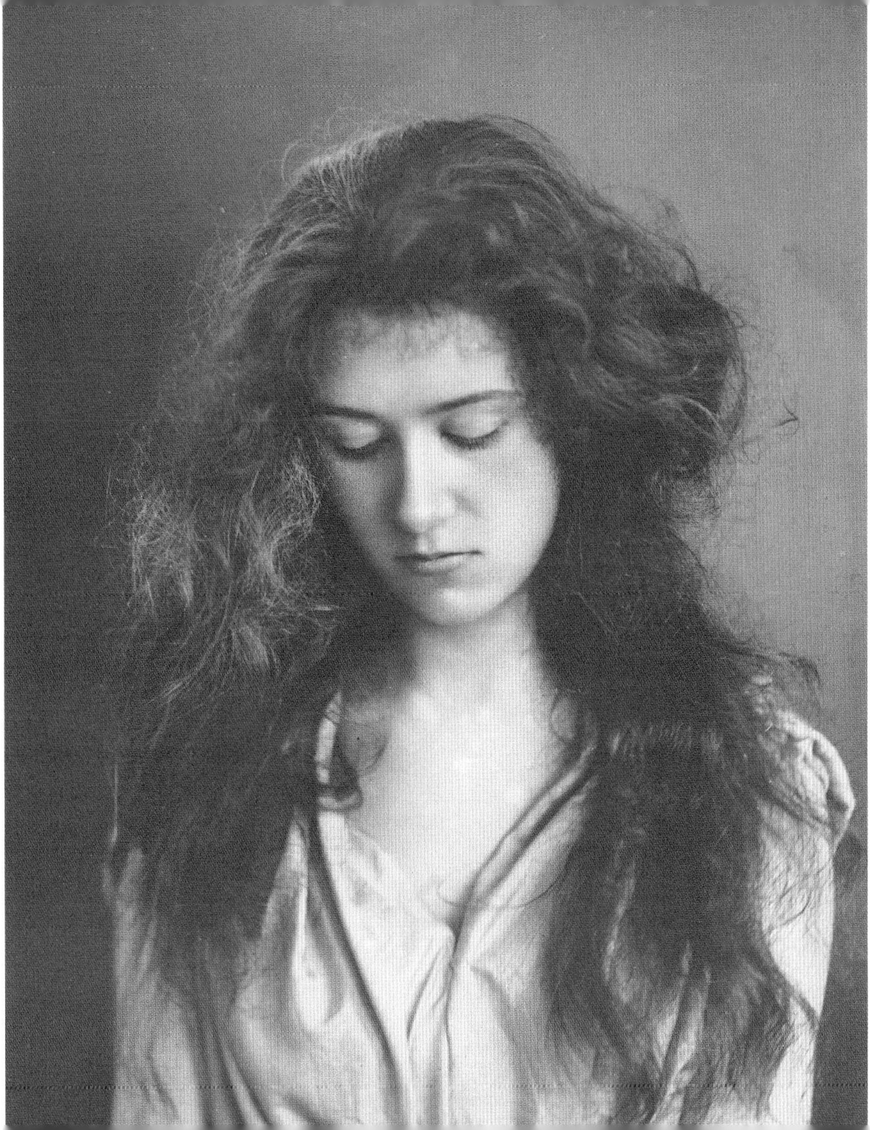

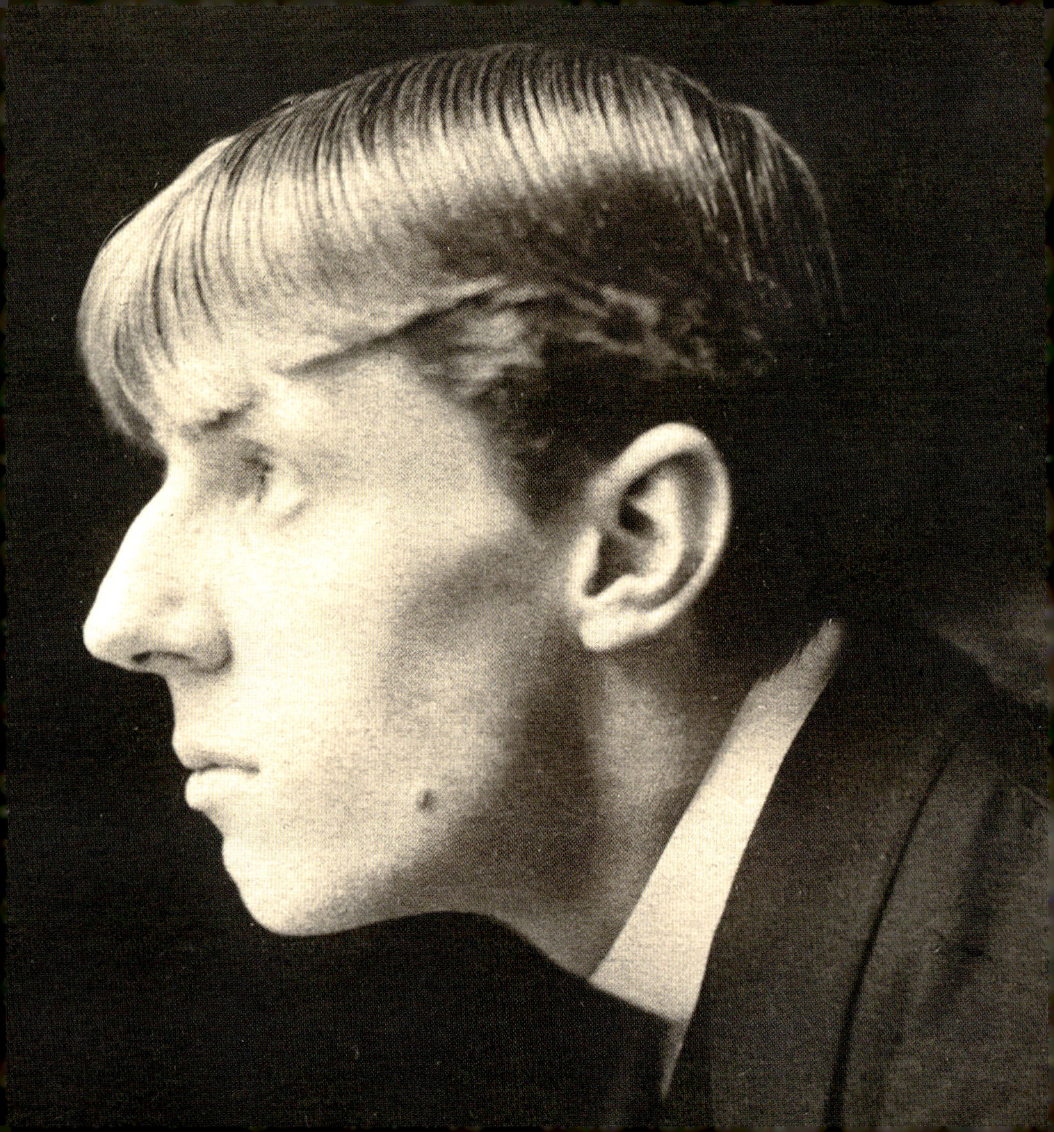

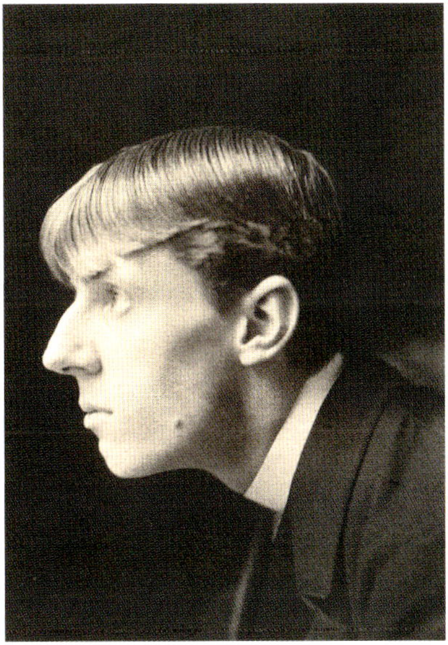

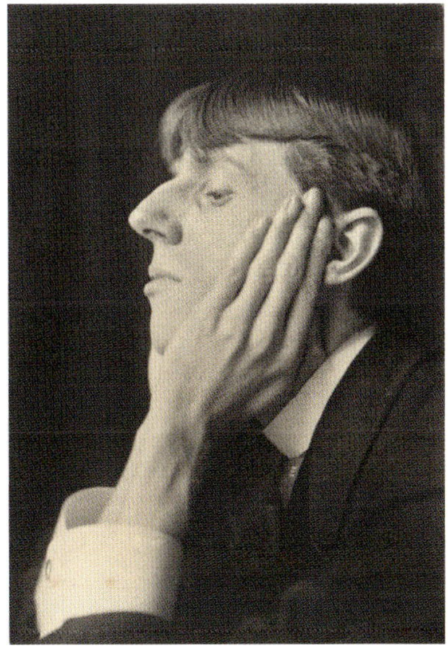

OPPOSITE AND ABOVE

AUBREY BEARDSLEY

(1872–98)

Frederick Henry Evans, 1894

UNKNOWN MAN

Cavendish Morton, 1900s

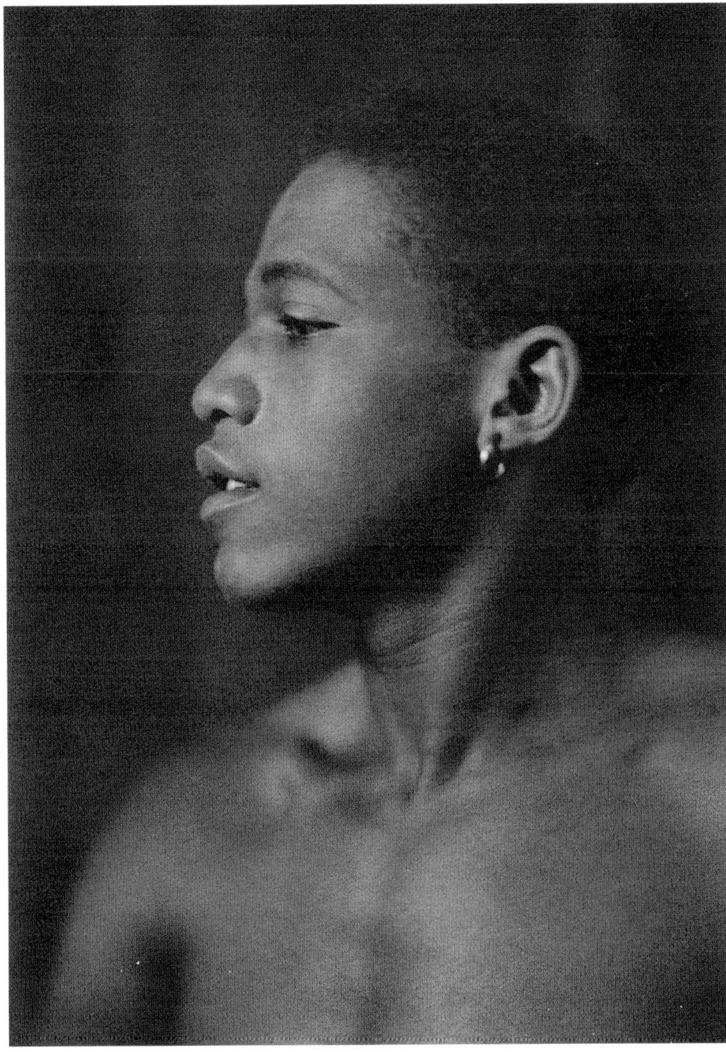

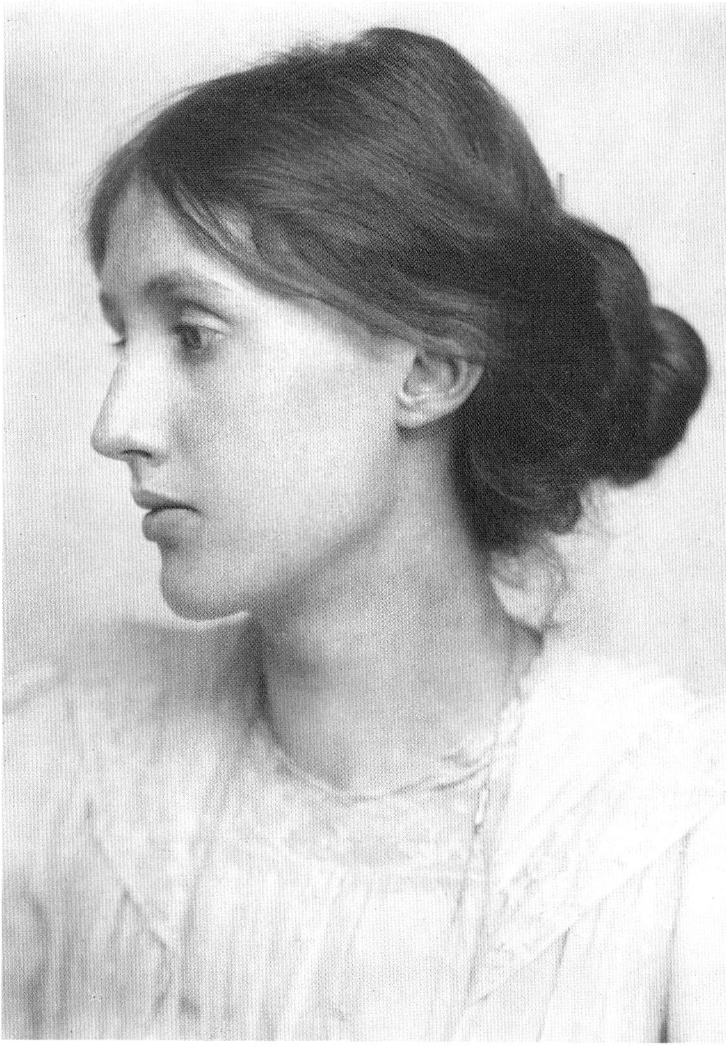

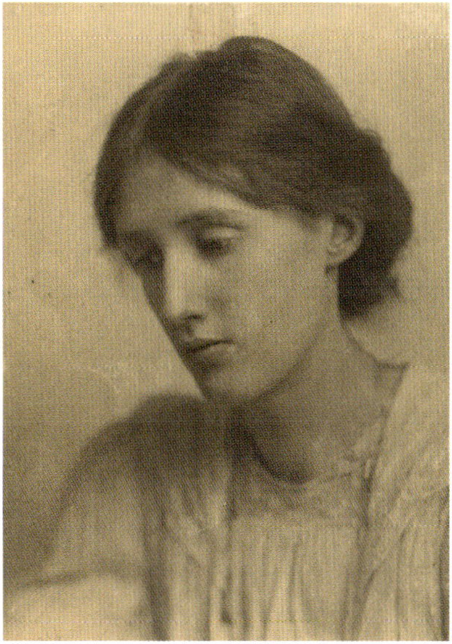

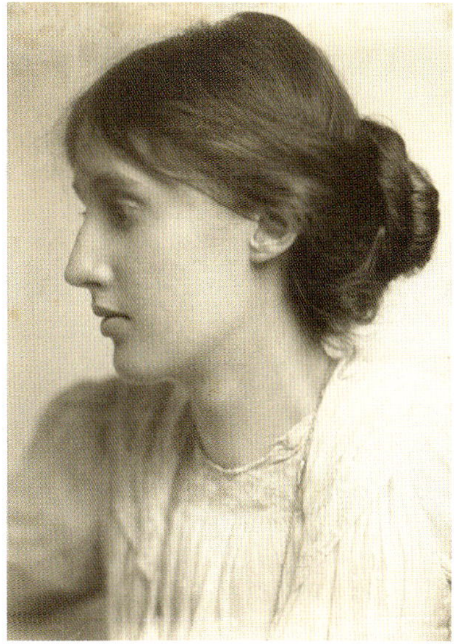

OPPOSITE AND ABOVE

VIRGINIA WOOLF

(1882–1941)

George Charles Beresford, 1902

HARLEY GRANVILLE-BARKER

(1877–1946)

Alvin Langdon Coburn, 1906

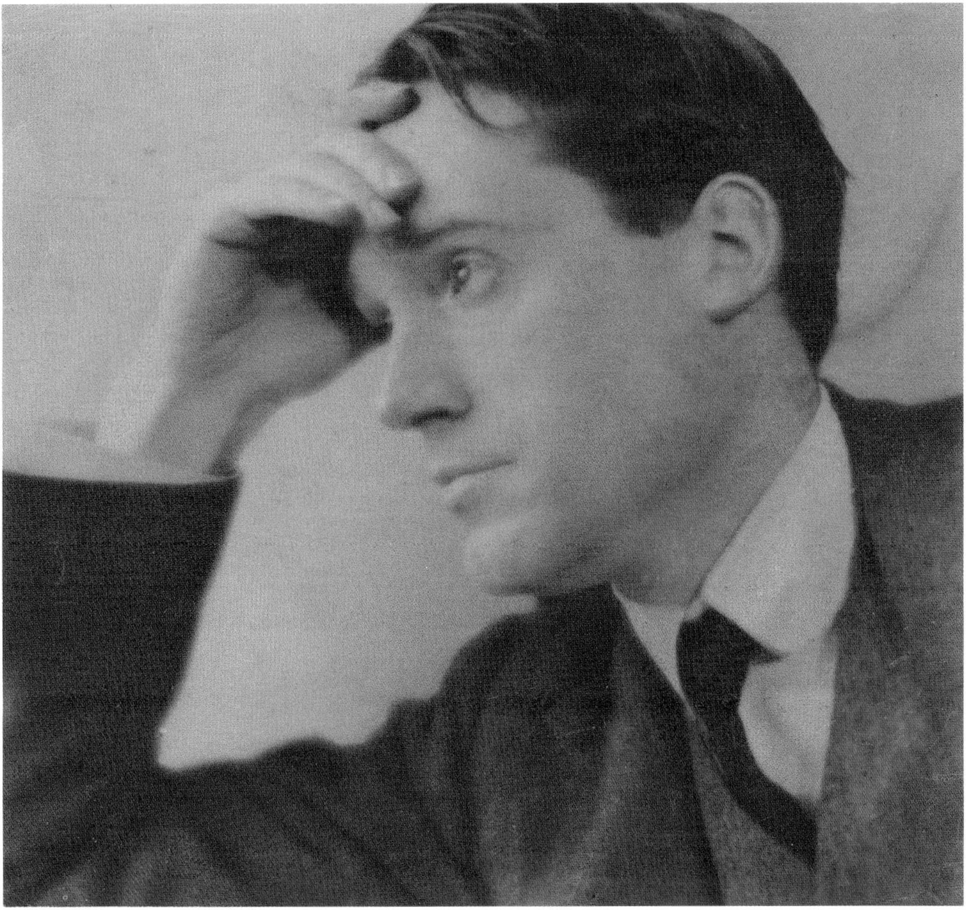

LEFT

GORDON CRAIG

(1872–1966)

Edward Steichen, 1908

OPPOSITE

LADY OTTOLINE MORRELL

(1873–1938)

Baron Adolph de Meyer, c.*1907*

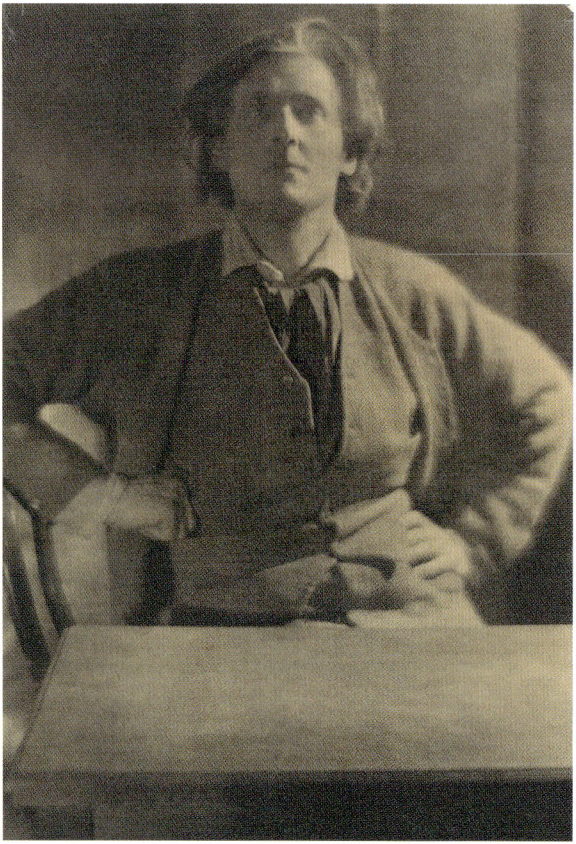

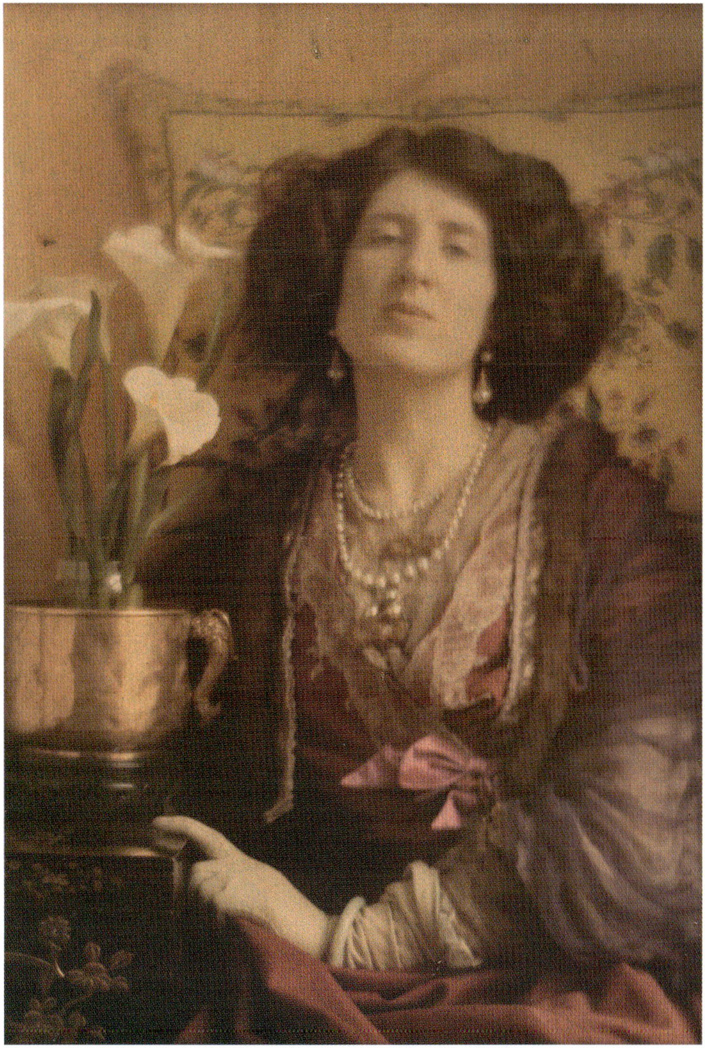

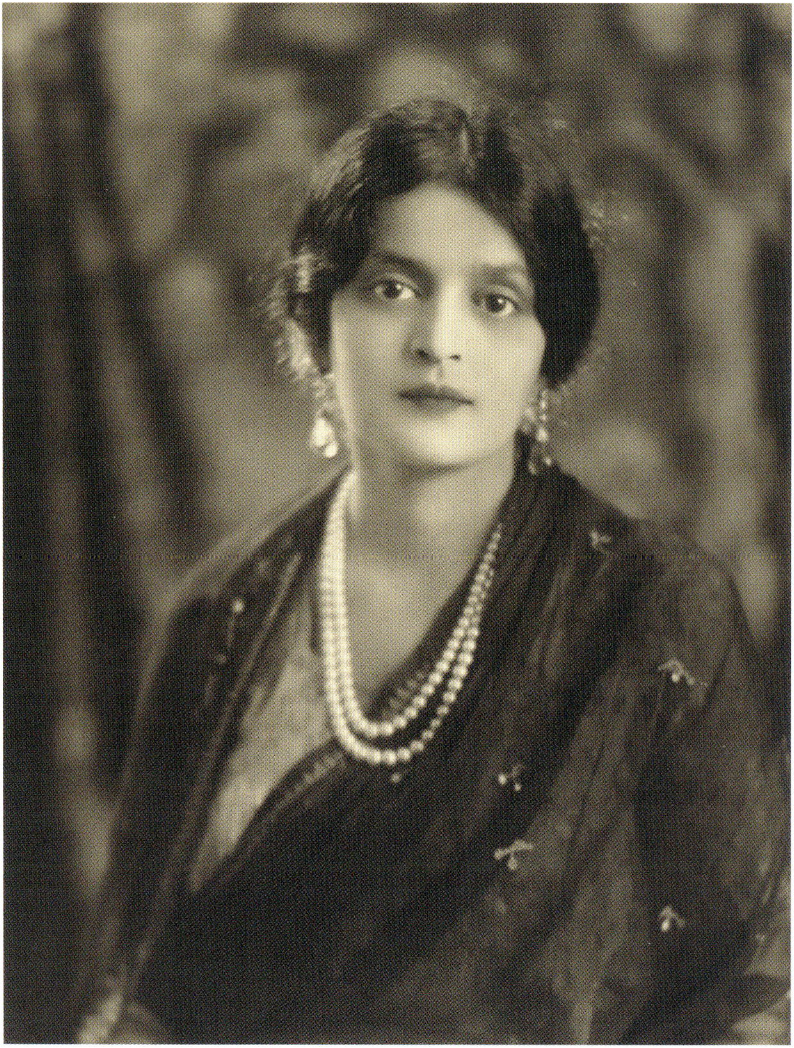

OPPOSITE

INDIRA, MAHARANI OF COOCH BEHAR

(1892–1968)

Bertram Park, c.1920

RIGHT

KATHARINE LEGAT

(1880–1963)

Olive Edis, mid-1910s

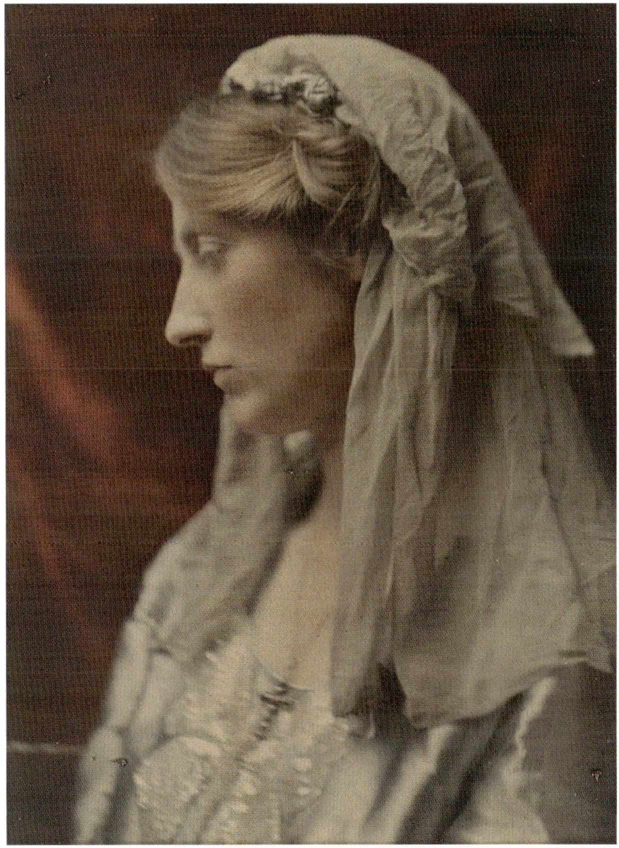

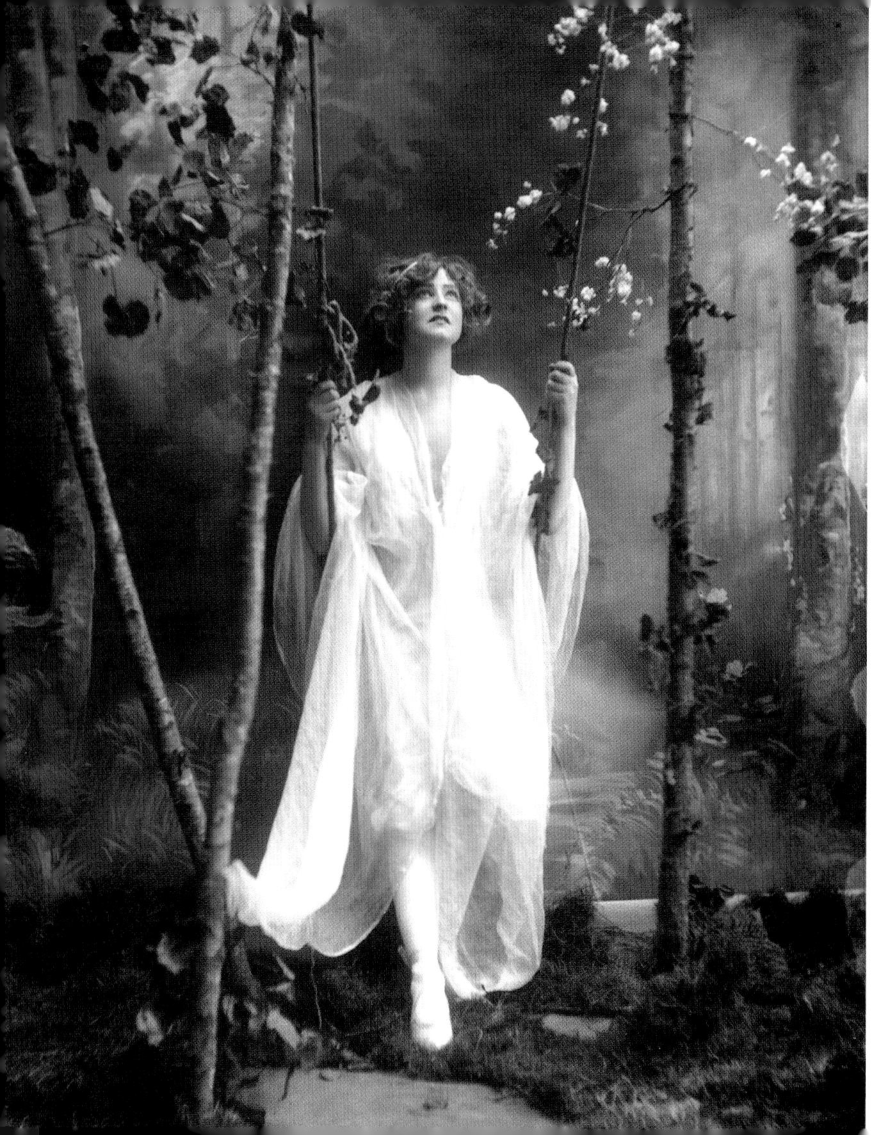

OPPOSITE AND BELOW

GABRIELLE RAY

(1883–1973)

Bassano Ltd, 1910

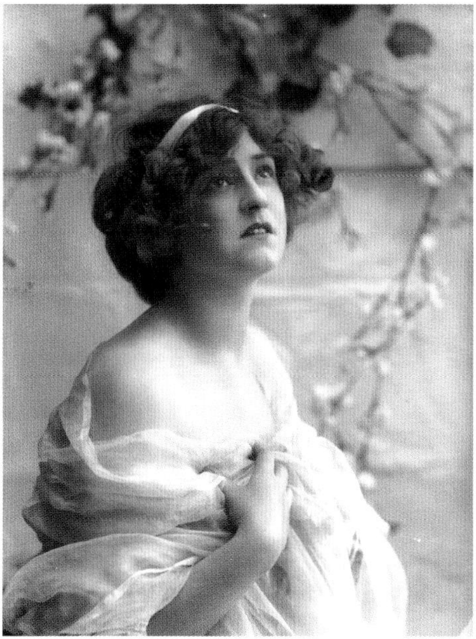

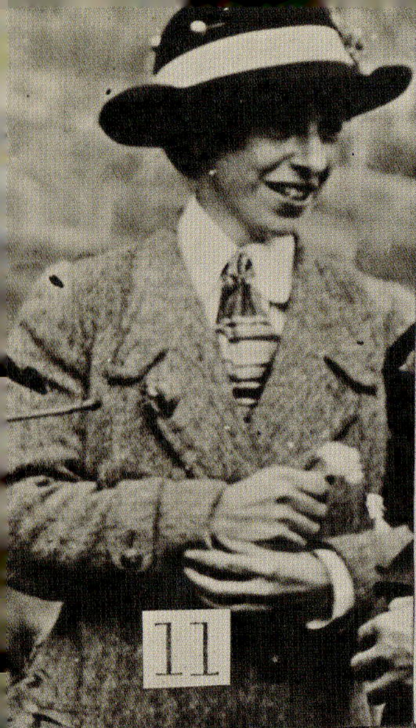

11

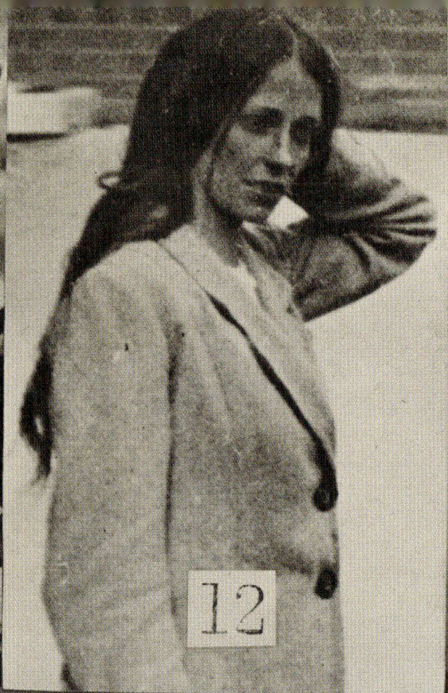

12

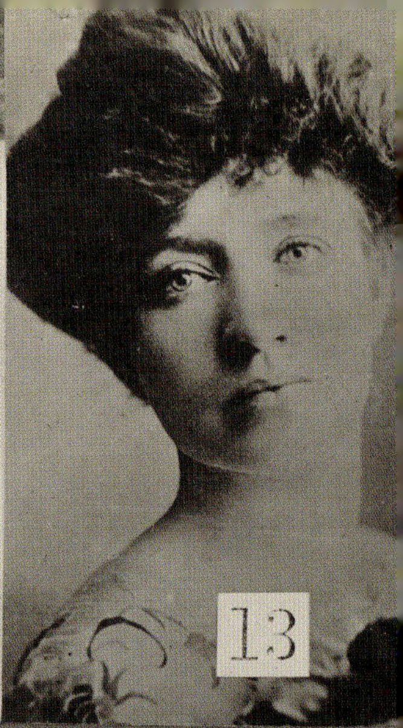

13

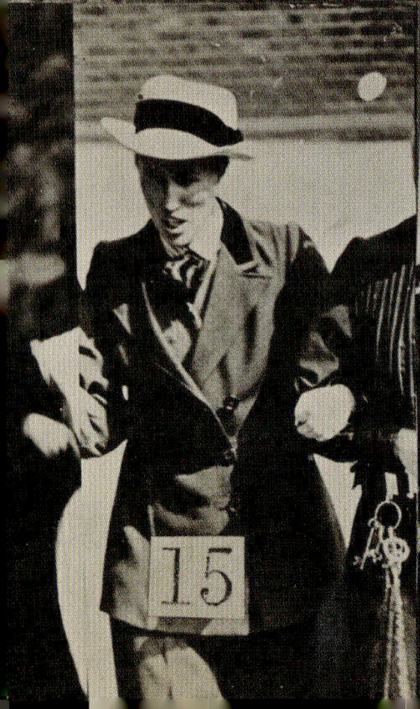

15

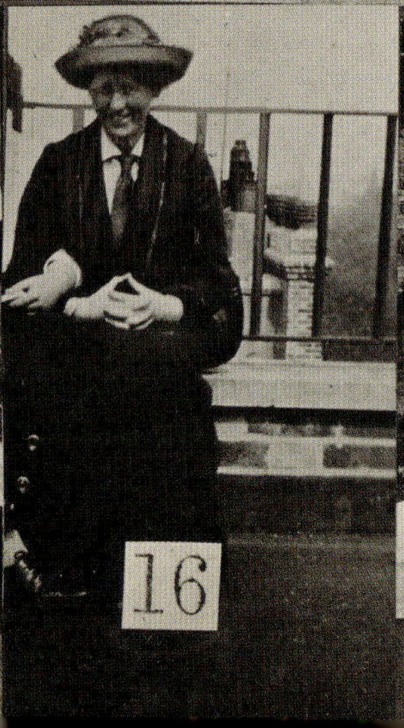

16

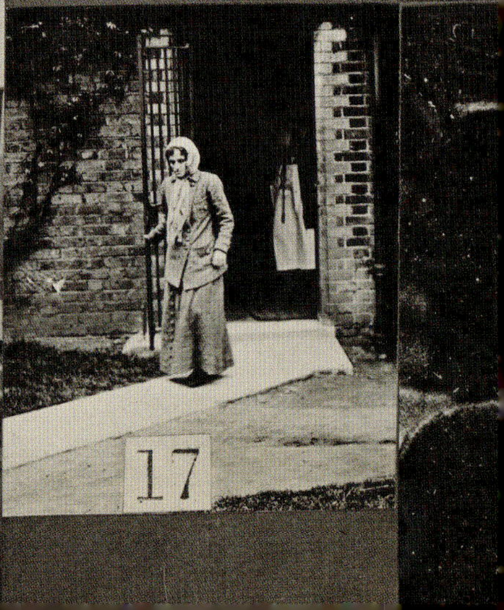

17

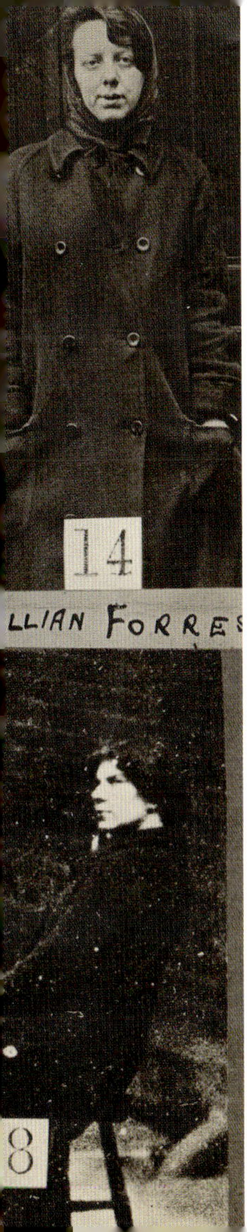

SURVEILLANCE PHOTOGRAPHS OF MILITANT SUFFRAGETTES

Criminal Records Office, 1914

WILLIAM STRANG

(1859–1921)

Malcolm Arbuthnot, 1914

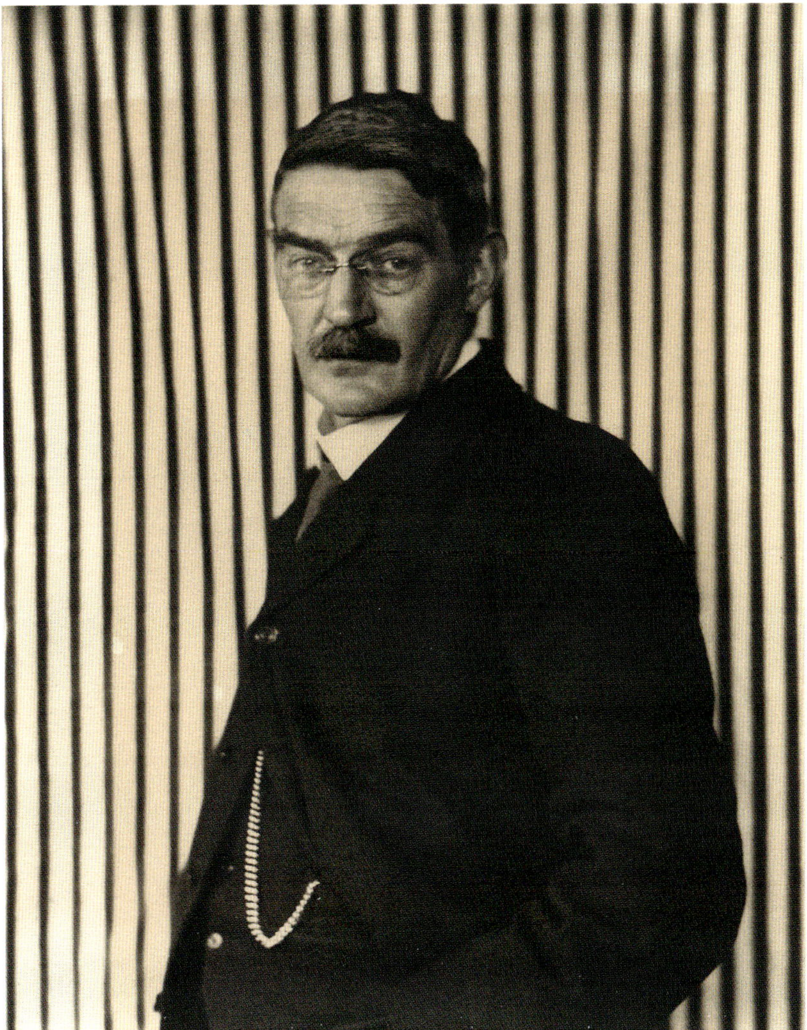

SIR CHARLES ('CHARLIE') CHAPLIN
(1889–1977)
James Abbe, 1922

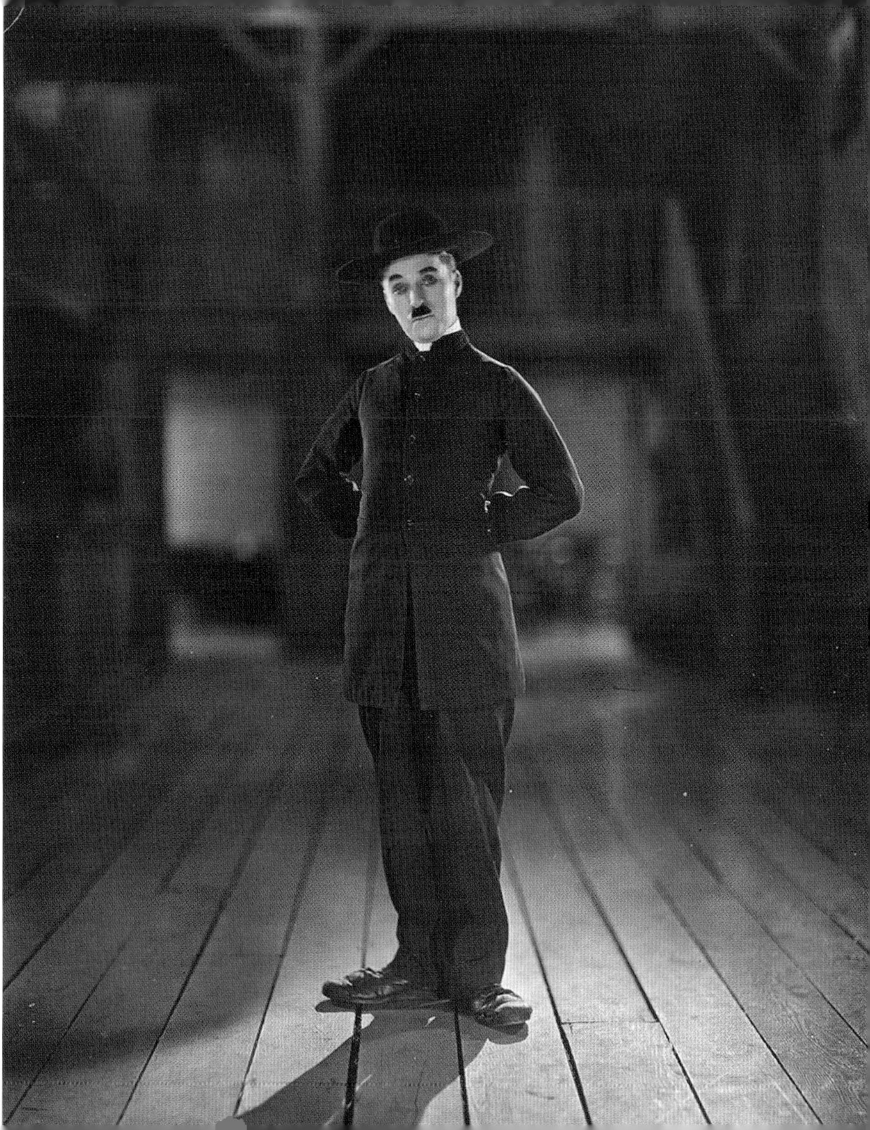

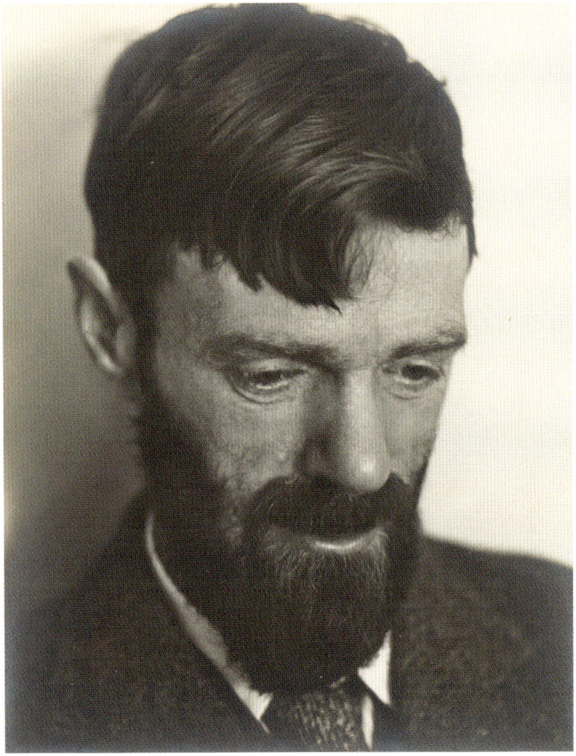

LEFT
D.H. LAWRENCE
(1885–1930)
Edward Weston, 1924

OPPOSITE
DAME GLADYS COOPER
(1888–1971)
Curtis Moffat, c.1924

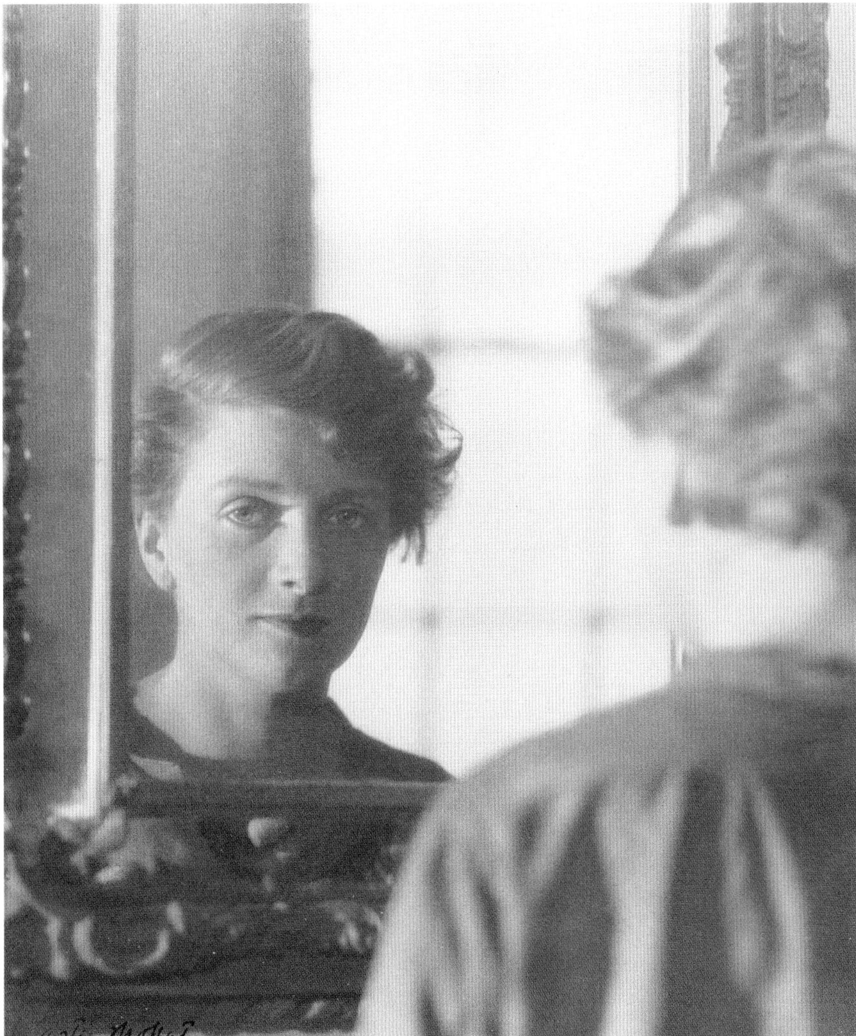

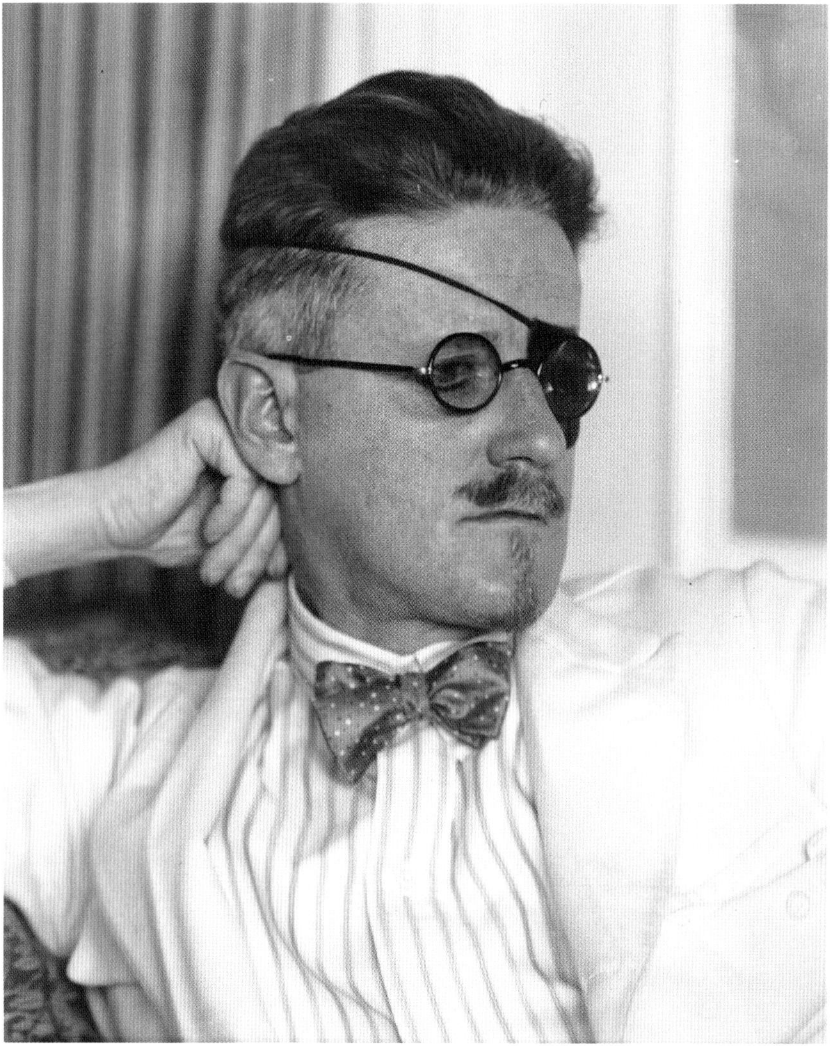

OPPOSITE

JAMES JOYCE

(1882–1941)

Berenice Abbott, 1926

BELOW

TILLY LOSCH

(1907–75)

E.O. Hoppé, 1928

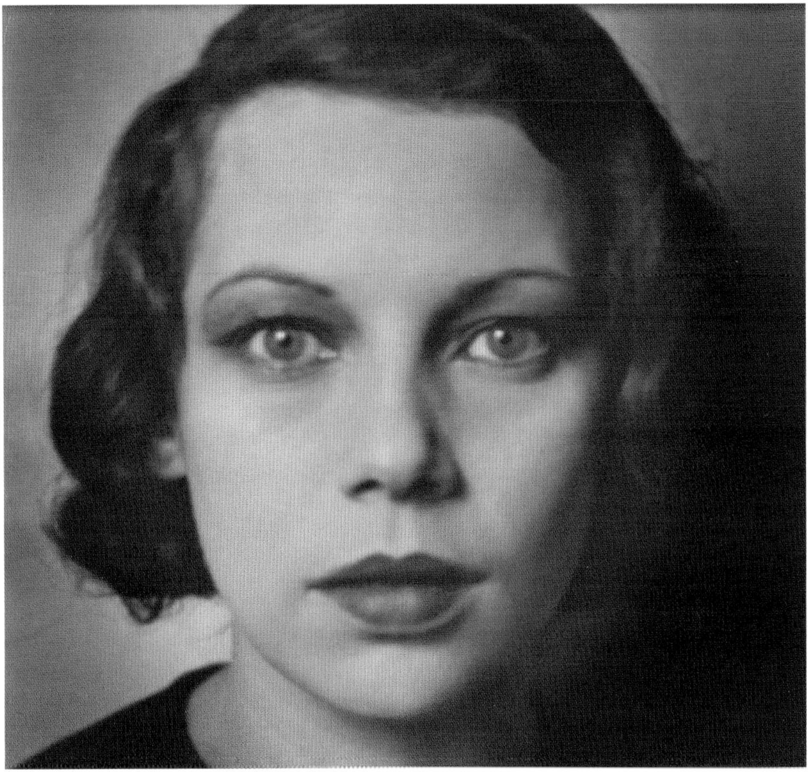

LILLIAN GISH

(1893–1993)

Cecil Beaton, 1929

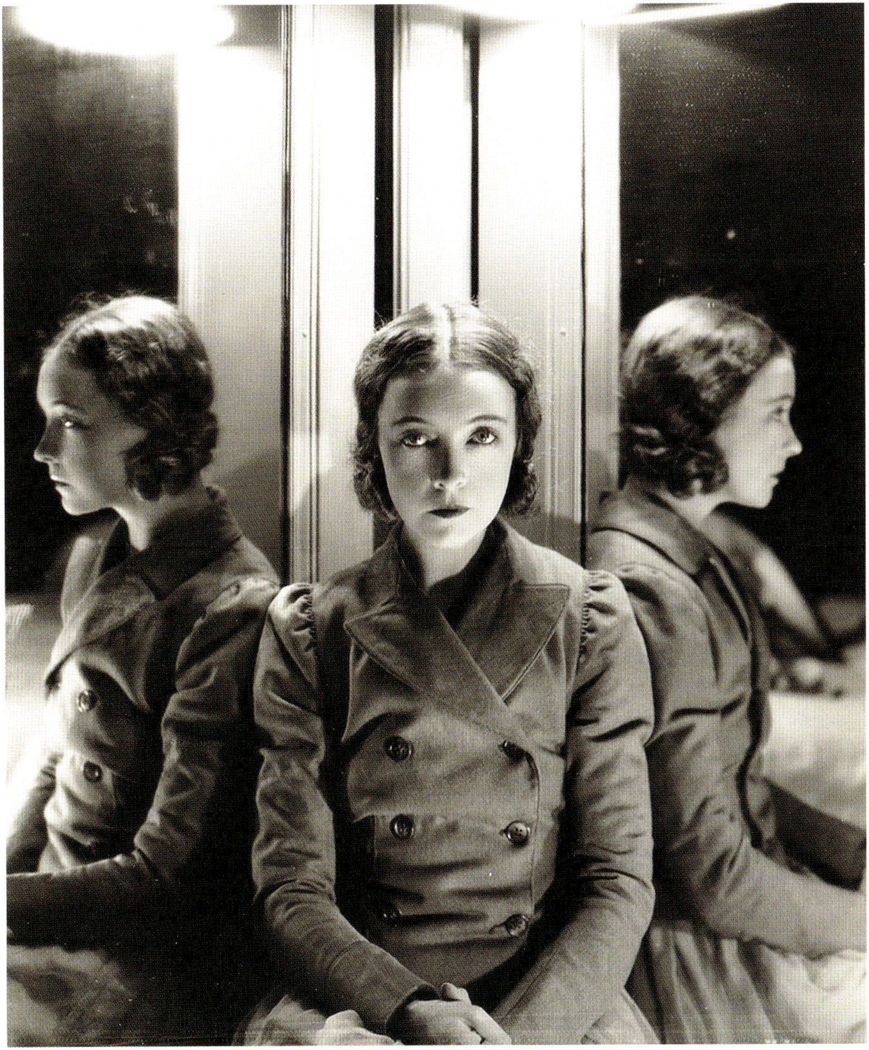

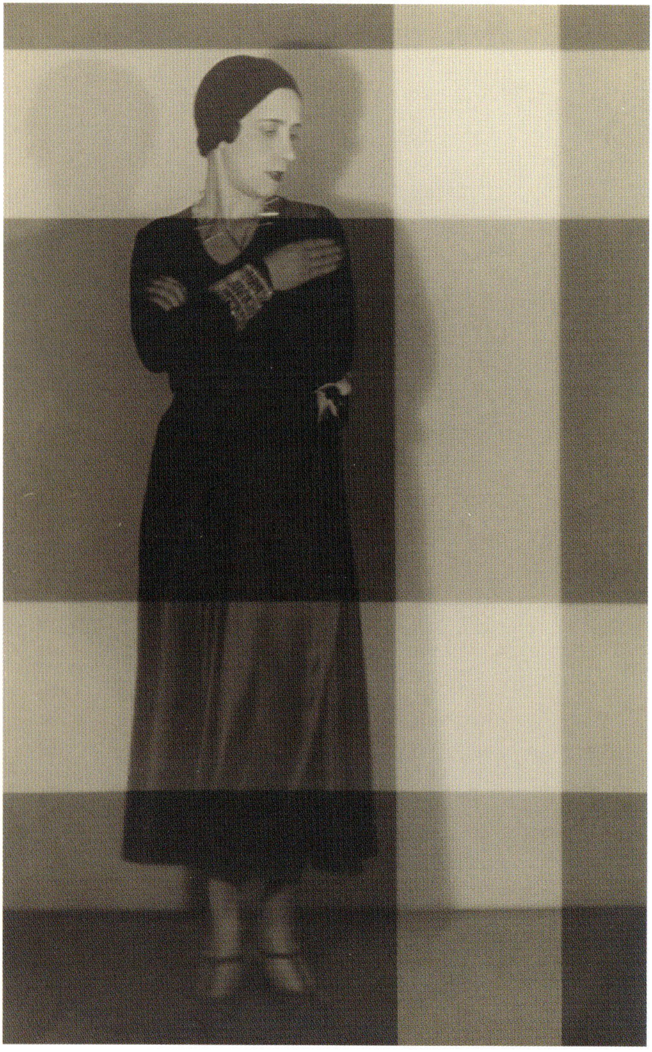

OPPOSITE

ELSA SCHIAPARELLI

(1890–1973)

Man Ray, c.1930

RIGHT

ANNA MAY WONG

(1905–61)

Dorothy Wilding, 1929

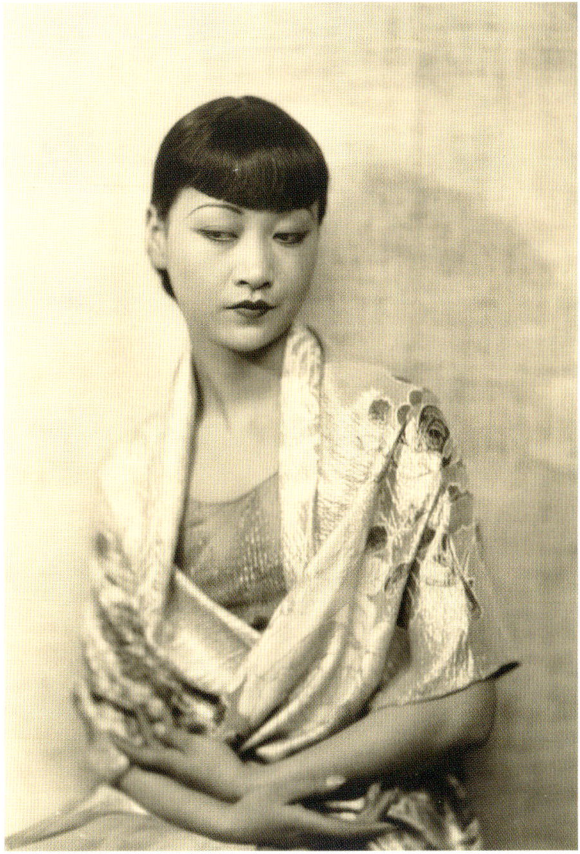

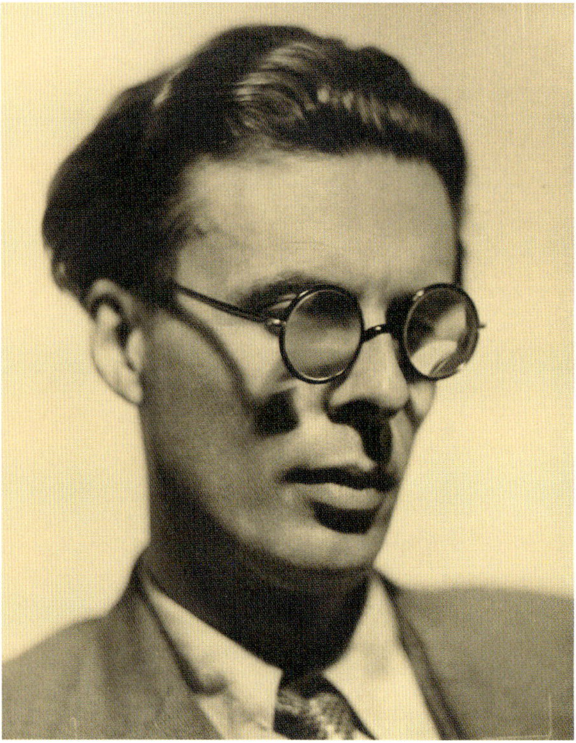

LEFT

ALDOUS HUXLEY

(1894–1963)

Howard Coster, 1934

OPPOSITE

PRIMROSE SALT

(1915–2005)

Paul Tanqueray, 1933

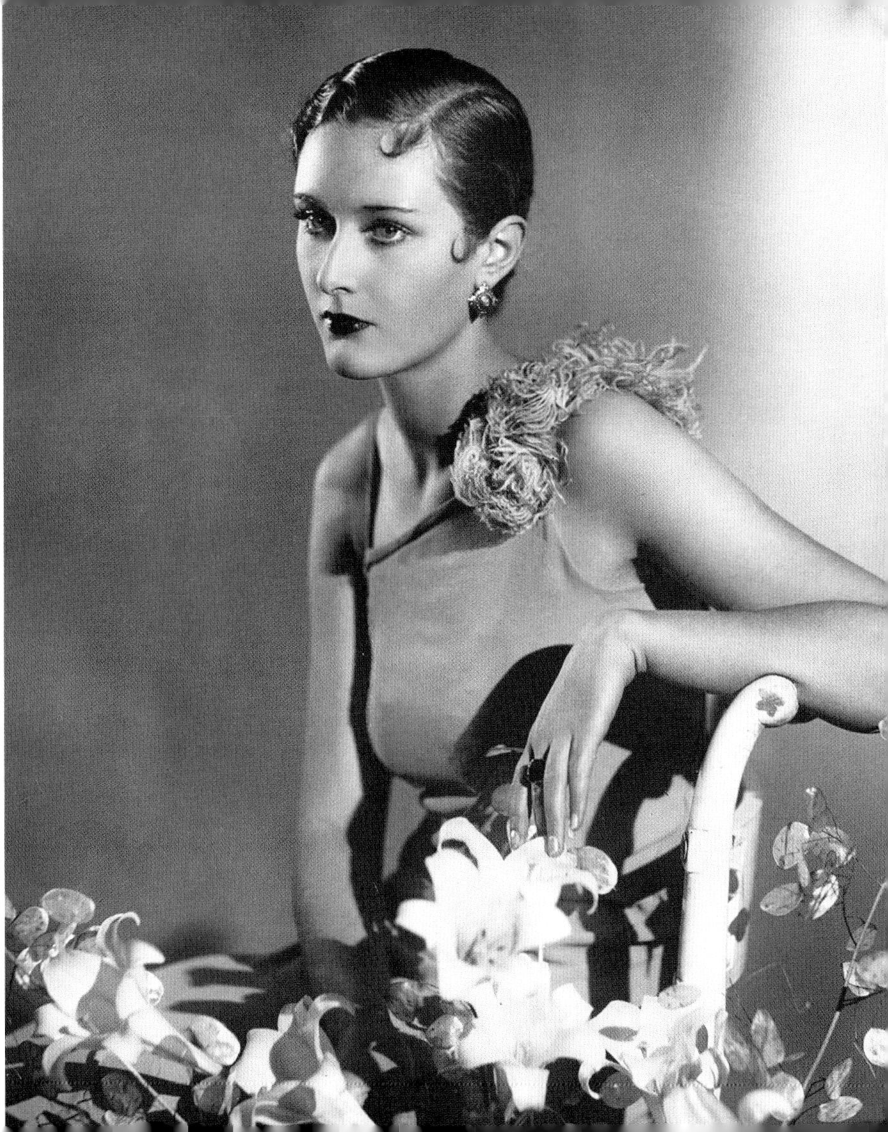

MARGOT ASQUITH,
COUNTESS OF OXFORD
AND ASQUITH

(1864–1945)

Lucia Moholy, 1935

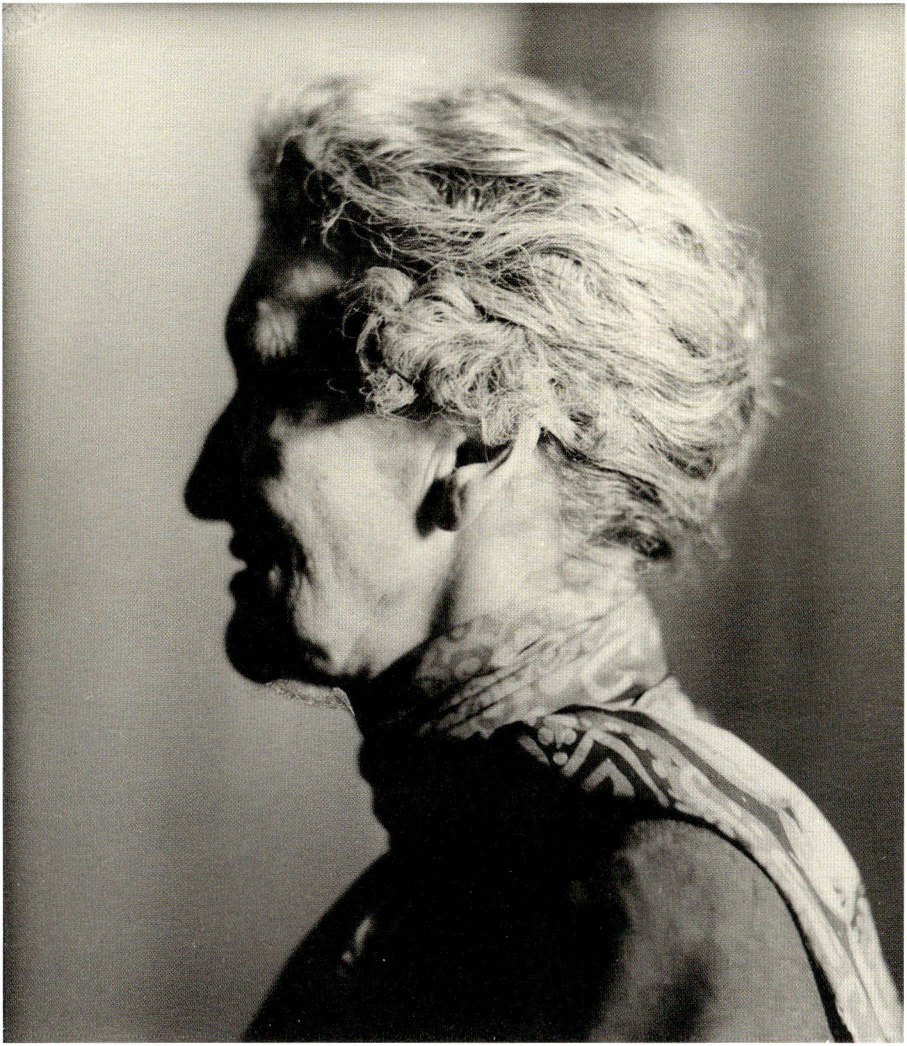

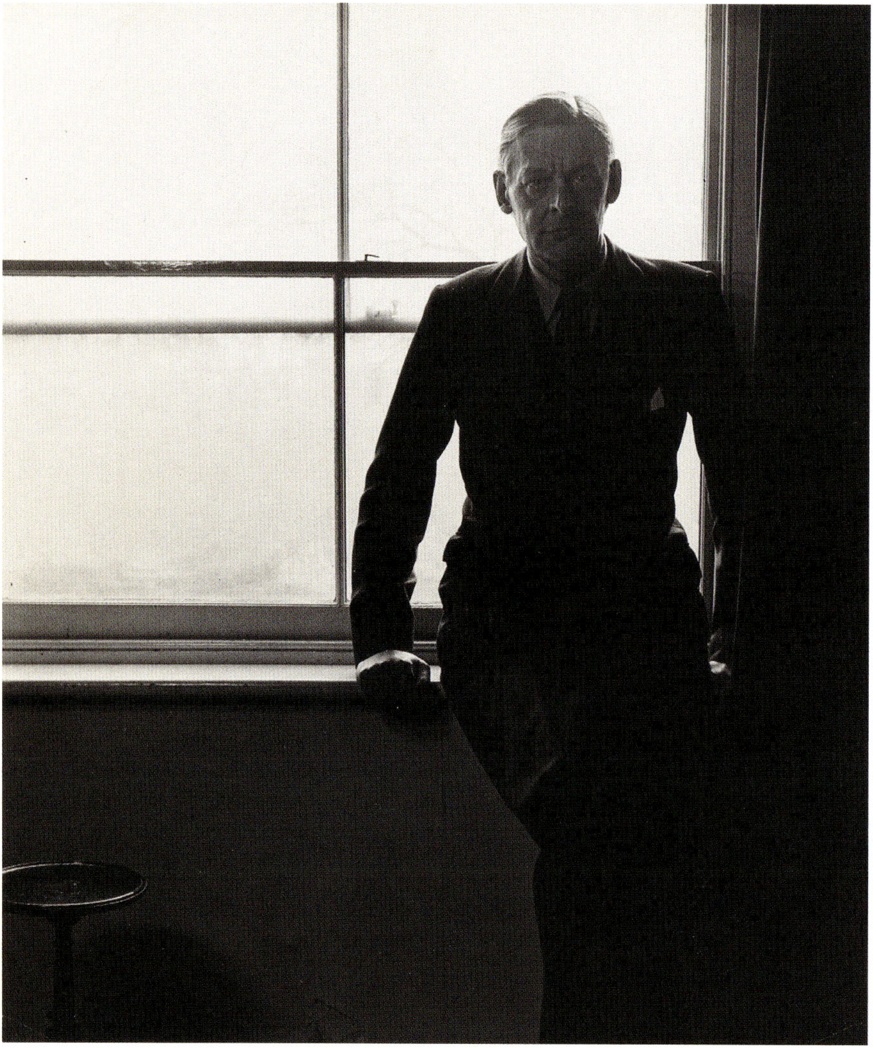

OPPOSITE

T.S. ELIOT (1888–1965)

Bill Brandt, 1945

BELOW

CHRISTOPHER ISHERWOOD (1904–86)
AND W.H. AUDEN (1907–73)

Louise Dahl-Wolfe, 1938

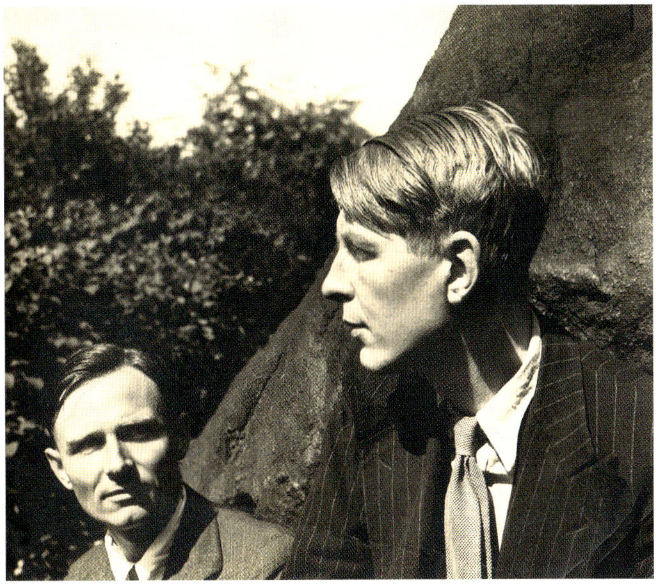

HUMPHREY JENNINGS

(1907–50)

Lee Miller, 1942

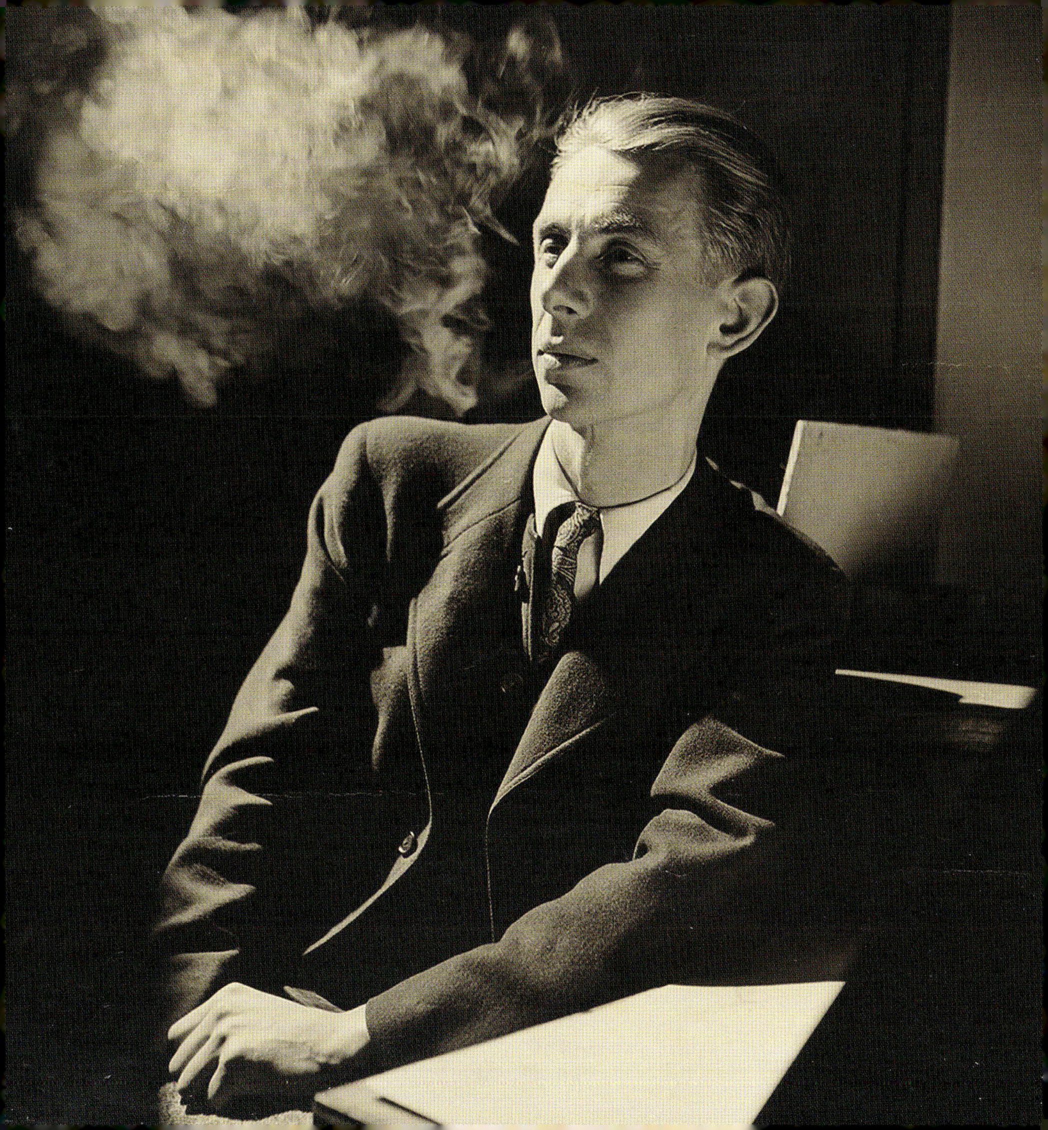

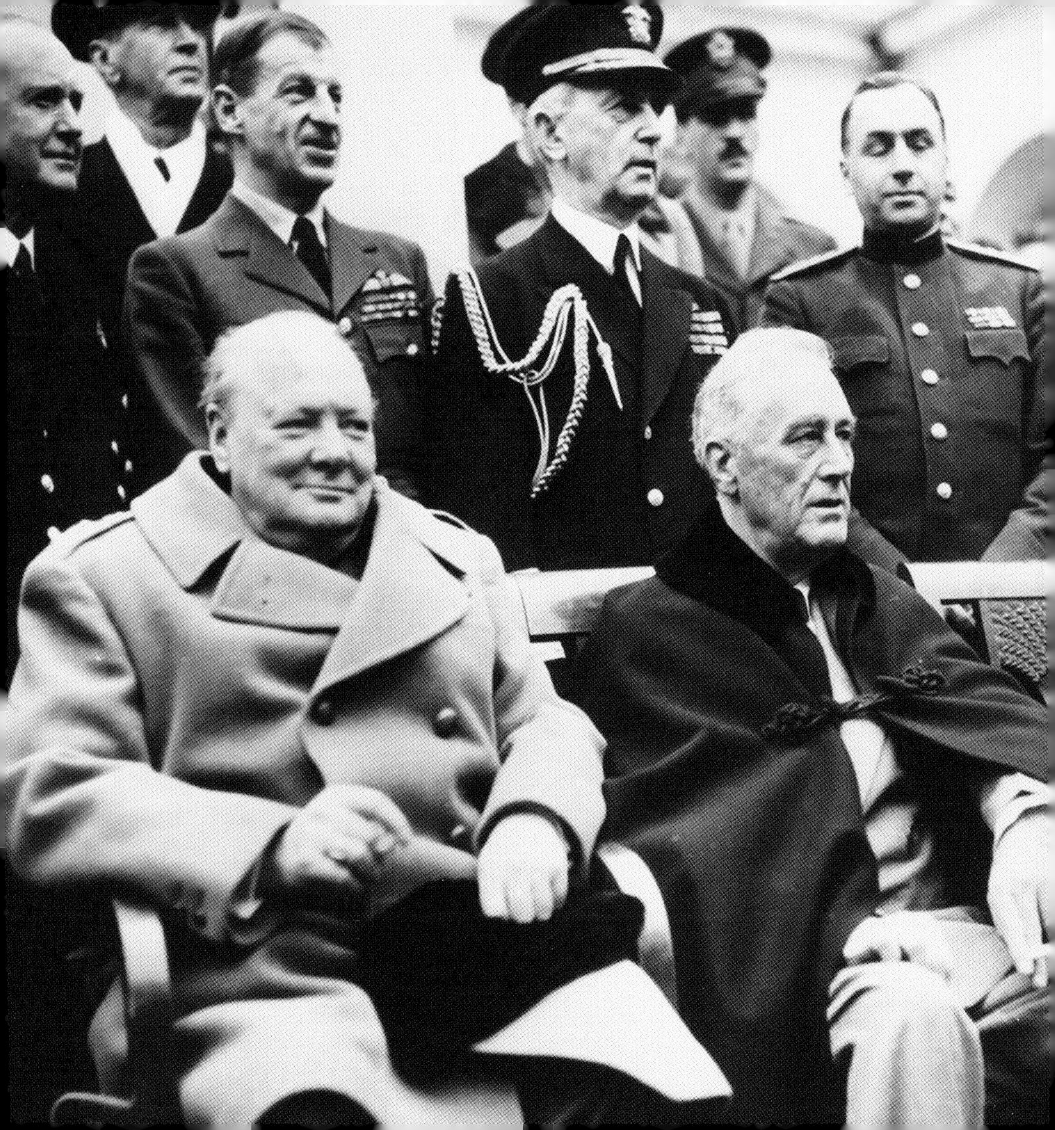

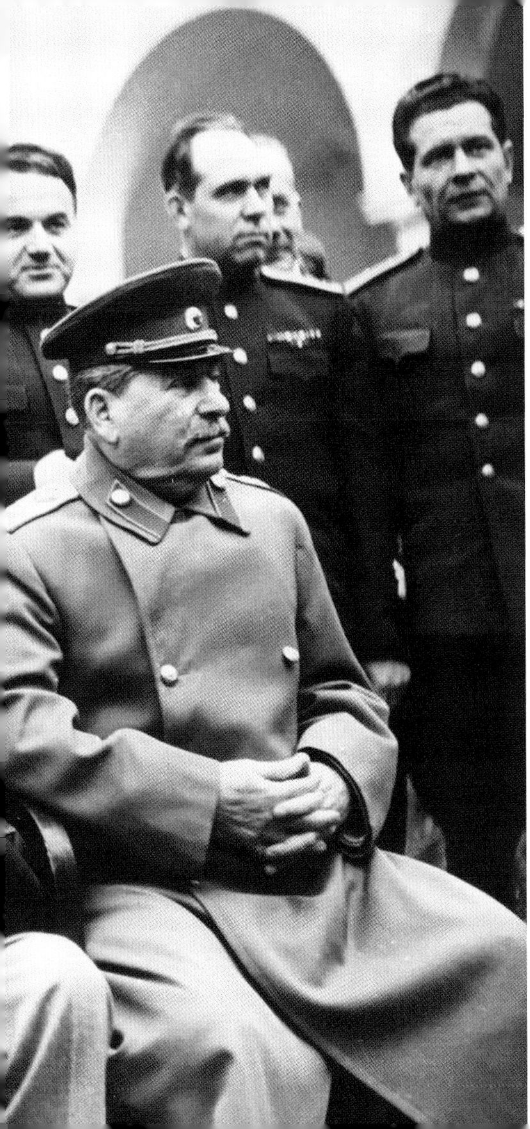

SIR WINSTON CHURCHILL (1874–1965), FRANKLIN ROOSEVELT (1882–1945) AND JOSEPH STALIN (1878–1953) AT THE YALTA CONFERENCE
Yevgeny Khaldei, 1945

SIR ALFRED HITCHCOCK

(1899–1980)

Irving Penn, 1947

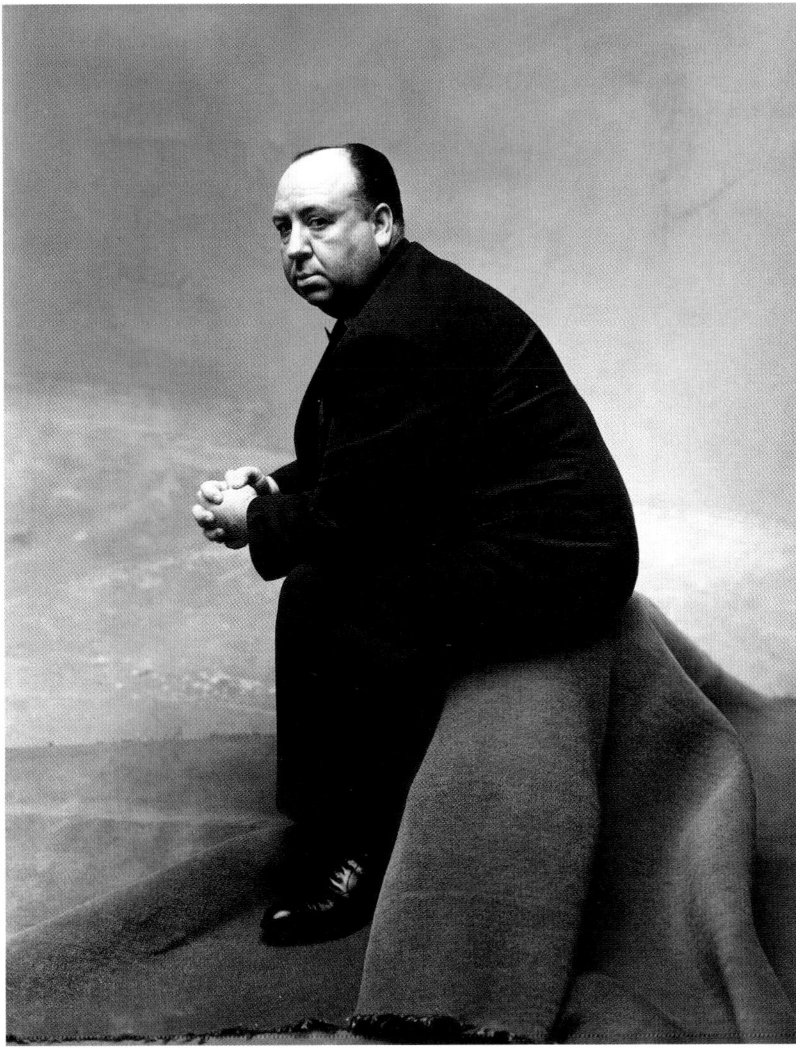

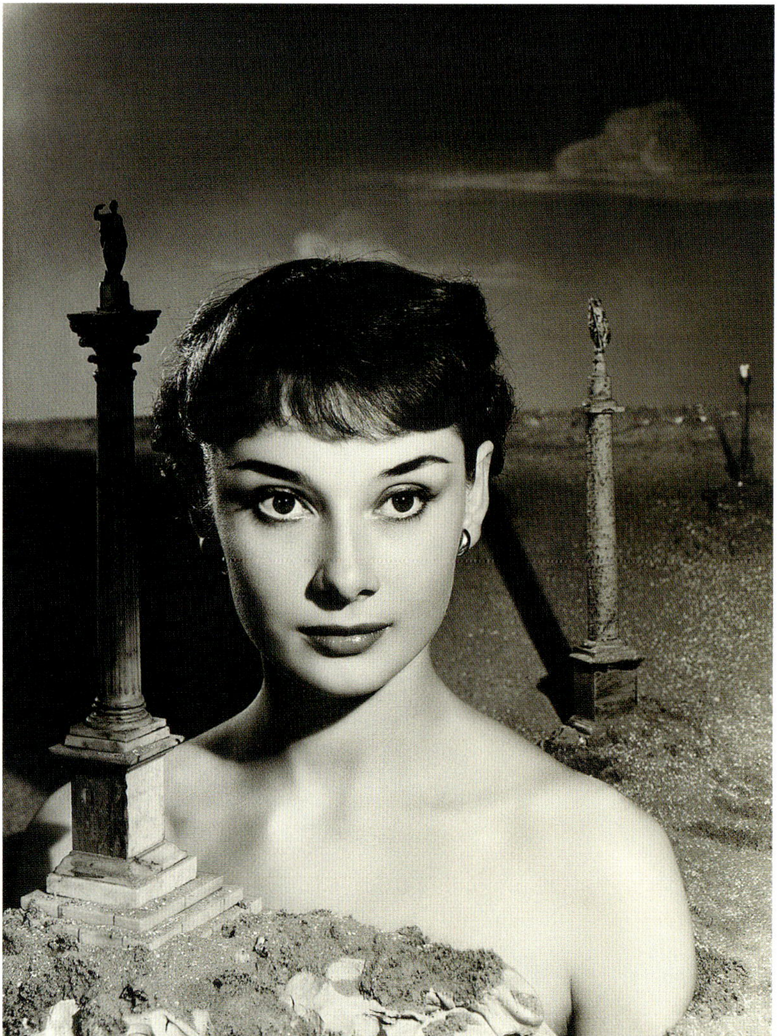

OPPOSITE

AUDREY HEPBURN

(1929–93)

Angus McBean, 1950

RIGHT

BETSY DRAKE (1923–2015)
AND CARY GRANT (1904–86)

Sanford H. Roth, early 1950s

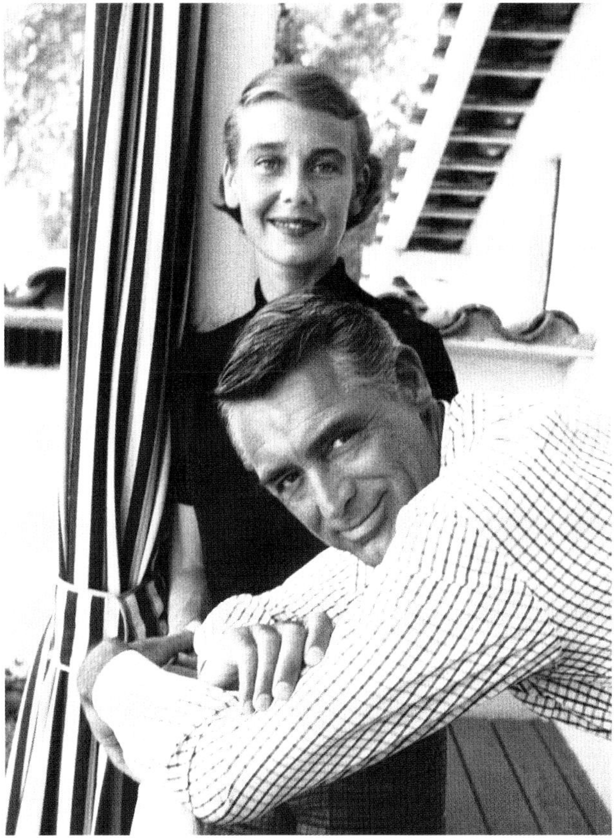

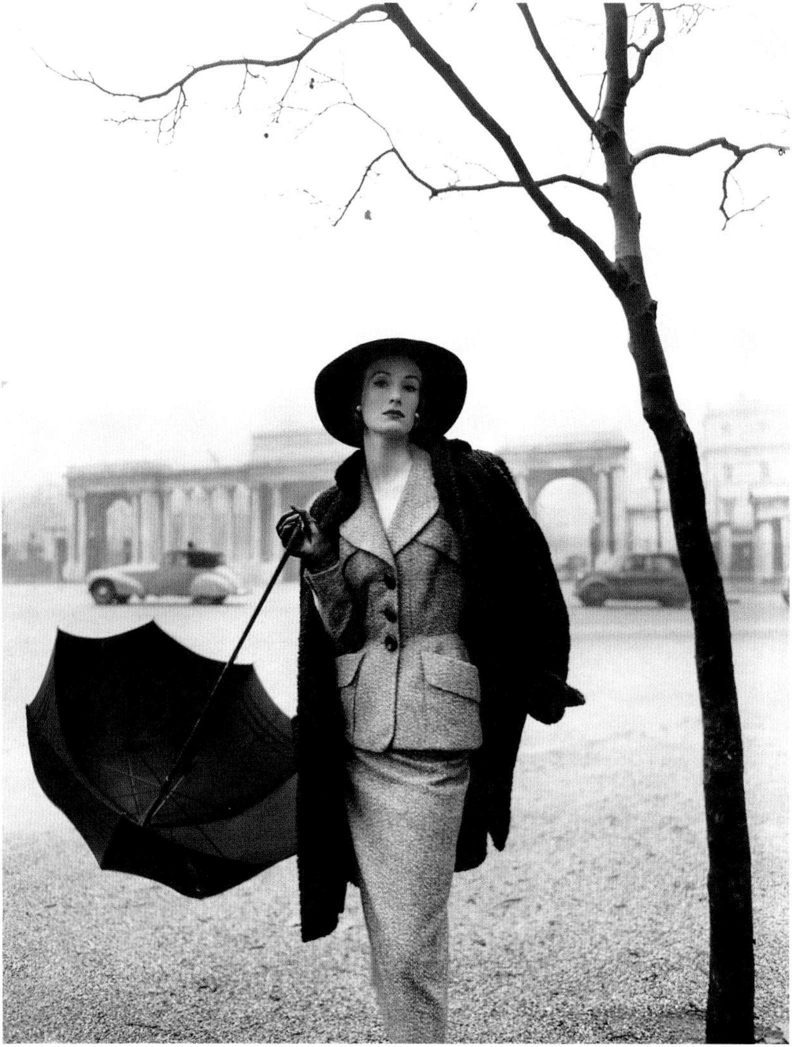

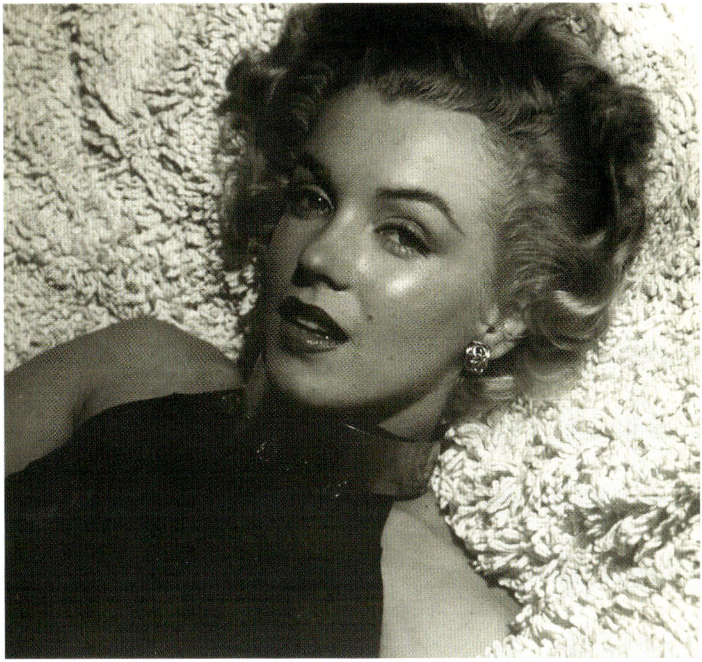

OPPOSITE

WENDA PARKINSON

(1923–87)

Norman Parkinson, 1951

ABOVE

MARILYN MONROE

(1926–62)

Antony Beauchamp, 1951

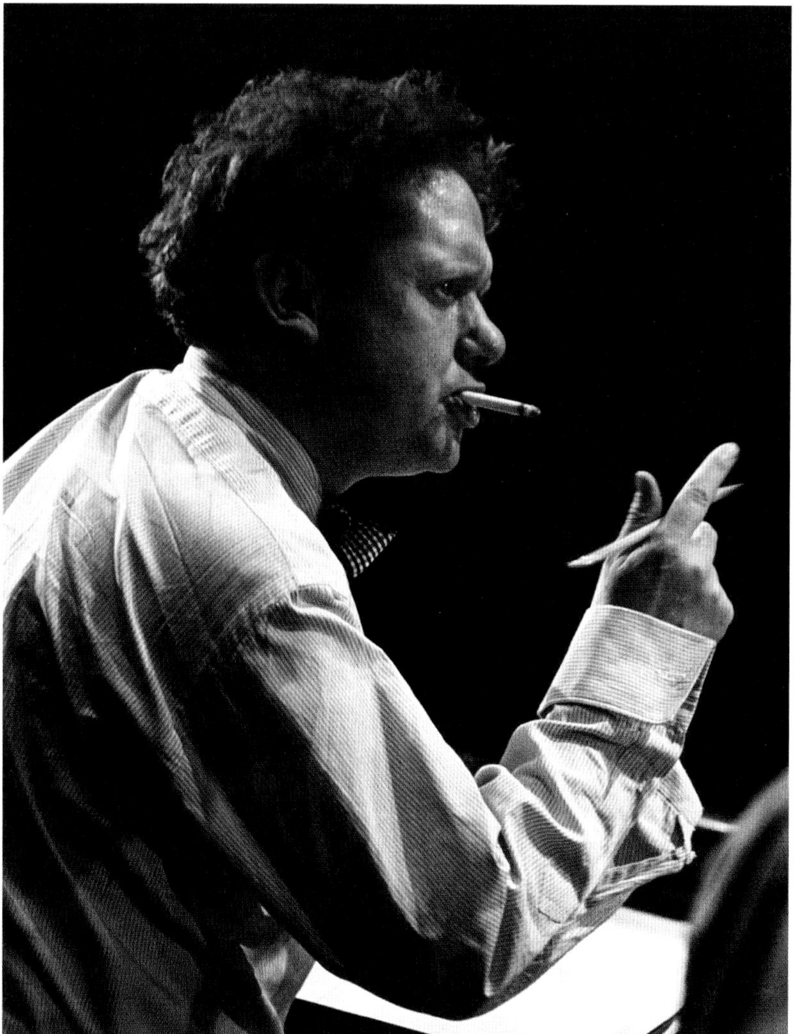

OPPOSITE

DYLAN THOMAS

(1914–53)

Rollie McKenna, 1953

RIGHT

ALAN TURING

(1912–54)

Elliott & Fry, 1951

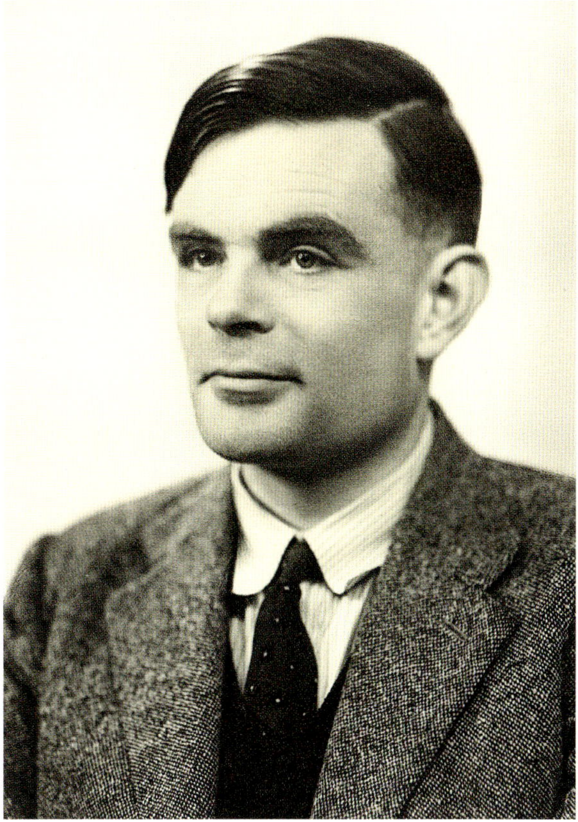

DAME MARGOT FONTEYN

(1919–91)

Yousuf Karsh, 1957

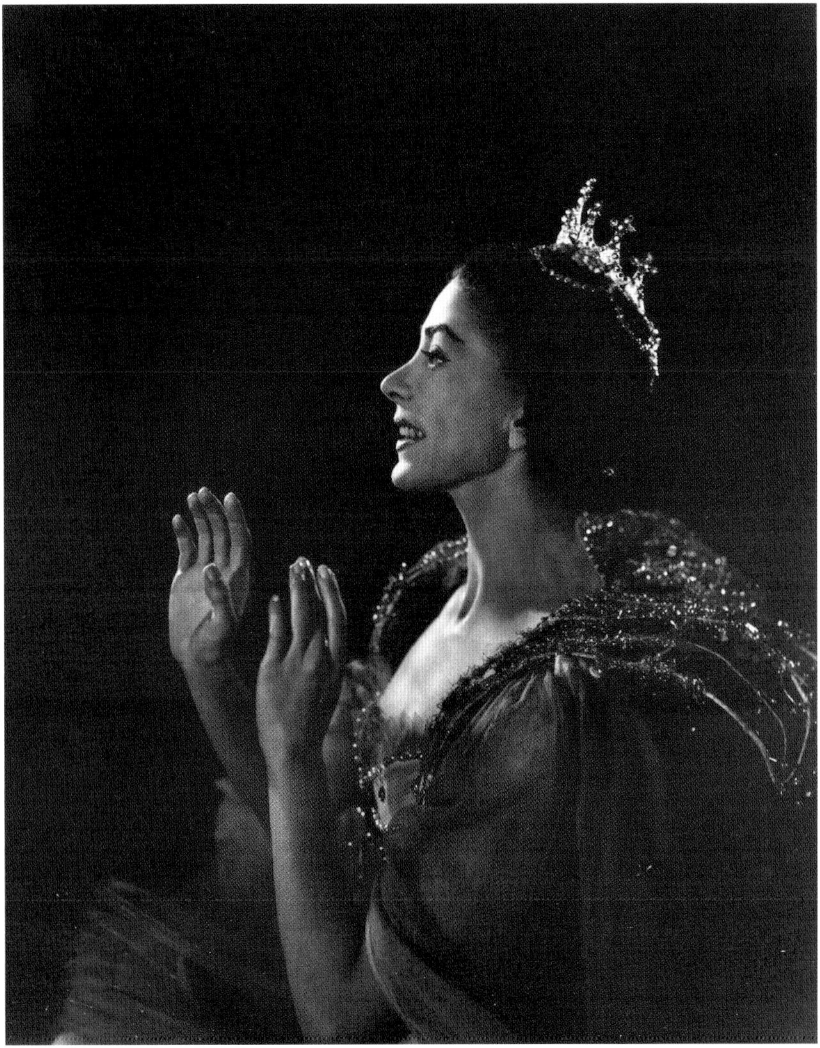

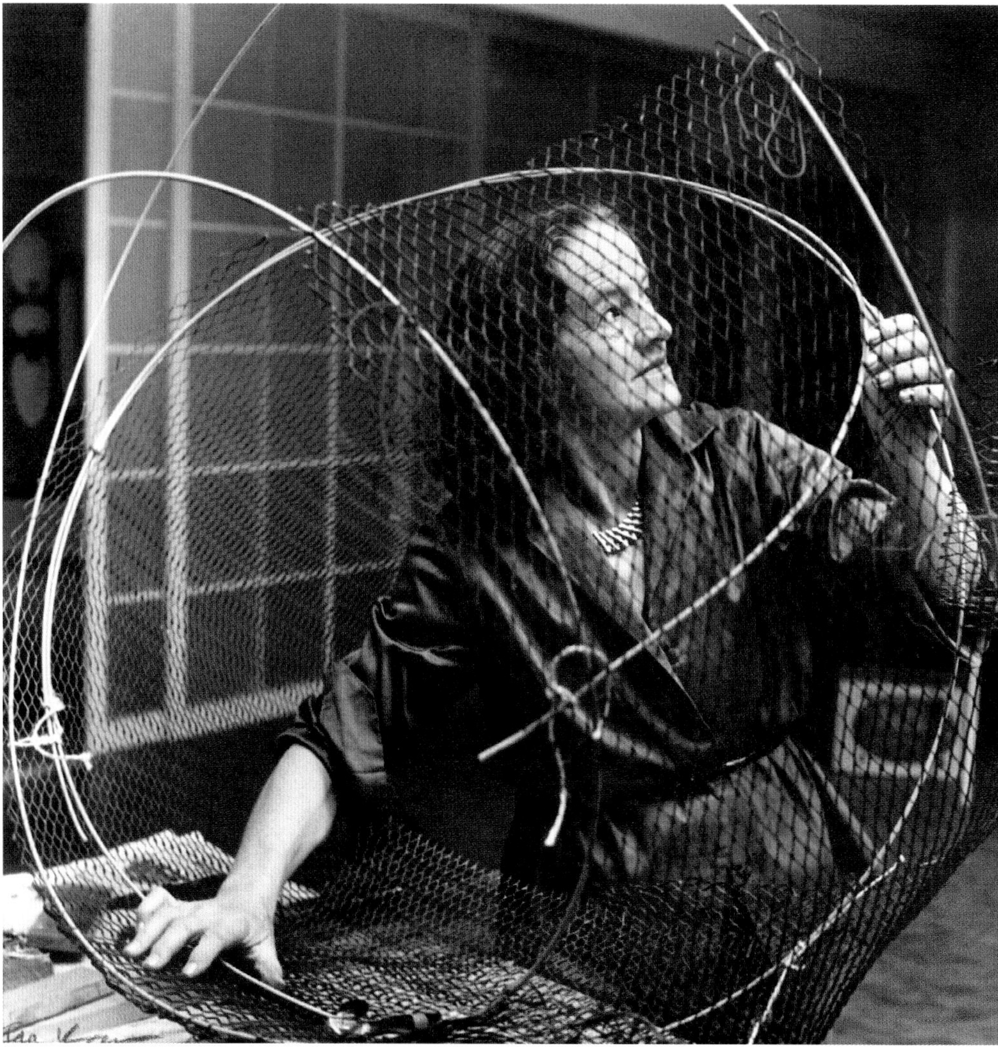

DAME BARBARA HEPWORTH

(1903–75)

Ida Kar, 1961

SIR MICHAEL CAINE

(b.1933)

David Bailey, 1965

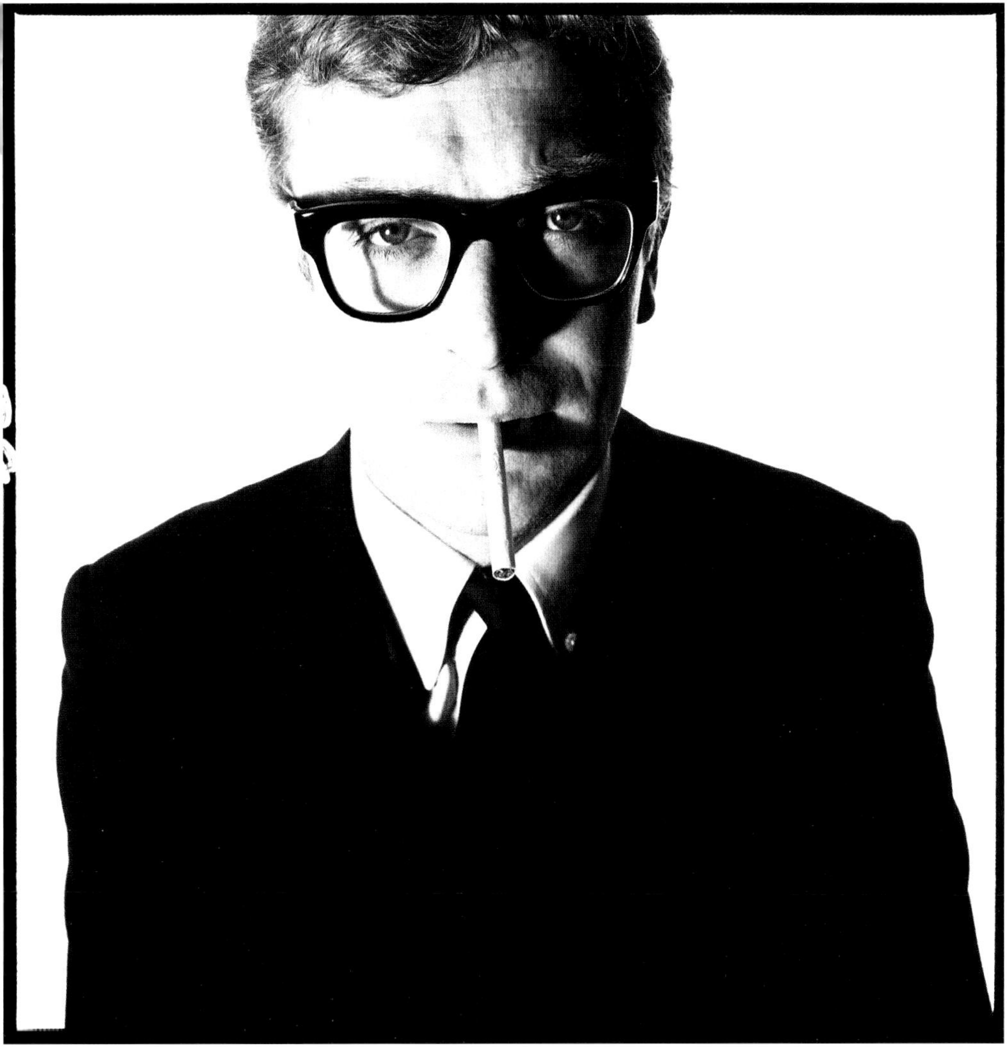

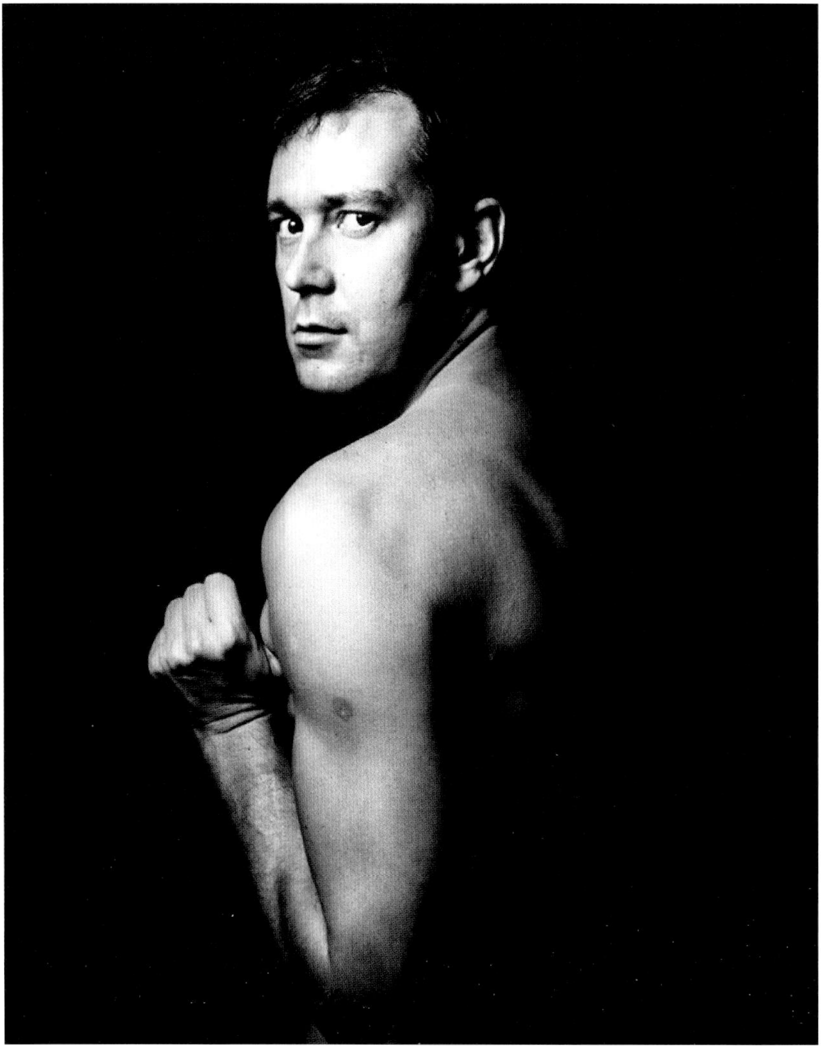

JOE ORTON

(1933–67)

Lewis Morley, 1965

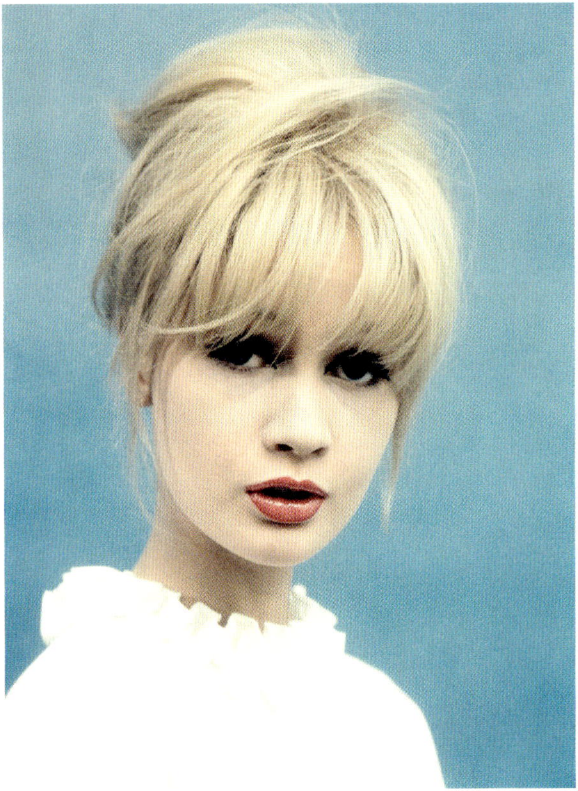

CELIA HAMMOND

(b.1941)

Sandra Lousada, 1962

THE WHO
ROGER DALTREY (b.1944),
KEITH MOON (1946–78), JOHN
ENTWISTLE (1944–2002) AND
PETE TOWNSHEND (b.1945)
Tony Frank, 1965

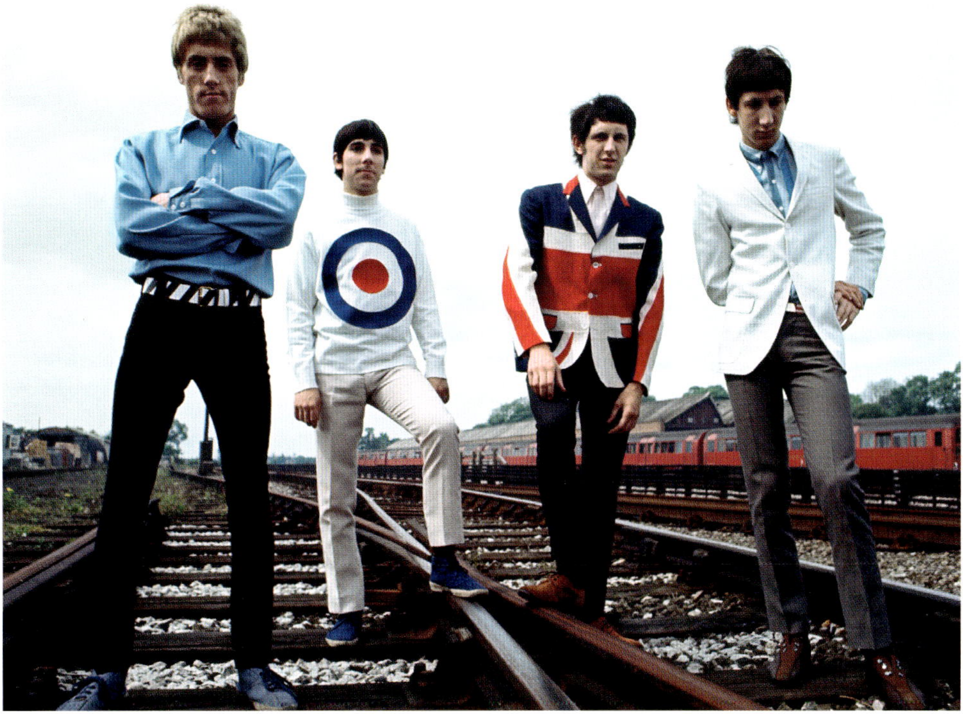

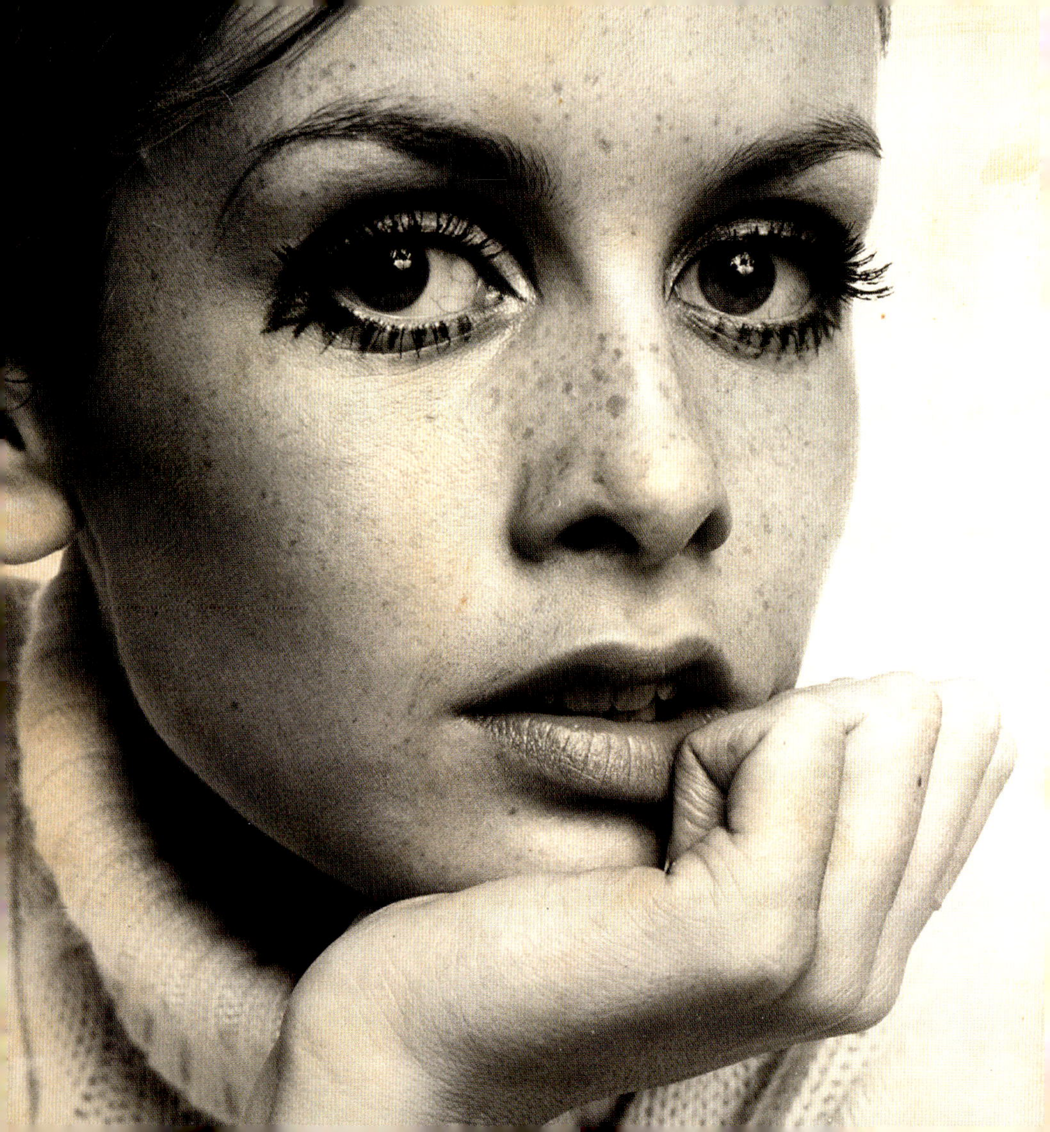

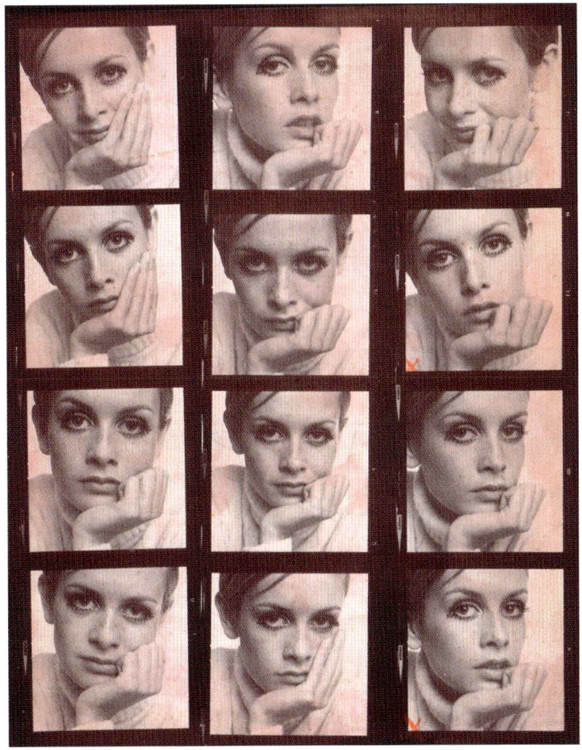

OPPOSITE AND ABOVE

TWIGGY

(b.1949)

Ronald Traeger, 1967

THE BEATLES
SIR PAUL MCCARTNEY (b.1942),
SIR RINGO STARR (b.1940),
GEORGE HARRISON (1943–2001)
AND JOHN LENNON (1940–80)
Linda McCartney, 1967

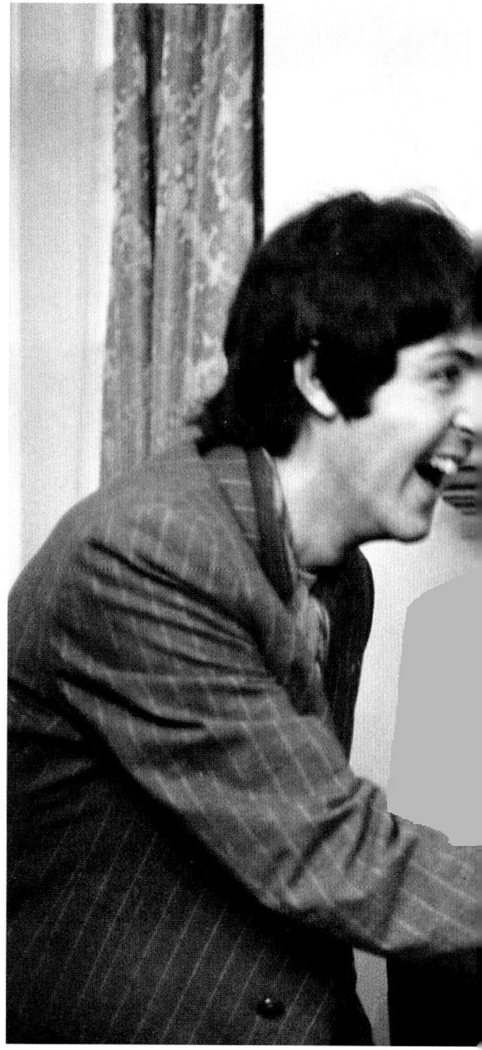

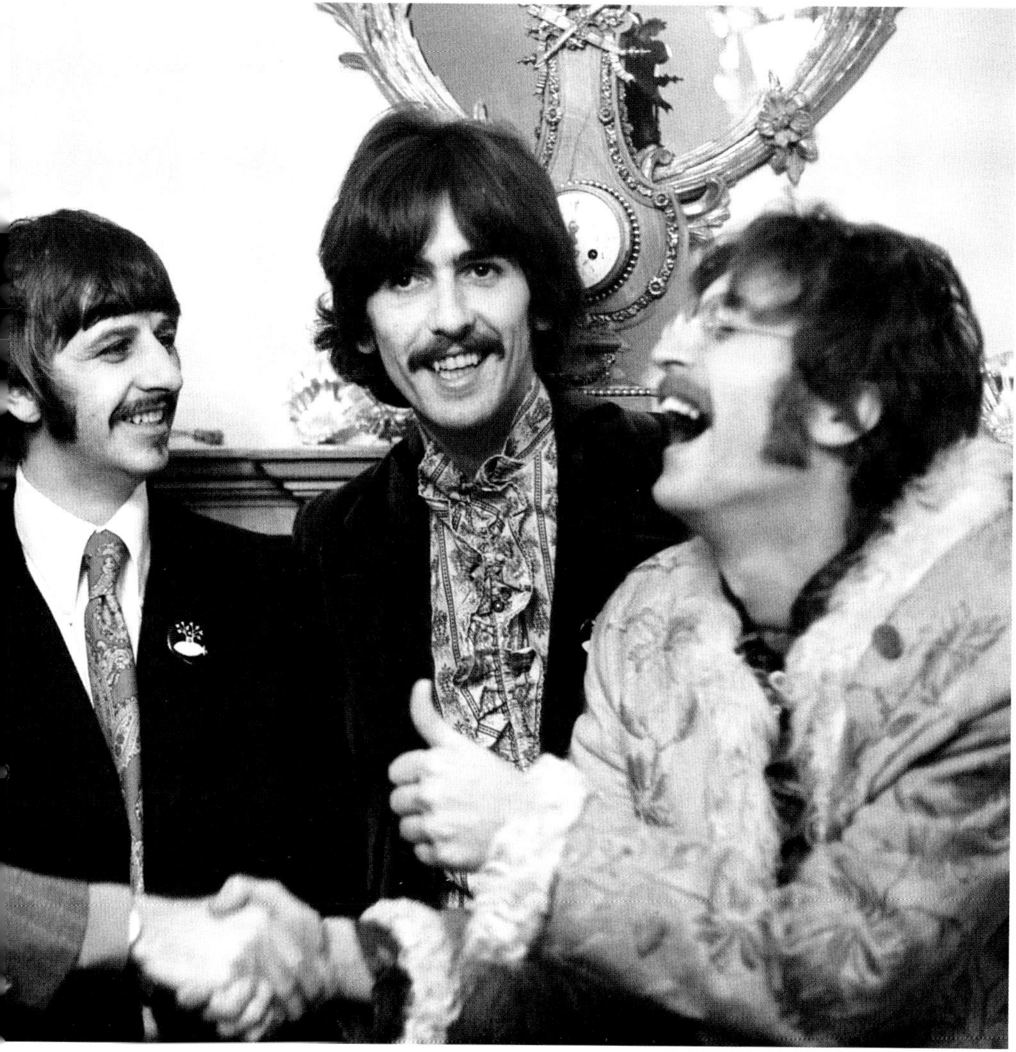

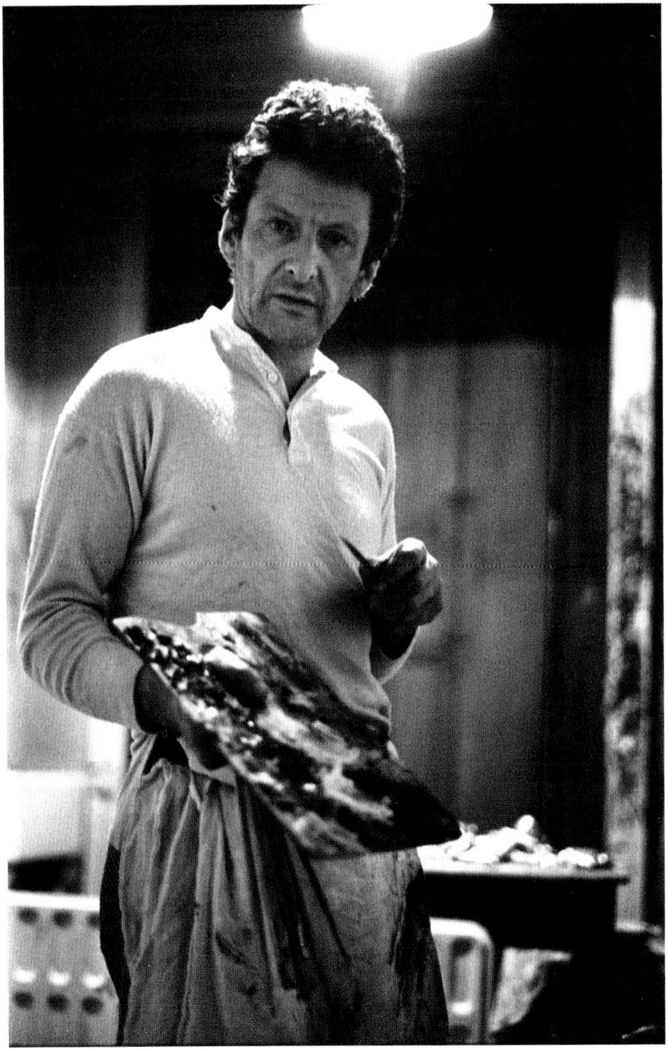

LUCIAN FREUD

(1922–2011)

Harry Diamond, 1969

THE SEX PISTOLS
STEVE JONES (b.1955),
GLEN MATLOCK (b.1956),
JOHNNY ROTTEN
(JOHN LYDON) (b.1956),
AND PAUL COOK (b.1956)
Peter Vernon, 1976

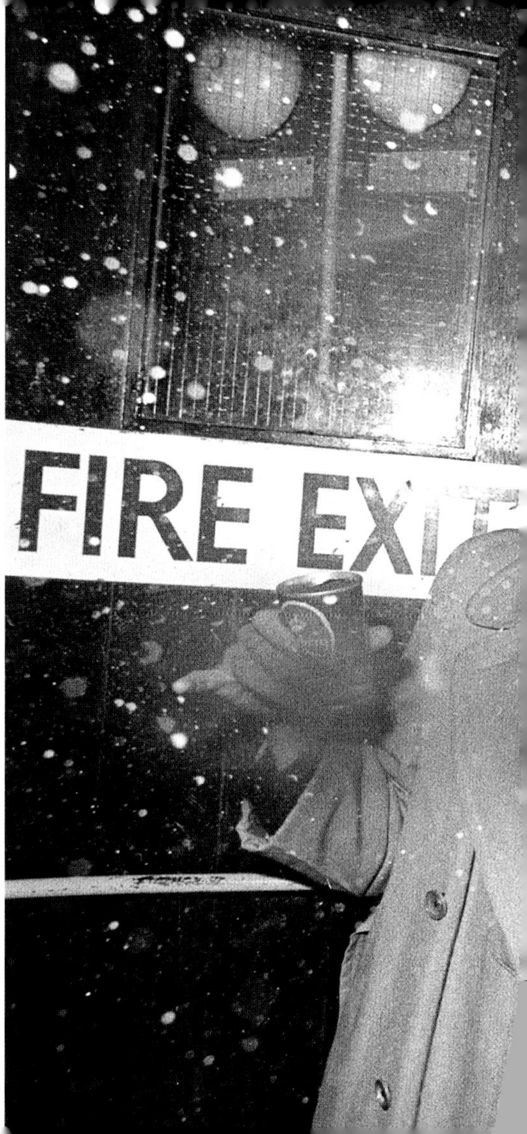

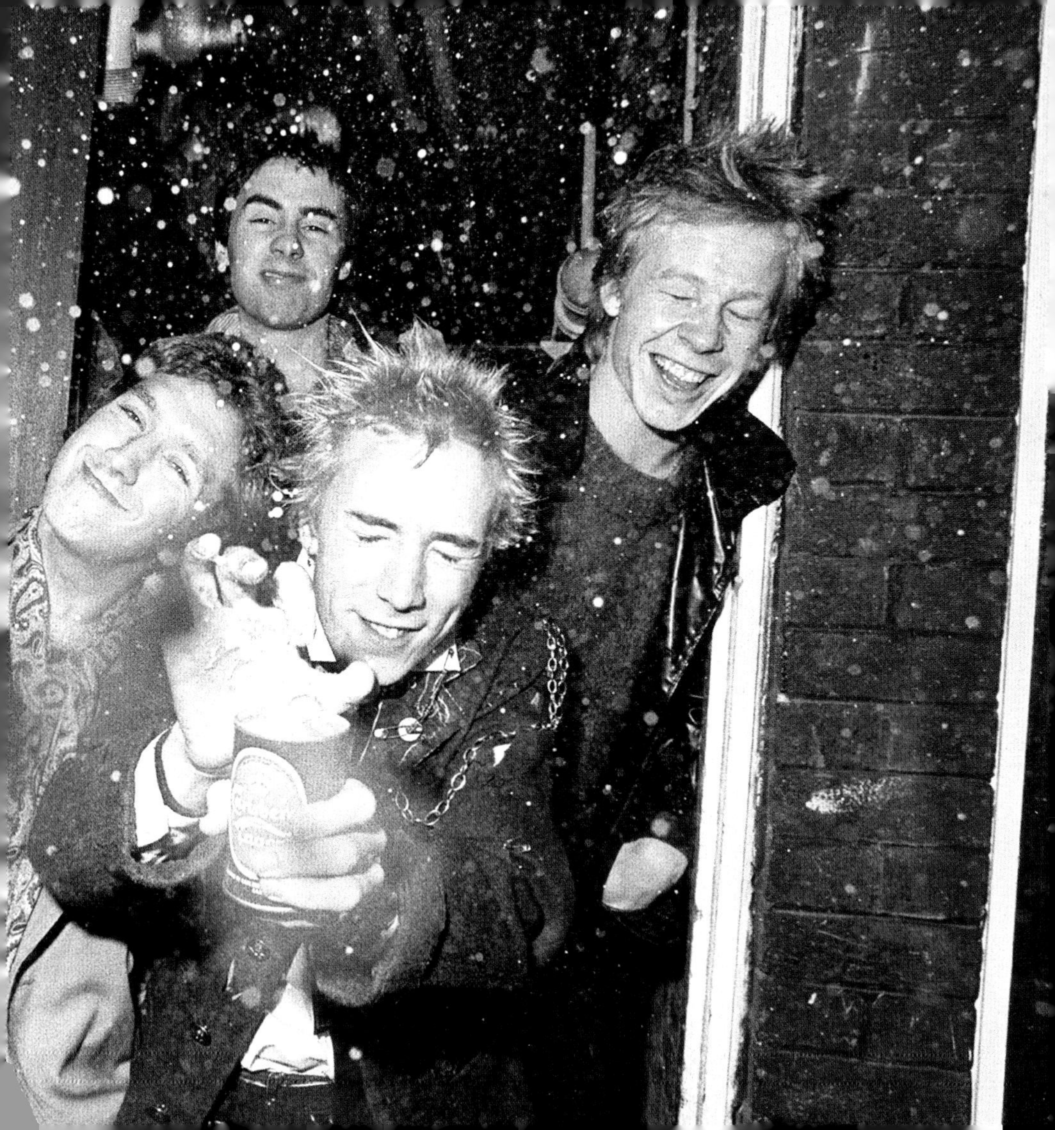

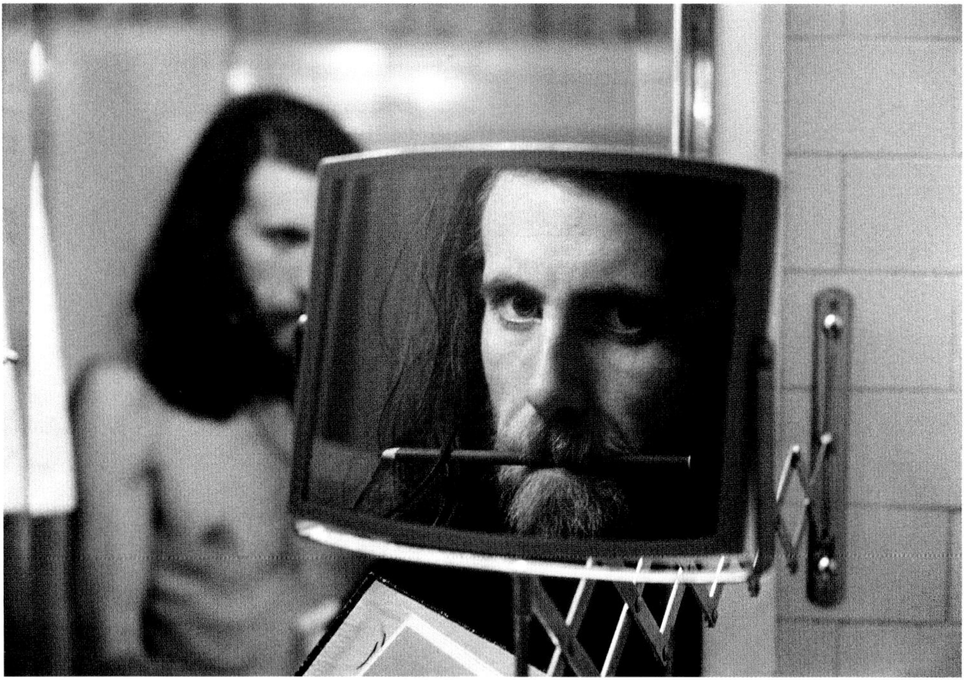

ABOVE
GRAHAM NASH
(b.1942)
Graham Nash, 1974

OPPOSITE
GLENDA JACKSON
(b.1936)
Mayotte Magnus, 1977

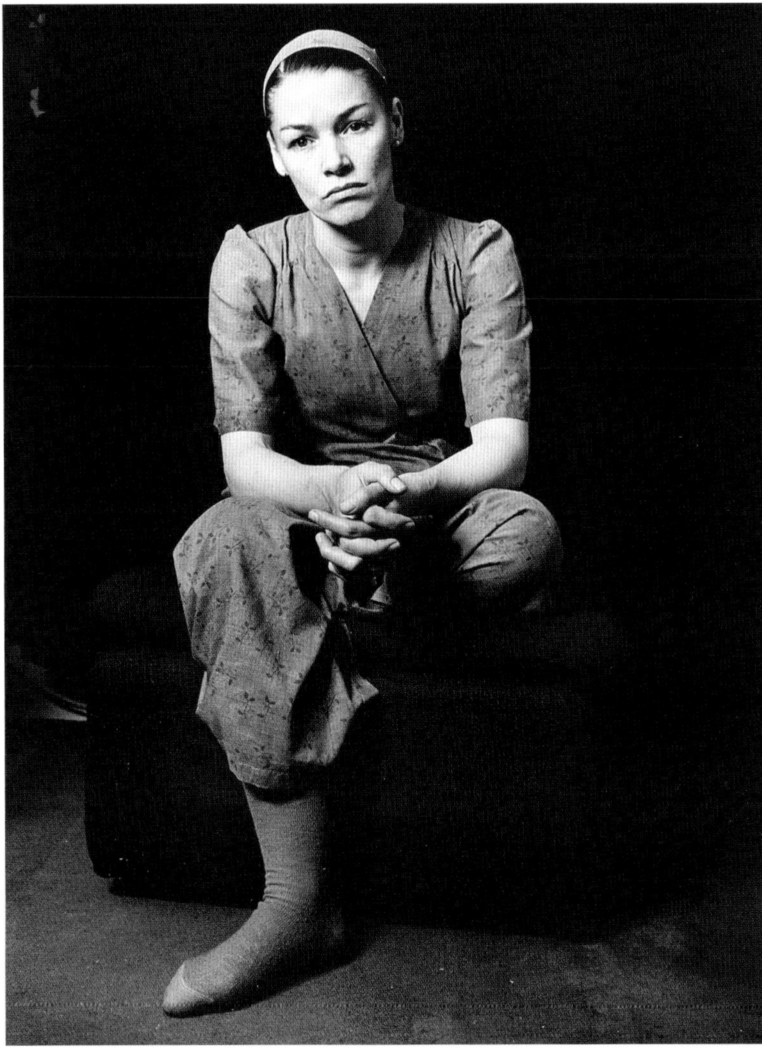

DAVID HOCKNEY

(b.1937)

Bernard Lee ('Bern') Schwartz, 1977

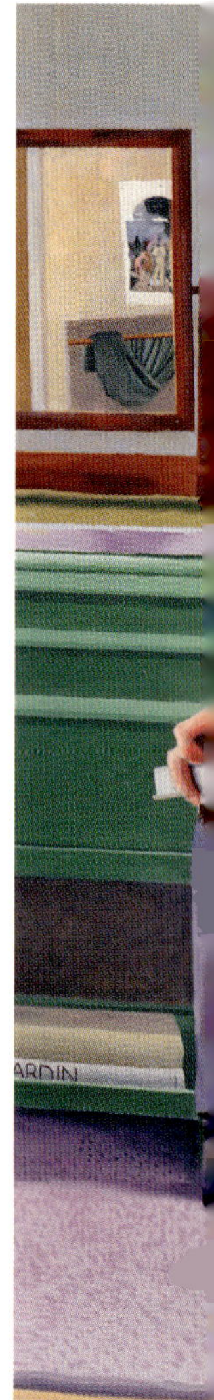

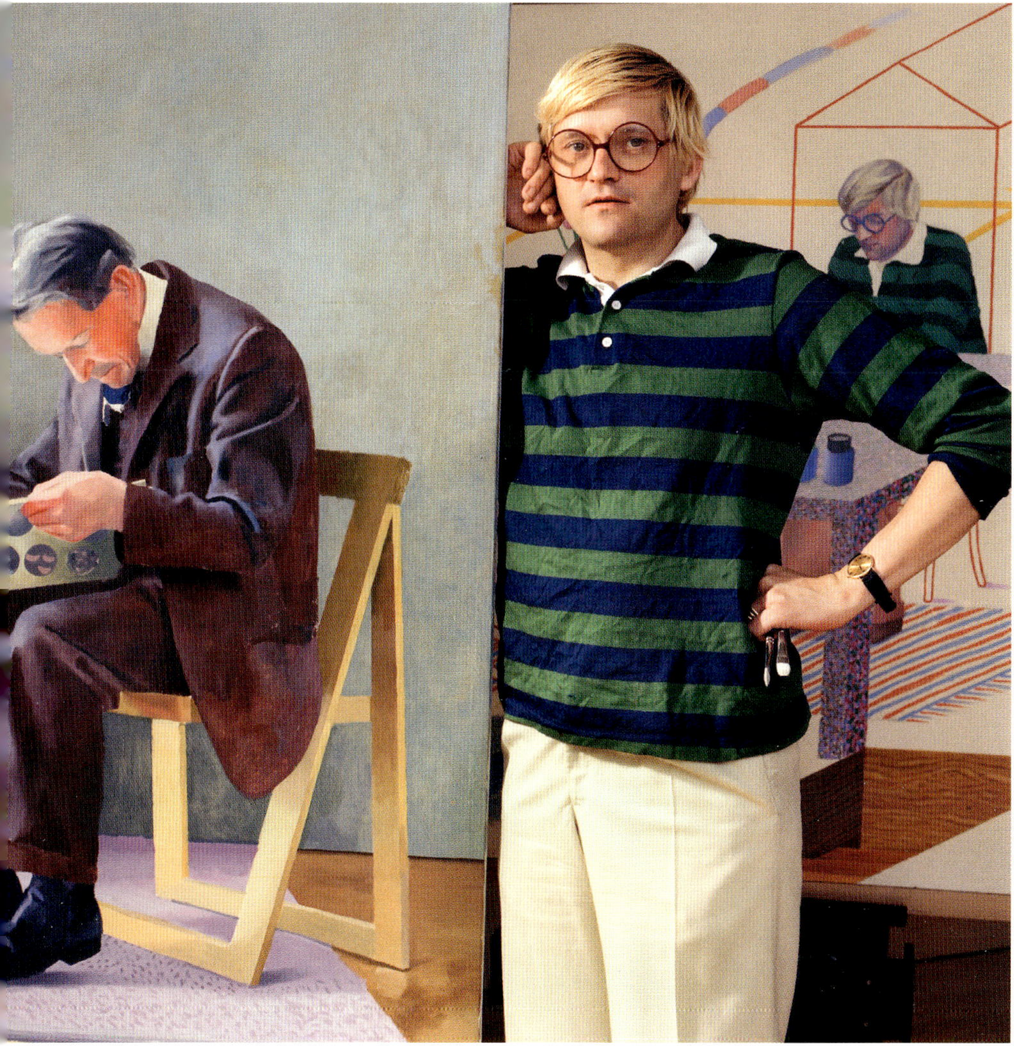

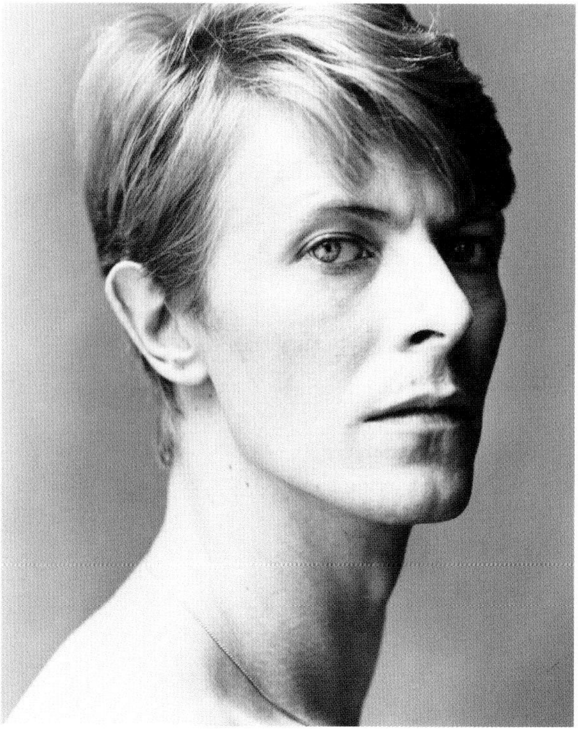

LEFT

DAVID BOWIE

(1947–2016)

Antony Armstrong Jones, 1st Earl of Snowdon, 1978

OPPOSITE

KATE BUSH

(b.1958)

Thomas Patrick John Anson, 5th Earl of Lichfield, 1980

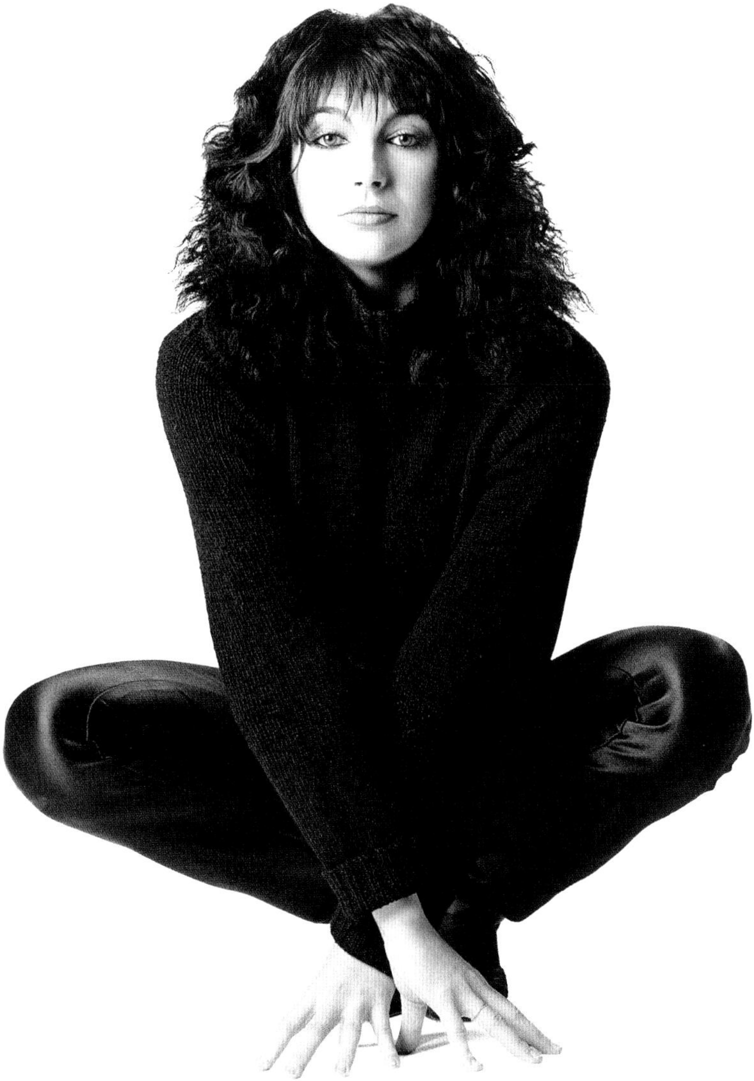

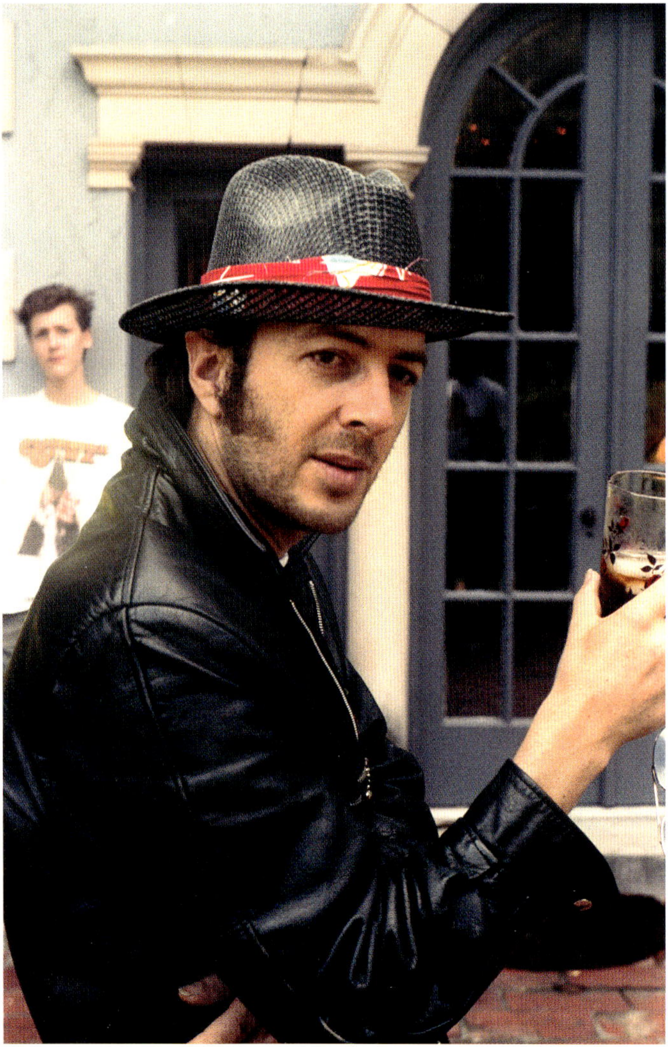

JOE STRUMMER

(1952–2002)

William Eggleston, c.*1980*

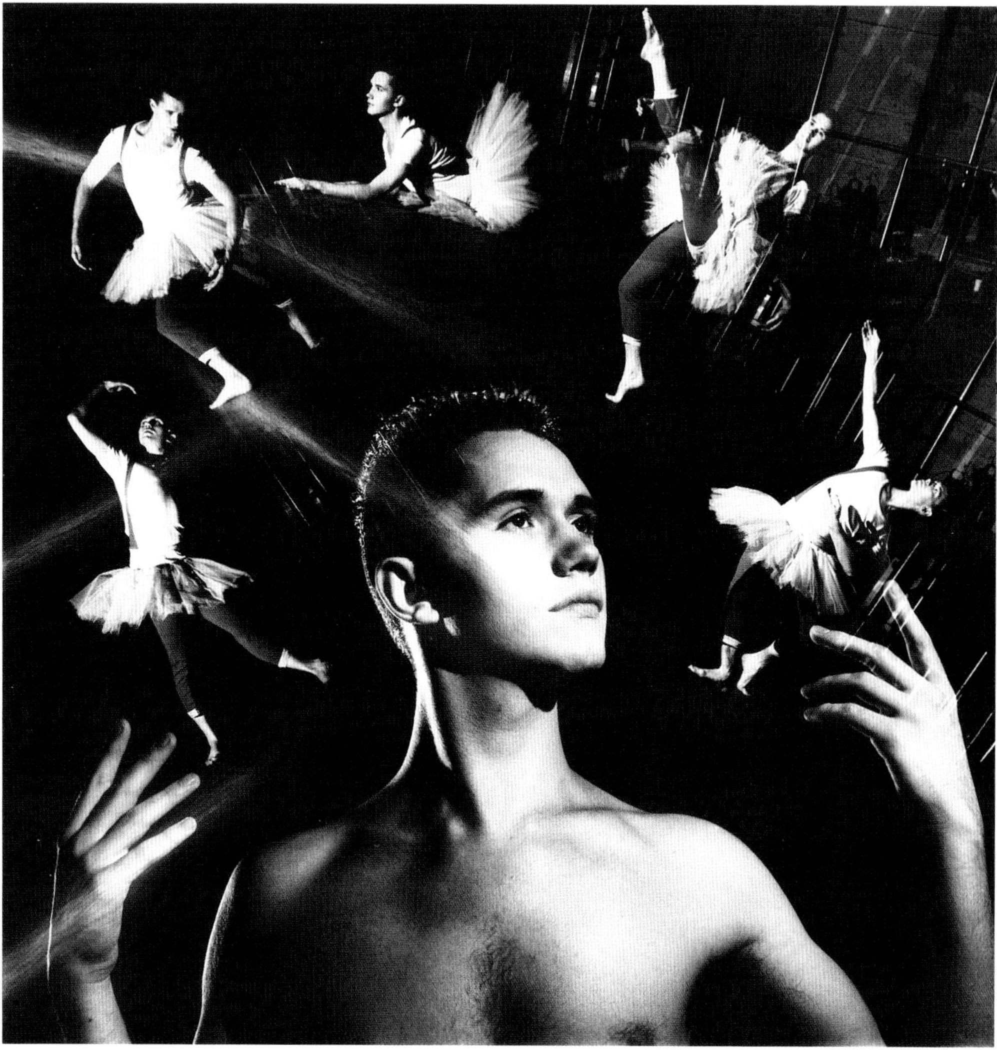

OPPOSITE

MICHAEL CLARK

(b.1962)

Chris Garnham, 1984

RIGHT

HANIF KUREISHI

(b.1954)

Jillian Edelstein, 1989

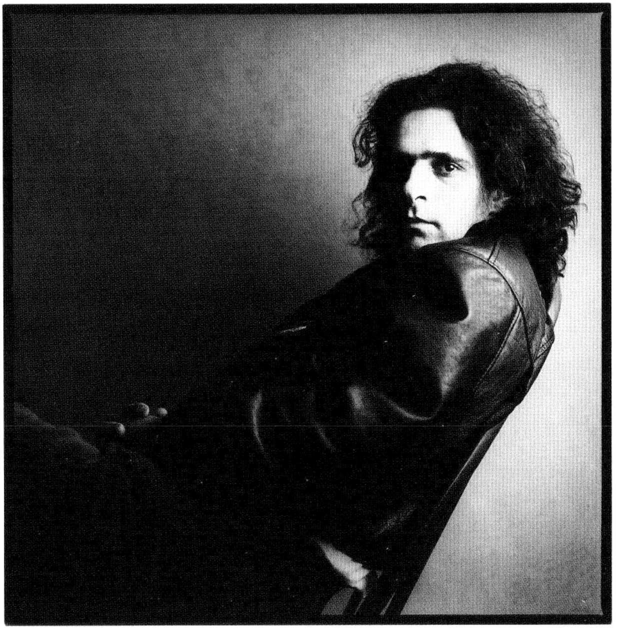

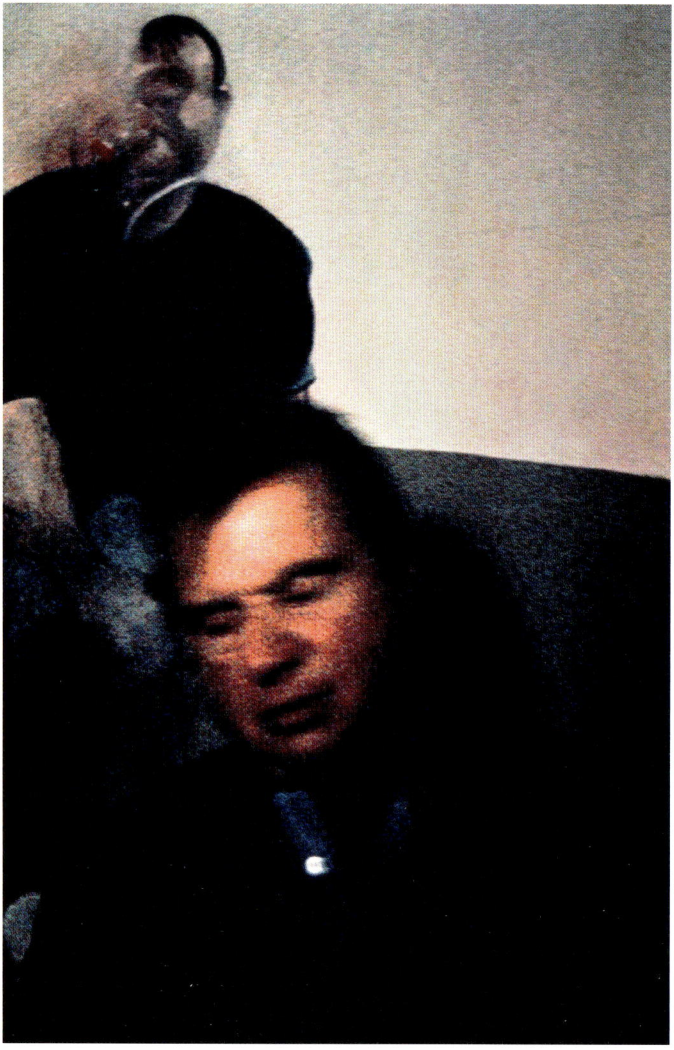

FRANCIS BACON

(1909–92)

Guy Bourdin, 1986

MORRISSEY

(b.1959)

Nick Knight, 1985

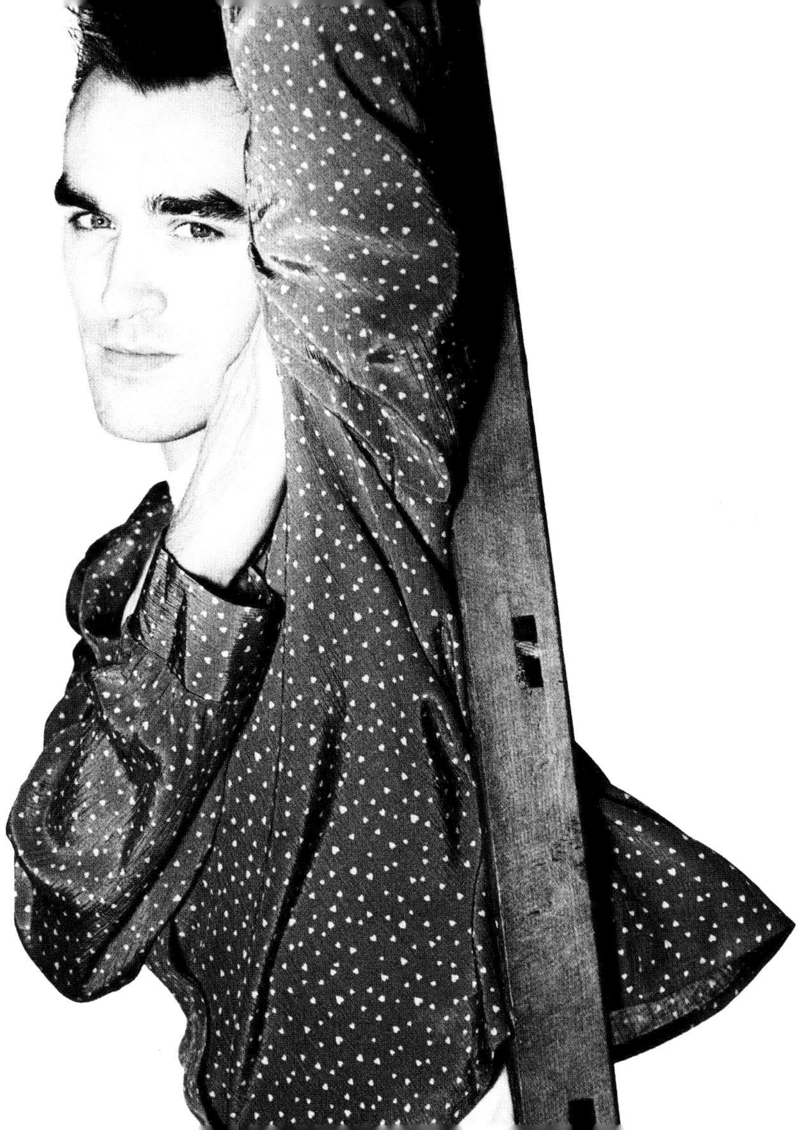

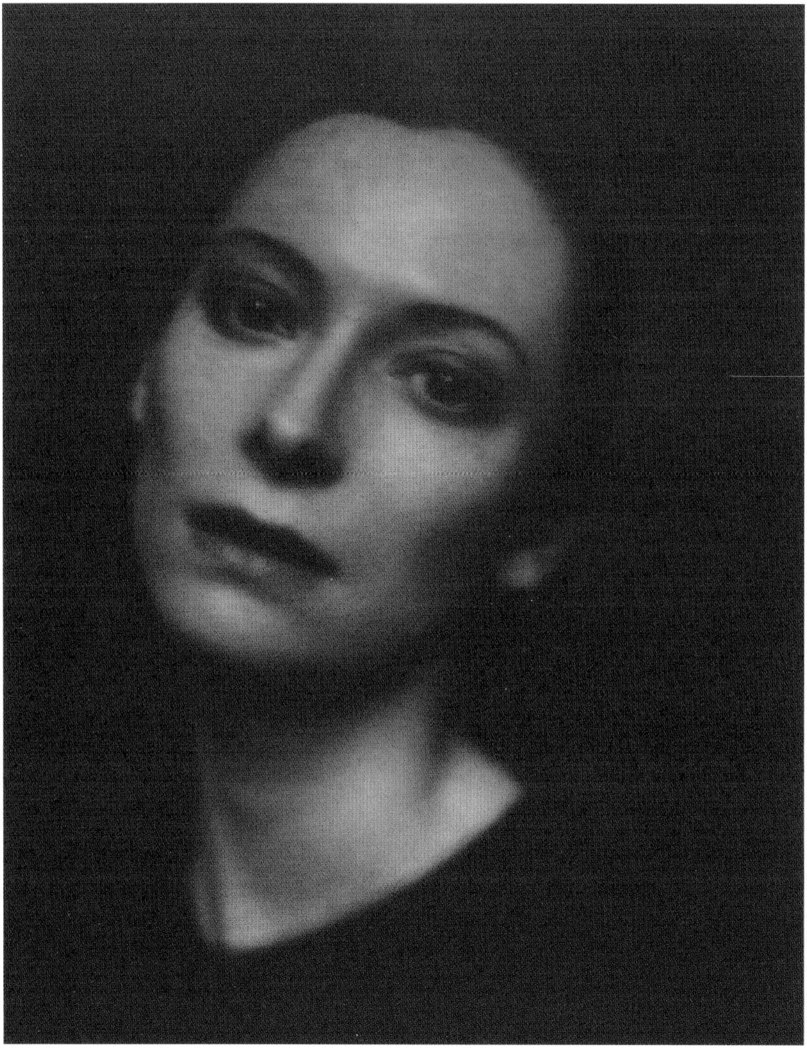

TILDA SWINTON

(b.1961)

The Douglas Brothers, 1992

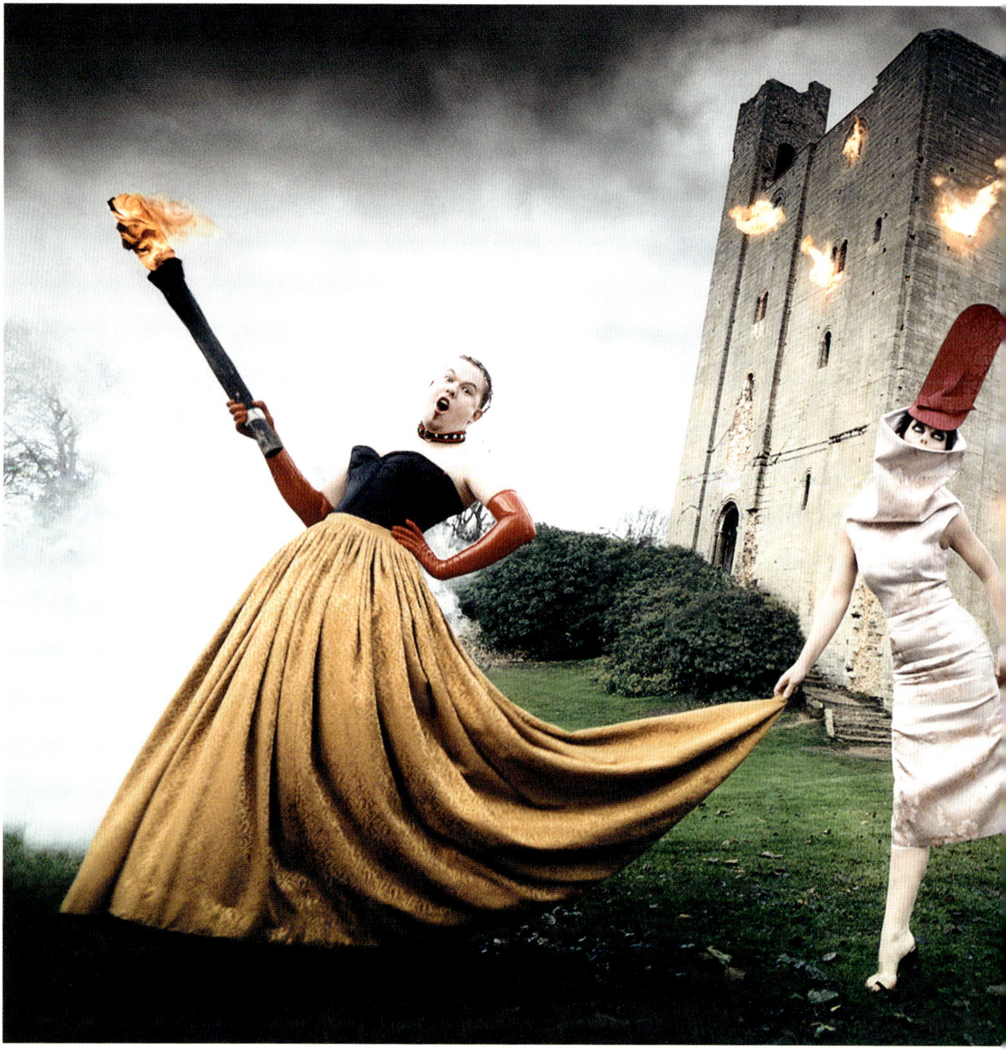

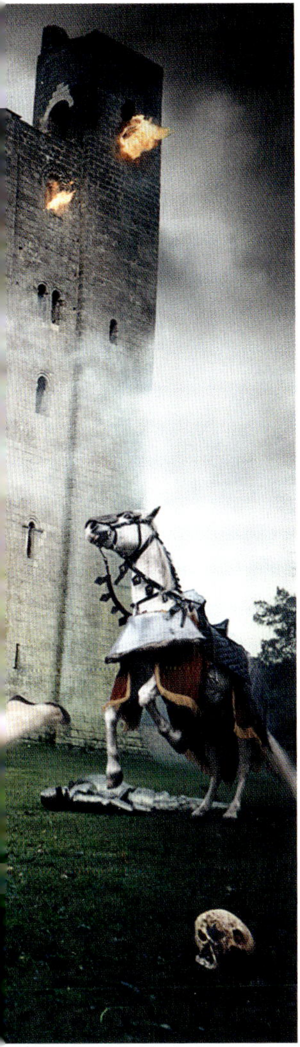

ALEXANDER MCQUEEN (1969–2010) AND ISABELLA BLOW (1958–2007)
David LaChapelle, 1996

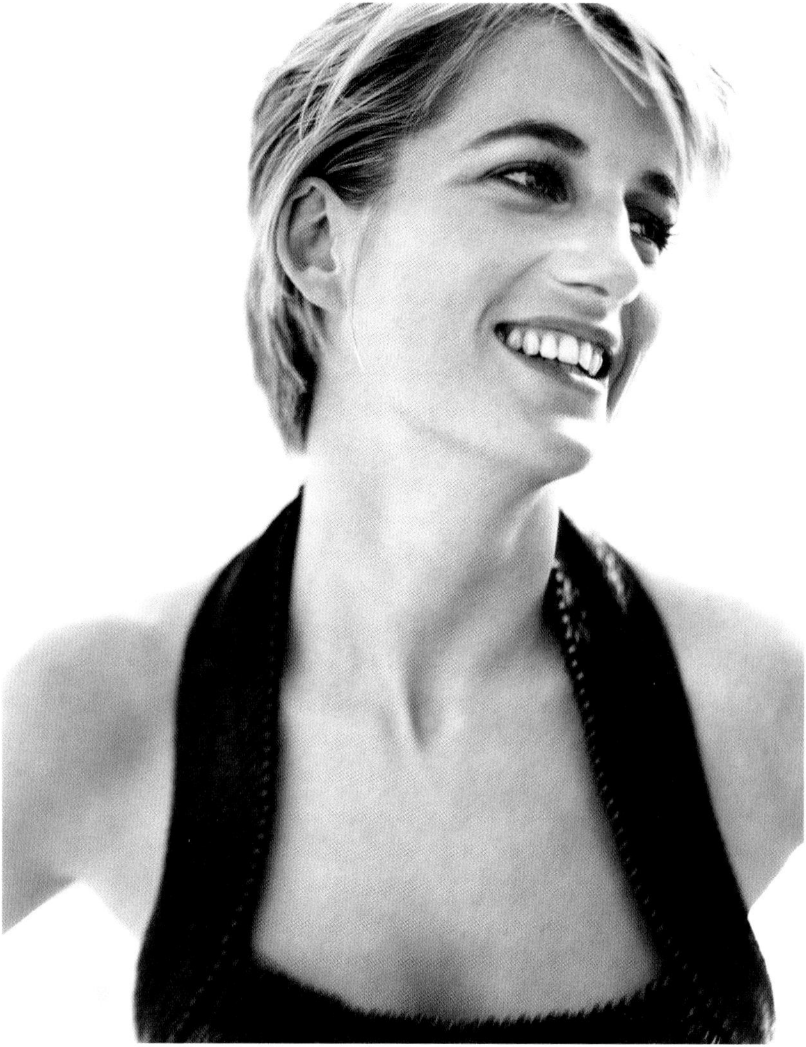

DIANA, PRINCESS OF WALES
(1961–97)
Mario Testino, 1997

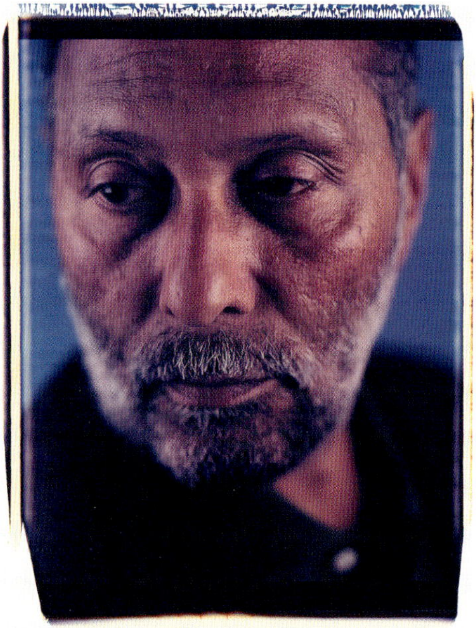

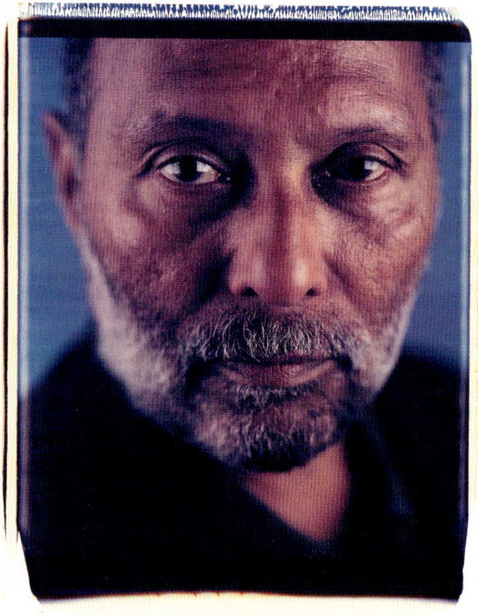

ABOVE

STUART HALL

(1932–2014)

Dawoud Bey, 1998

OPPOSITE

J.K. ROWLING

(b.1965)

Neil Wilder, 1999

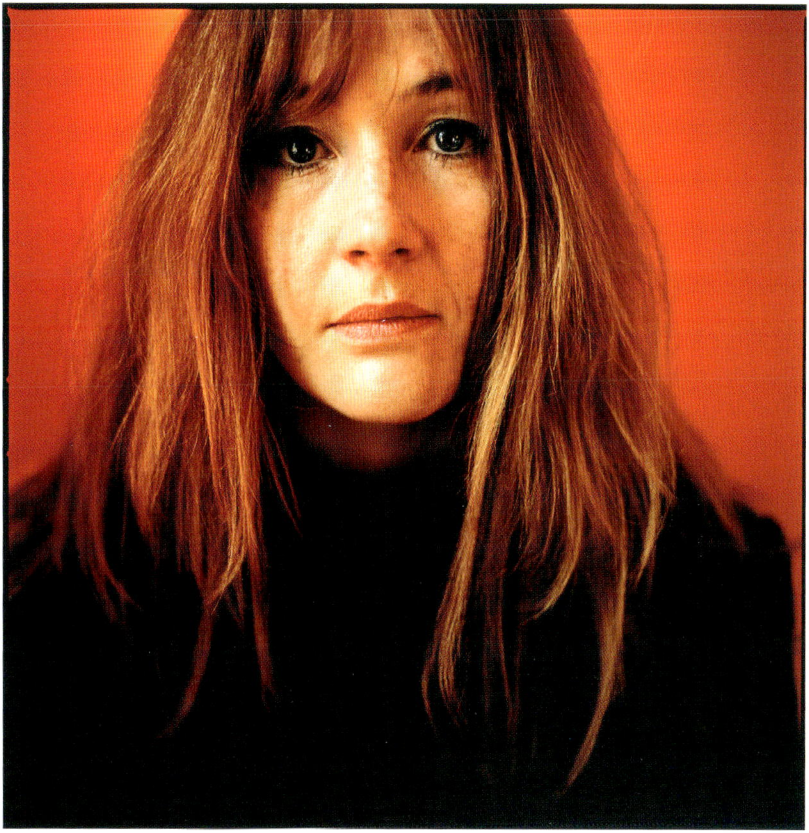

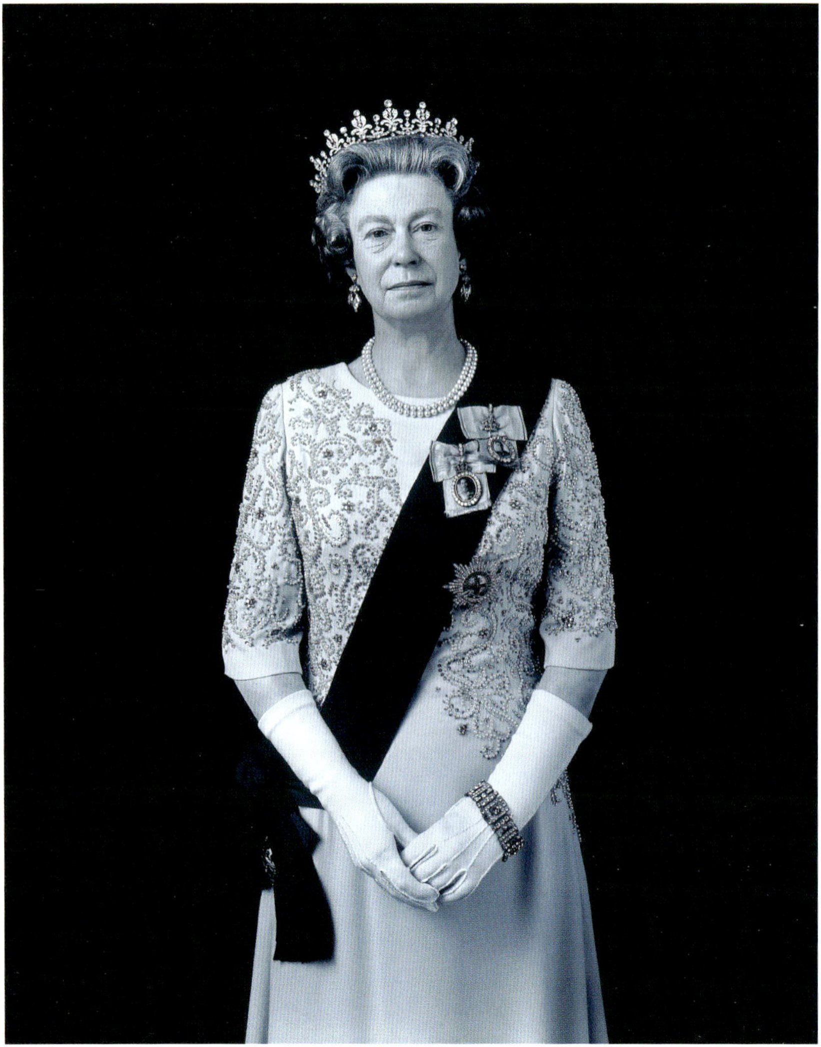

QUEEN ELIZABETH II

(b.1926)

Hiroshi Sugimoto, 1999

PETER SAVILLE

(b.1955)

Wolfgang Tillmans, 2002

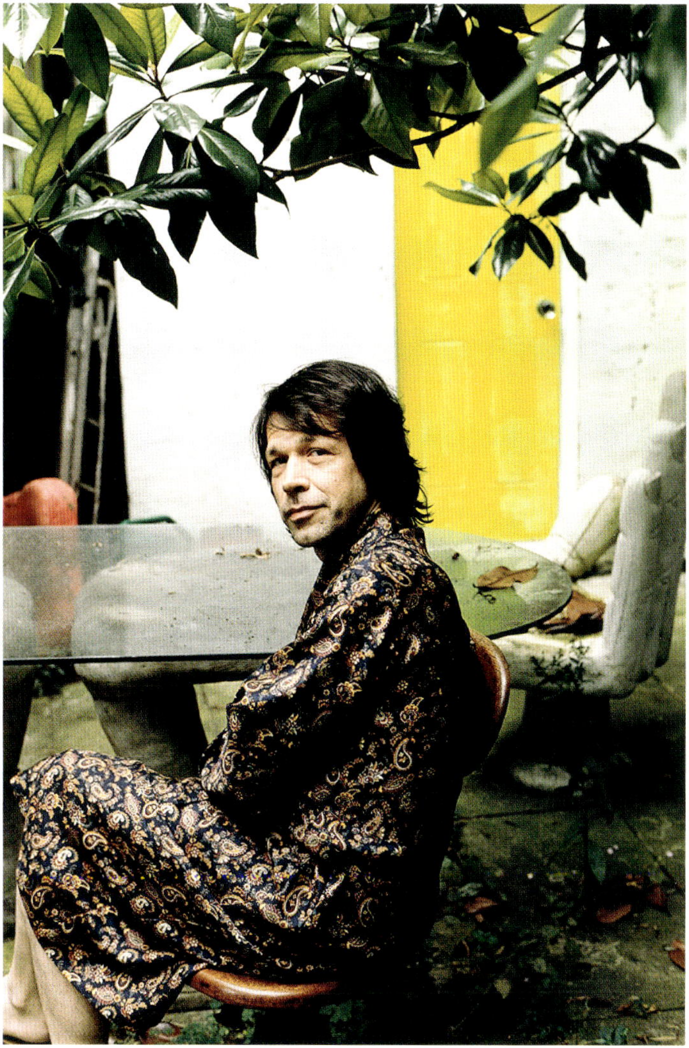

LEFT

STELLA MCCARTNEY

(b.1971)

Mary McCartney, 1998

OPPOSITE

LILY ALLEN

(b.1985)

Nadav Kander, 2008

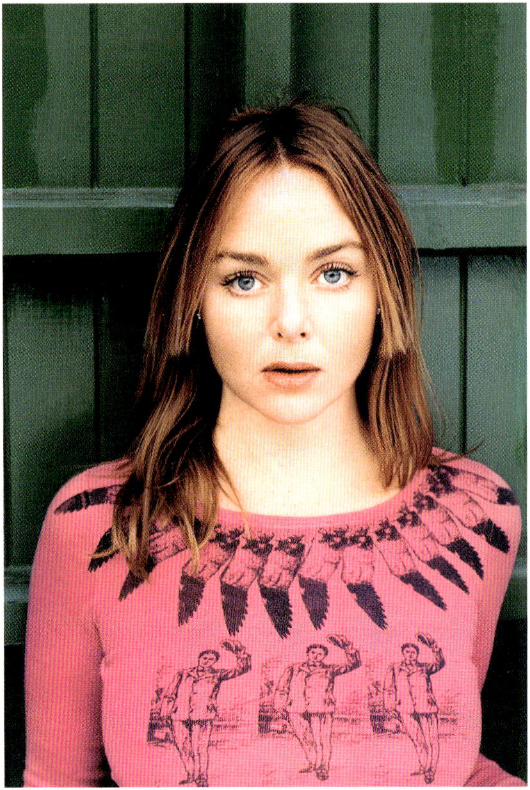

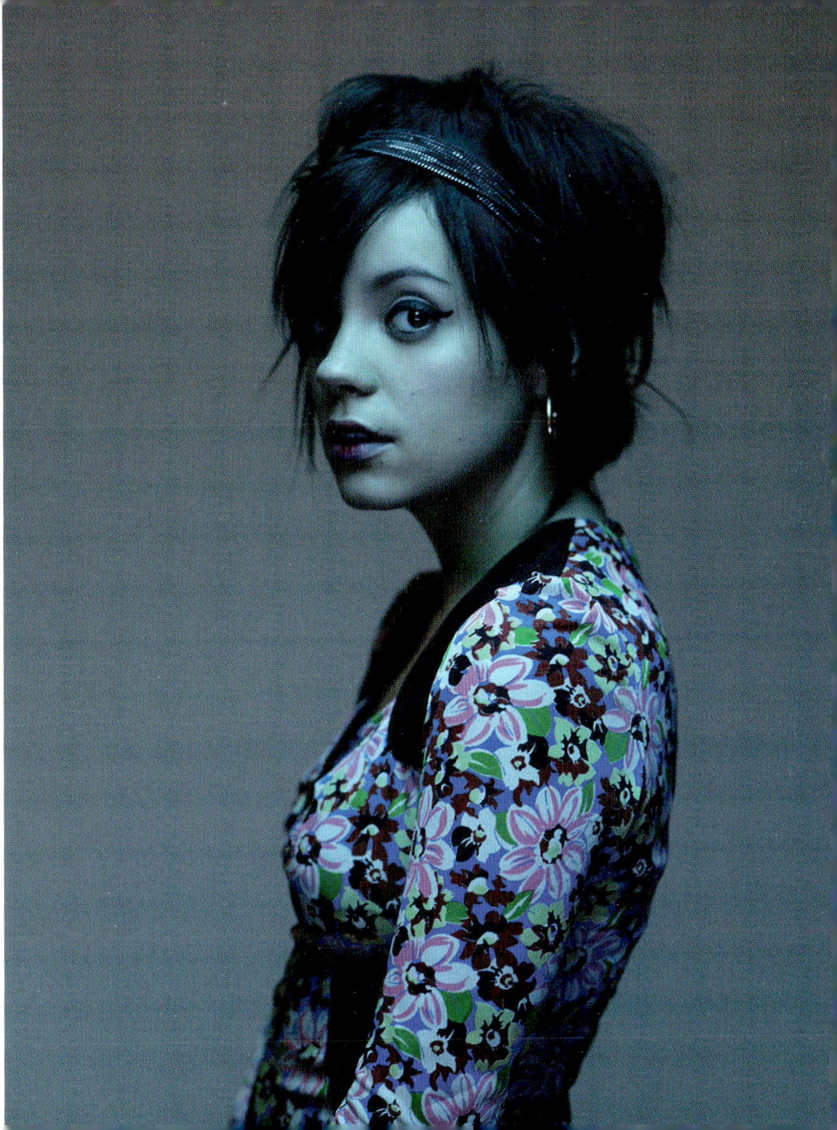

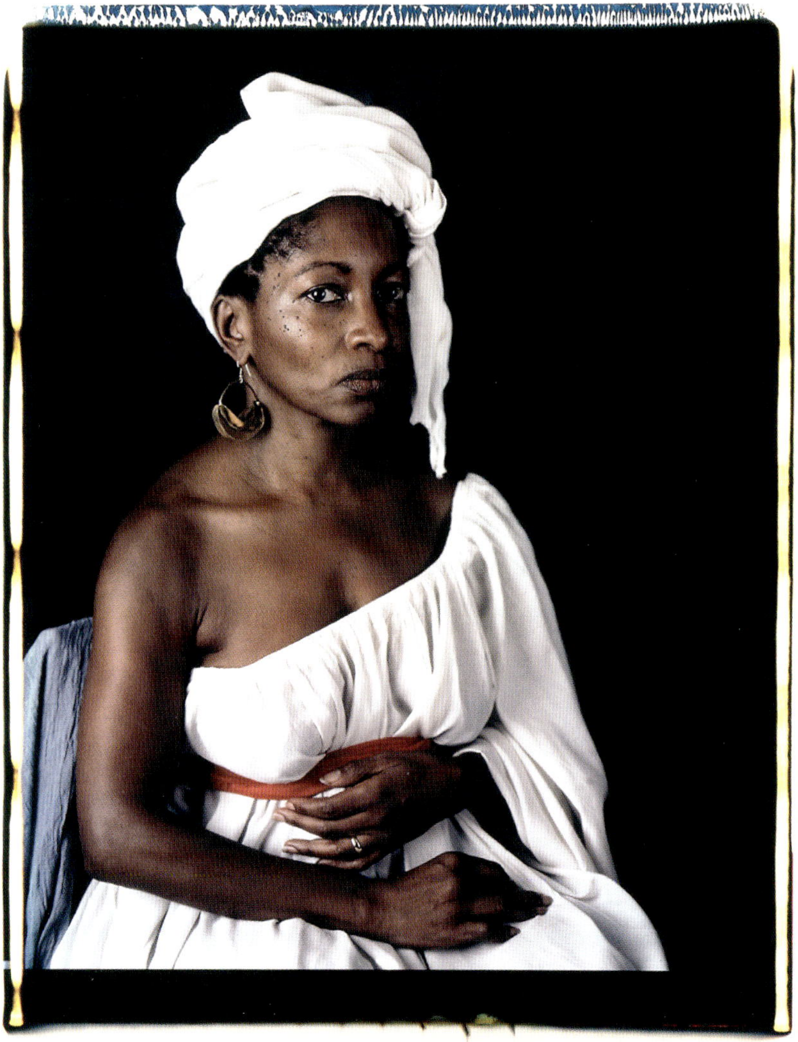

OPPOSITE

BONNIE GREER

(b.1948)

Maud Sulter, 2002

RIGHT

BENEDICT CUMBERBATCH

(b.1976)

Spencer Murphy, 2010

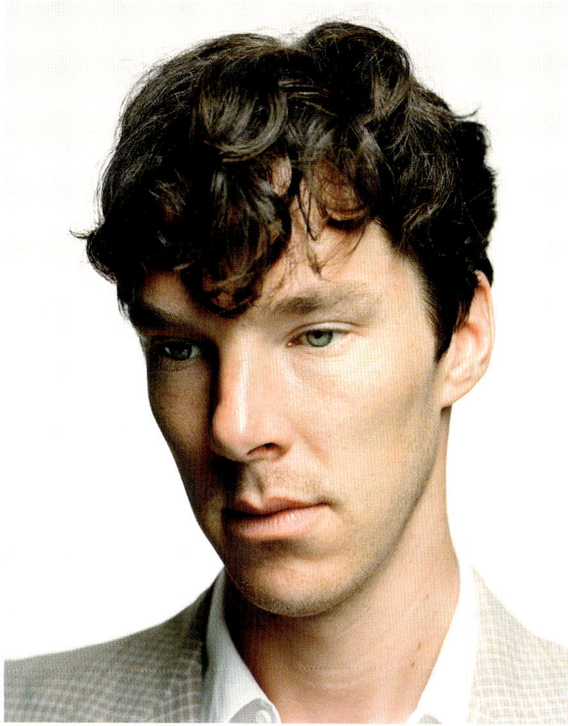

AMY WINEHOUSE

(1983–2011)

Charles Moriarty, 2003

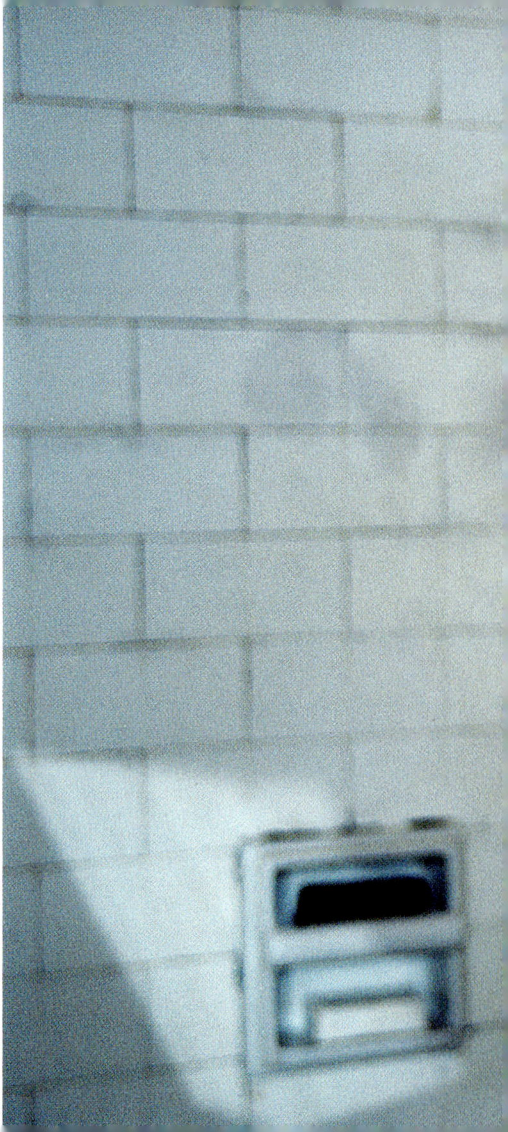

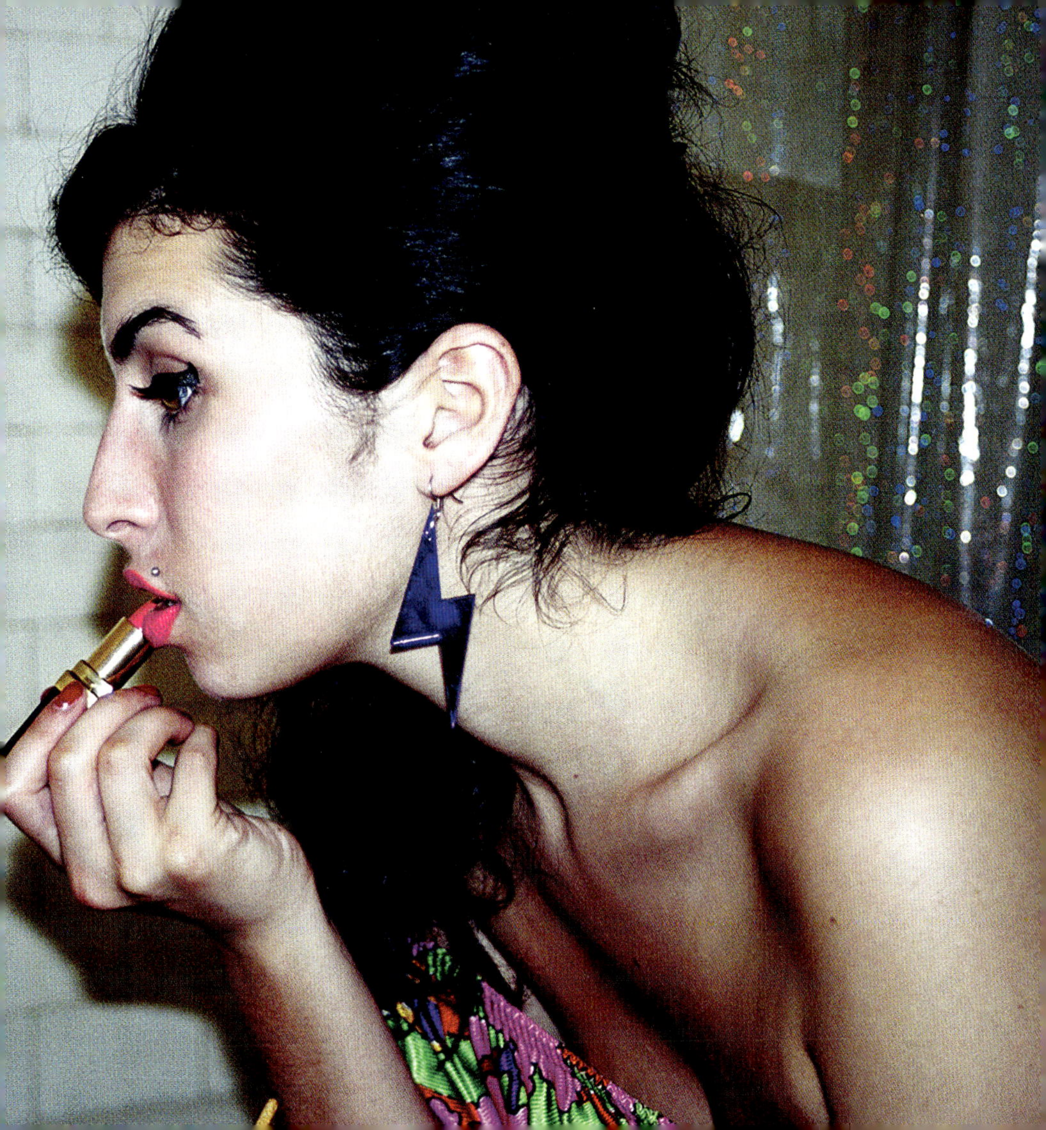

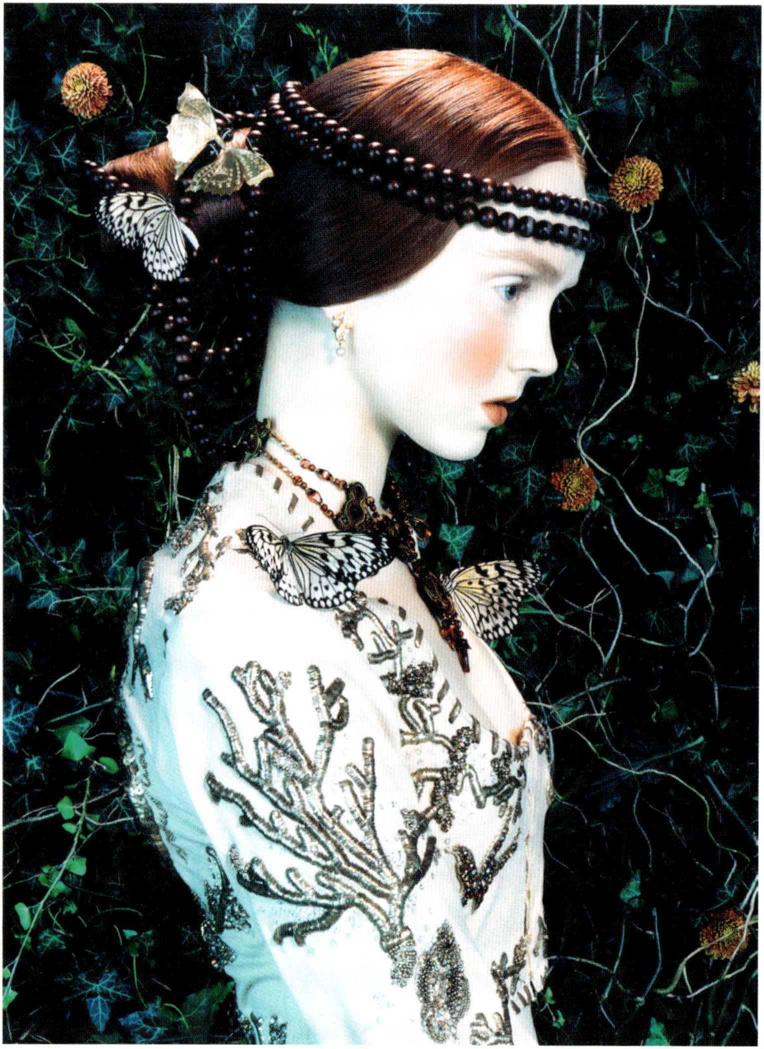

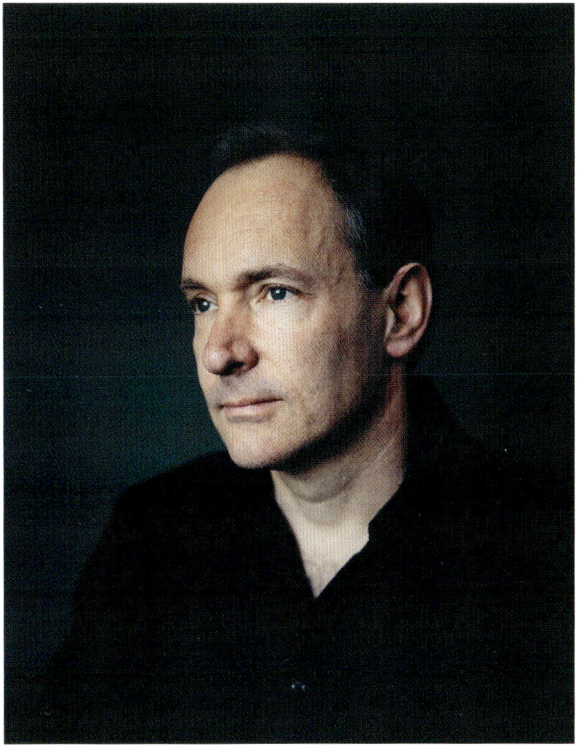

OPPOSITE

LIKE A PAINTING
(LILY COLE)
(b.1987)
Miles Aldridge, 2005

RIGHT

SIR TIM BERNERS-LEE
(b.1955)
Adam Broomberg and Oliver Chanarin, 2005

KATE MOSS

(b.1974)

Corinne Day, 2006

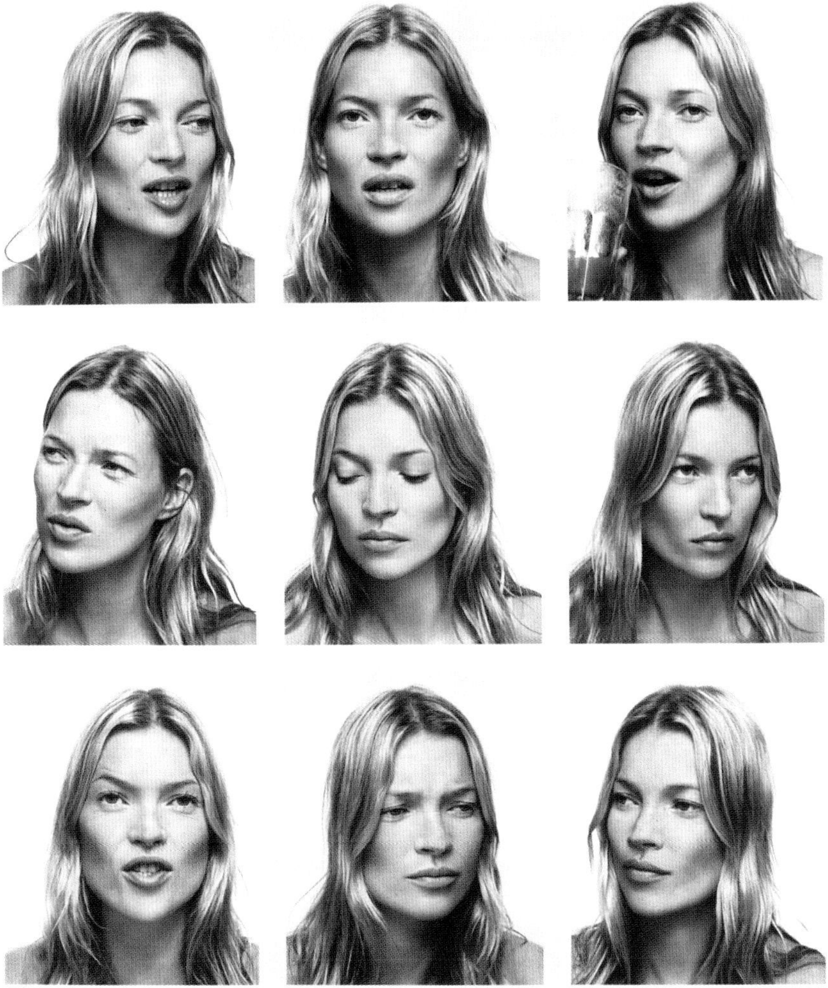

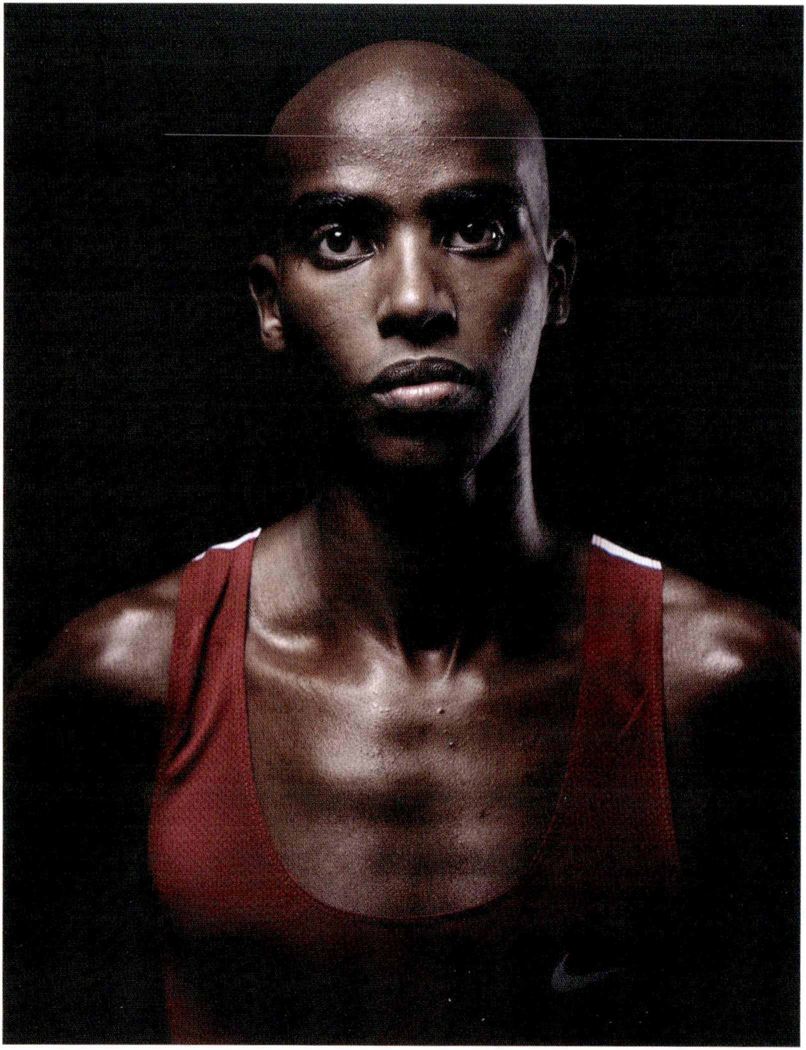

OPPOSITE

SIR MO FARAH

(b.1983)

Kate Peters, 2012

RIGHT

ADELE

(b.1988)

Julian Broad, 2008

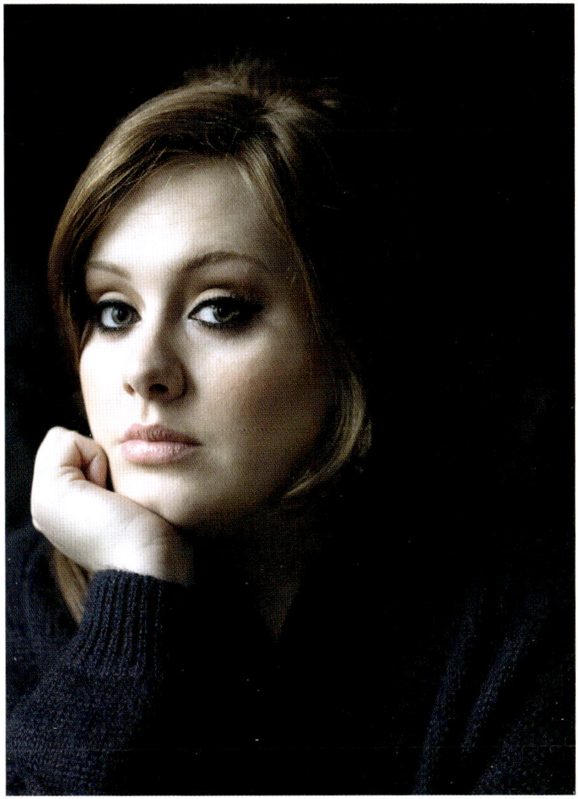

HANNAH WHELAN (b.1992),
JENNIFER PINCHES (b.1994),
BETH TWEDDLE (b.1985) AND
REBECCA TUNNEY (b.1996)
Anderson & Low, 2011

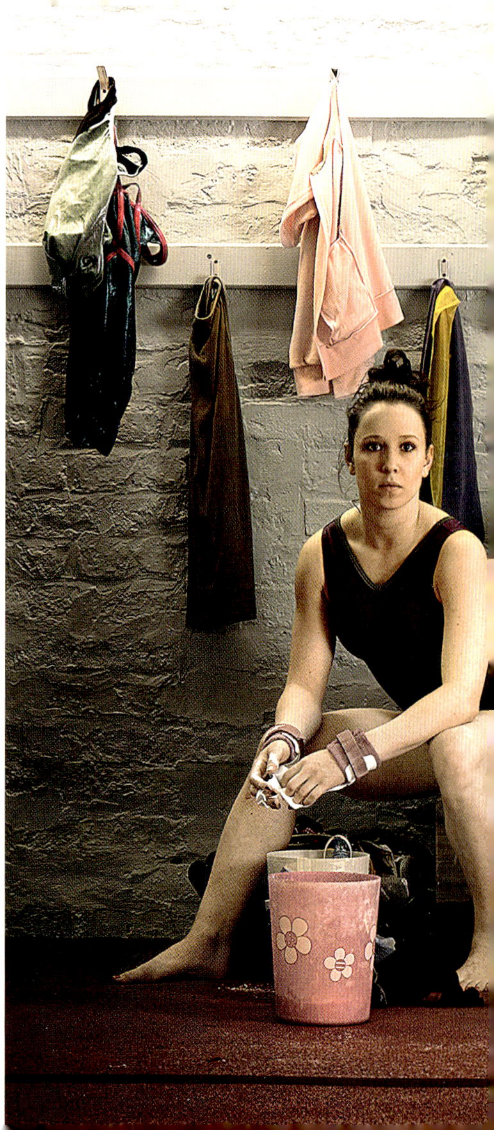

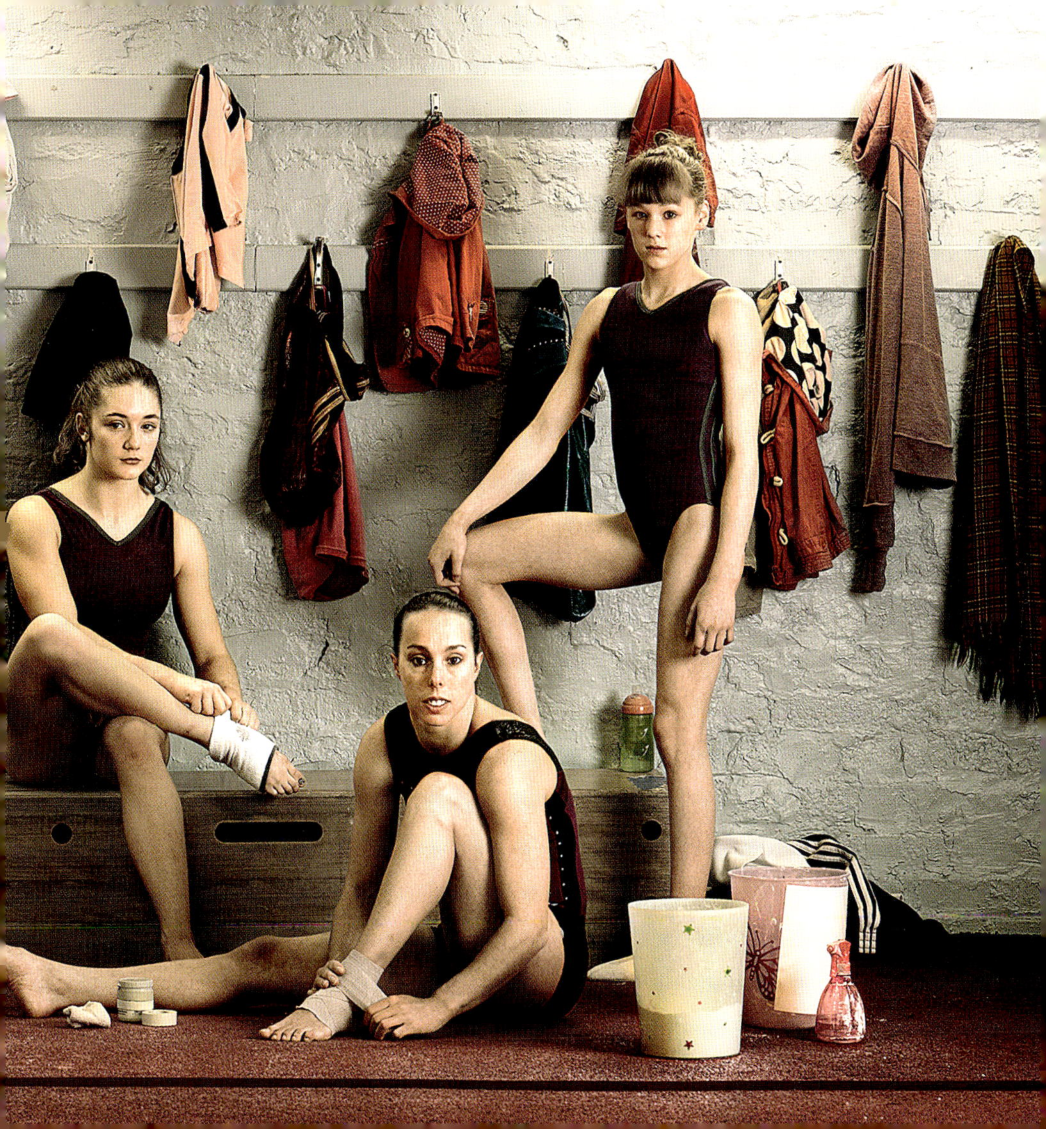

BELOW

SIR DAVID ATTENBOROUGH

(b.1926)

Sam Barker, 2015

OPPOSITE

CATE BLANCHETT

(b.1969)

Rineke Dijkstra, 2008

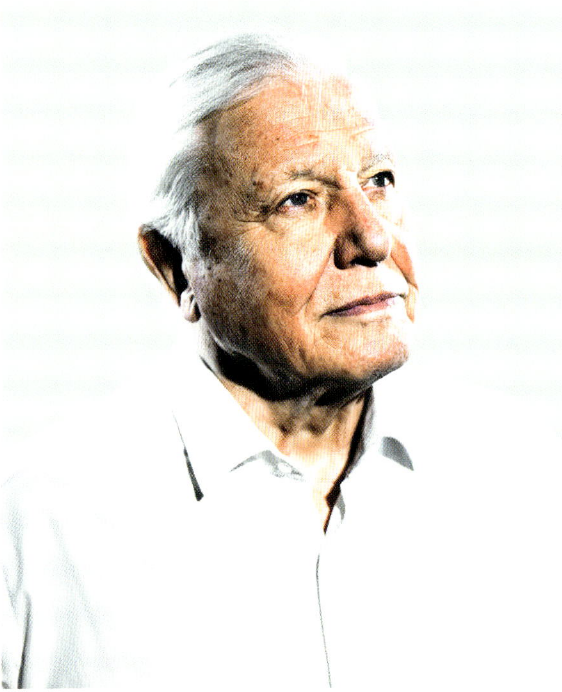

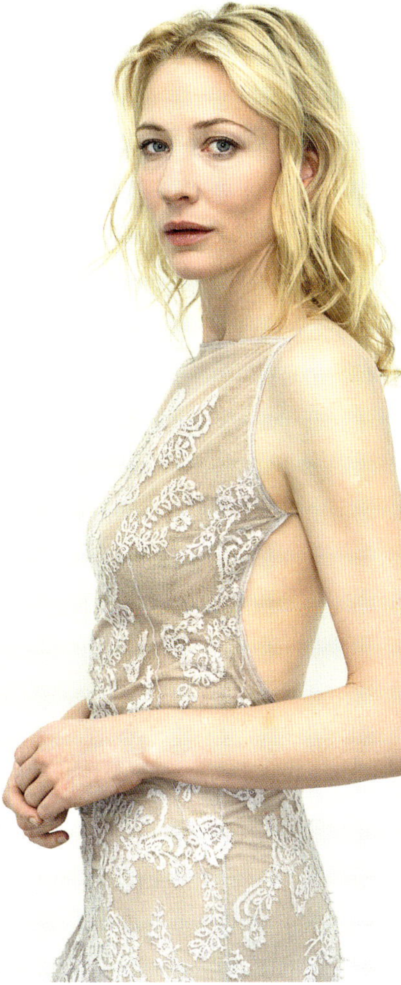

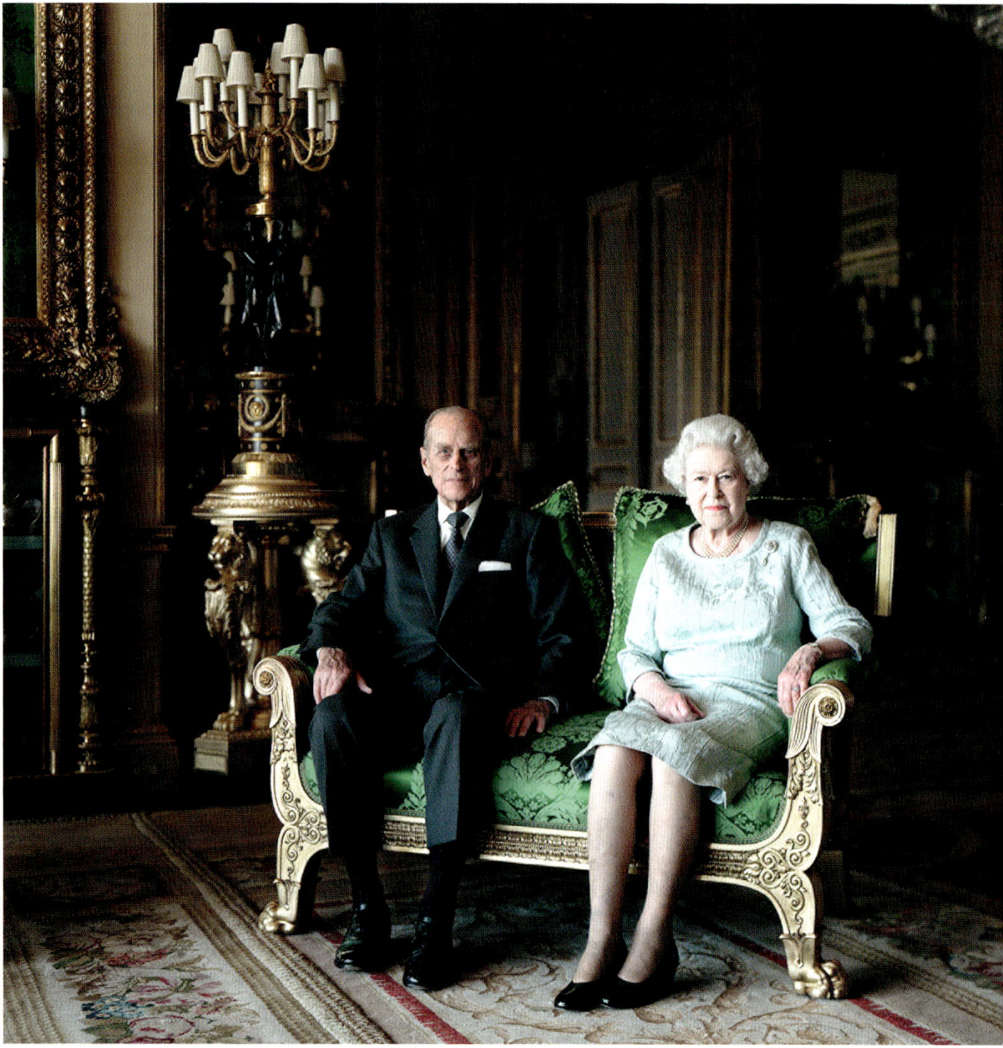

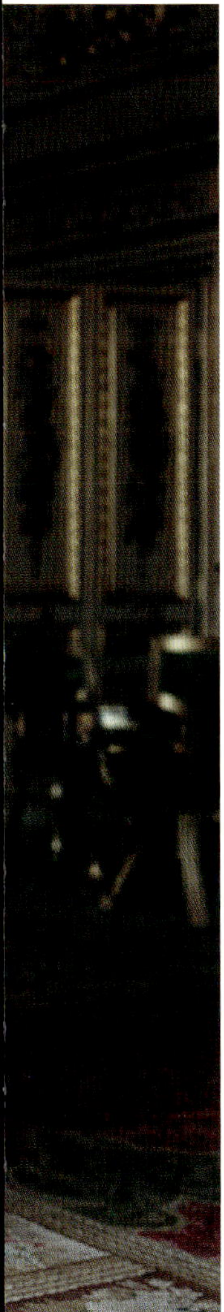

QUEEN ELIZABETH II (b.1926) *AND THE DUKE OF EDINBURGH* (b.1921), *WINDSOR CASTLE, 2011*
Thomas Struth, 2011

DAME VIVIENNE WESTWOOD

(b.1941)

Juergen Teller, 2014

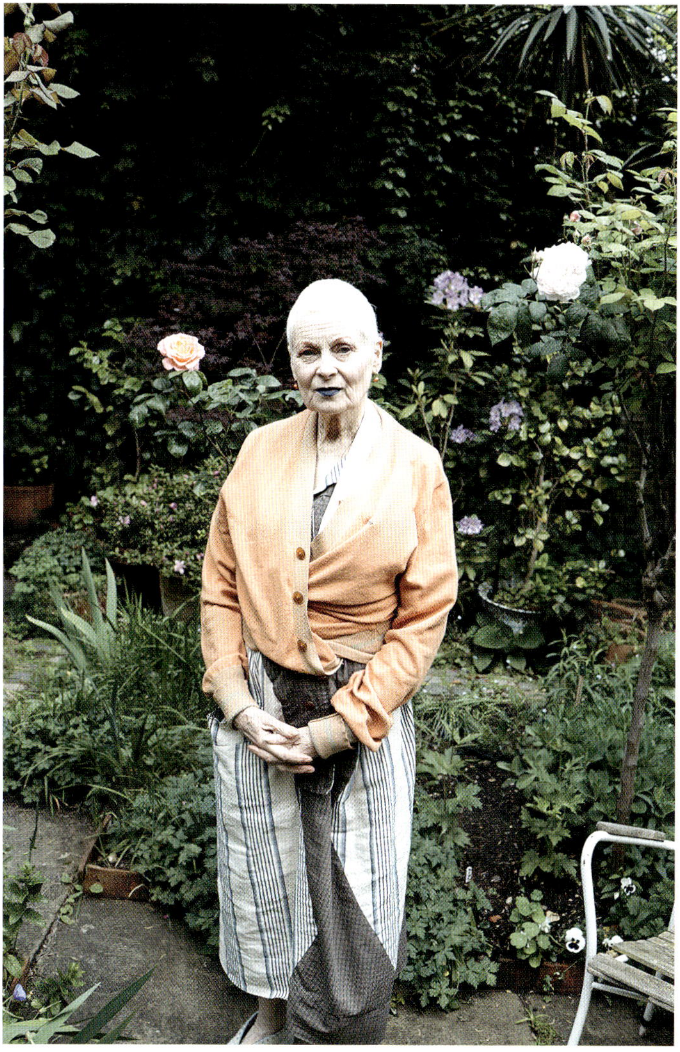

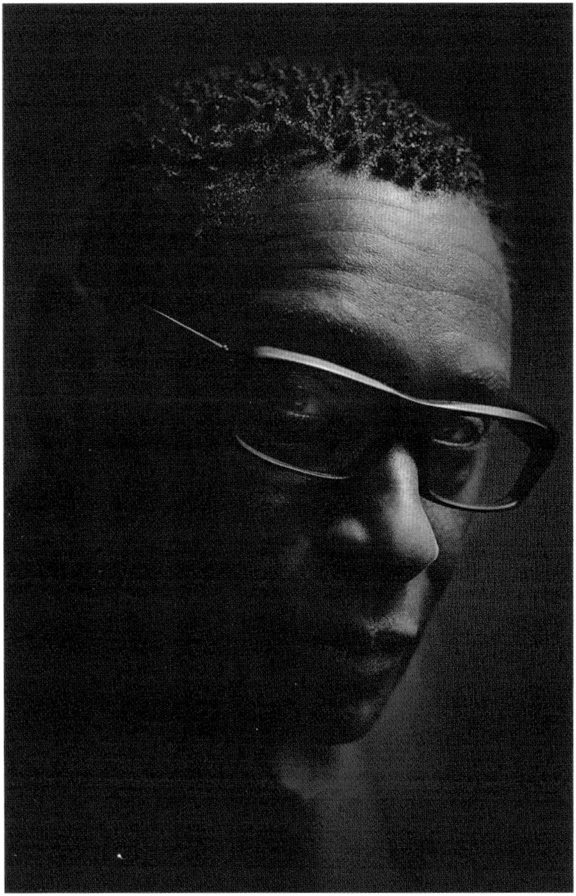

LEFT

DAVID HAREWOOD

(b.1965)

Simon Frederick, 2016

OPPOSITE

THANDIE NEWTON

(b.1972)

Simon Frederick, 2016

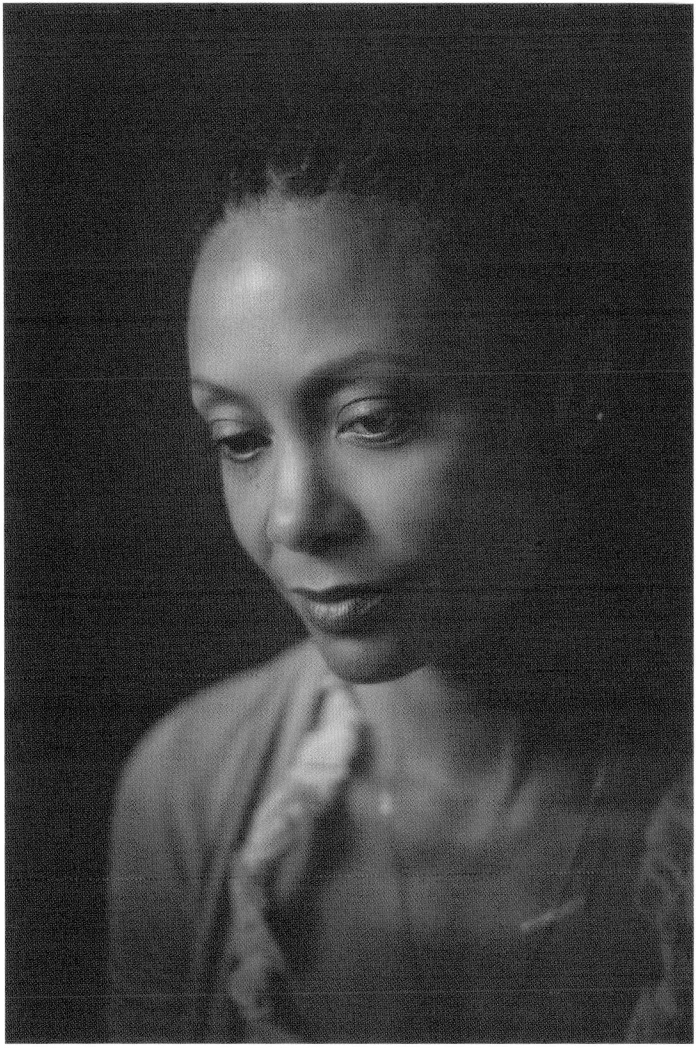

INVOCATION

Adam Fuss, 2013

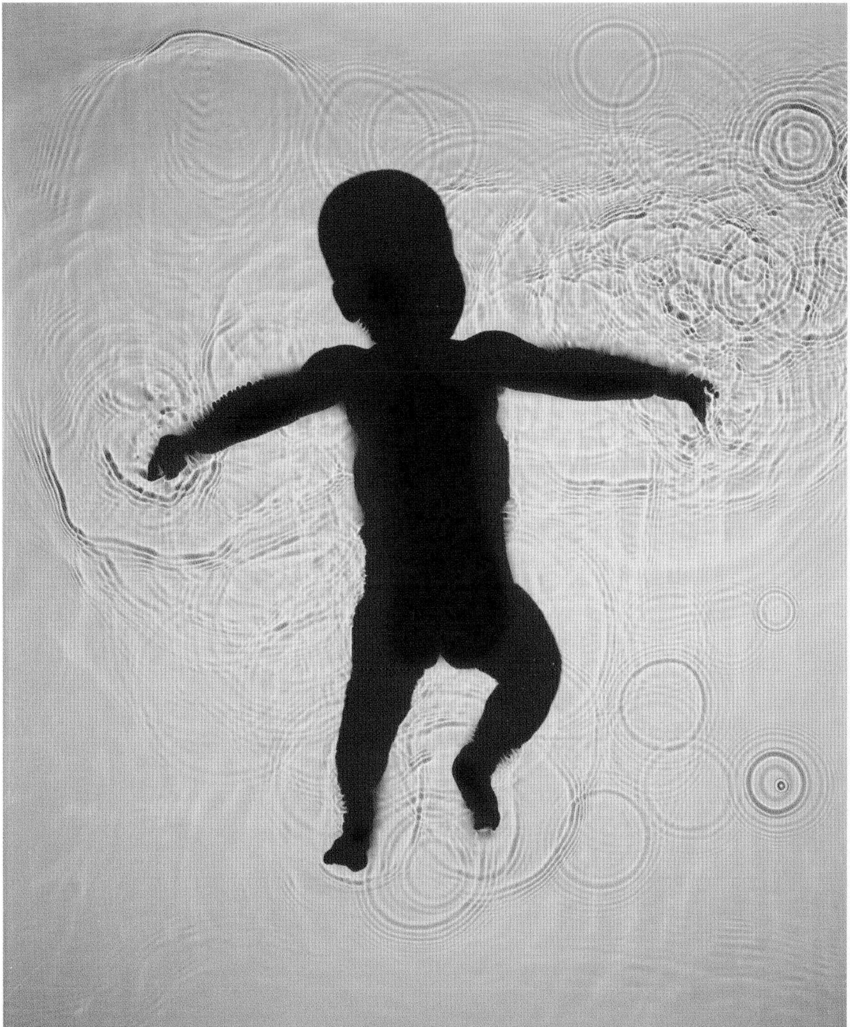

CAPTIONS

UNKNOWN CHILDREN
Marcus Adams, mid-1910s
Platinum print, 116 x 112mm
• NPG x199435
A work of understated beauty, this portrait by Marcus Adams (1875–1959) is notable for its carefully considered use of light and composition. The unusual juxtaposition of the girls' faces presents them as equals, while the light draws attention to details such as the sheen of the delicately tied satin bow, or the curl of hair resting on the intricate lace dress – a thread that symbolically connects the two young sitters in this image. Adams was a renowned photographer of children, taking the first official photograph of the future Queen Elizabeth II in 1926.

VIVIEN LEIGH
Madame Yevonde, 1936
Colour dye-transfer print, printed later, 484 x 317mm • NPG P742 (detail)
British actress Vivien Leigh (1913–67) became a household name playing Scarlett O'Hara in the Hollywood film *Gone with the Wind* (1939). Her marriage the following year to Laurence Olivier placed her at the heart of British theatre. Among many successes was her portrayal on stage and screen of Blanche DuBois in *A Streetcar Named Desire* (1951), which earned her a second Oscar. In this portrait, society photographer Madame Yevonde (1893–1975) exploits the intense colours produced by the Vivex process. This involved three quarter-plate negatives, separated into the colours magenta, cyan and yellow and recombined in printing. Yevonde stated: 'If we are going to have colour photographs, for heaven's sake let's have a riot of colour, none of your wishy-washy hand-tinted effects.'

ISABELLA BEETON
Maull & Polyblank, 1857
Hand-coloured albumen print, 184 x 149mm • NPG P3
Isabella Mayson (1836–65) married the editor and publisher Samuel Beeton in 1856 and worked with her husband as a journalist, writing fashion articles and notes on housekeeping for his periodicals. She was also the author of *Mrs Beeton's Book of Household Management* (1861). An essential guide to running a household, it enshrined Victorian ideas of a woman's role in the home, including advice on fashion, childcare, science and a large number of recipes. Revised and expanded many times, the book remains popular, but differs substantially from early editions. The National Portrait Gallery's albumen print was hand-coloured by Mrs Beeton's daughter, after the author died giving birth to her fourth child.

RUDYARD KIPLING
Walter Stoneman, 1924
Gelatin silver print, 160 x 114mm
• NPG x11899
Rudyard Kipling (1865–1936) was born in Bombay (now Mumbai), educated in England but returned to India and worked for *Civil and Military Gazette* in Lahore. His many publications include *Plain Tales from the Hills* (1888), *The Jungle Book* (1894) and *Kim* (1901). Later in life Kipling settled in Sussex, where he drew inspiration for fantasy books such as *Puck of Pook's Hill* (1906) and *Rewards and Fairies* (1910). The National Photographic Record began in 1917, during the First World War, at the instigation of Walter Stoneman (1876–1958), the chief photographer for the long-established firm of Russell & Sons. The Record was set up to

photograph every eminent British person. The portraits were mostly formulaic, half-length studio portraits, intended for reference purposes rather than display.

FREDERICK WILLIAM ROBERTSON
William Edward Kilburn, late 1840s
Hand-coloured, sixth-plate Daguerreotype, 70 x 57mm • NPG P1
Frederick William Robertson (1816–53), also known as Robertson of Brighton, was a charismatic Anglican preacher who served as perpetual curate of Trinity Chapel Brighton. He faced widespread political opposition for his embrace of democratisation across Europe, especially during the 'Spring of Nations' in 1848, around the time this photograph was made. Nevertheless, his appearances drew large and appreciative crowds, and his posthumously published sermons were widely read. William Edward Kilburn (1818–91) was one of the leading photographers in London at that time. He opened his portrait studio on Regent Street in 1846 and received a royal warrant in Daguerreotypy. He was famed for hand-coloured portraits such as this one, which were compared to painted portrait miniatures for their fineness and delicacy.

MISHAL HUSAIN
From *Today Everyday*
Nigel Shafran, 2017
Still from a single-channel video with audio component • NPG 7039
Running time: 14 mins (approx.)
Edited by Morena Mfuma and assisted by Jack Day
BBC Radio 4's daily current-affairs programme, *Today*, is one of the most popular radio shows in the country with over 7 million listeners a week. Launched on the BBC Home Service on 28 October 1957, it celebrated its sixtieth anniversary in 2017. Artist Nigel Shafran's *Today Everyday* features the five presenters of the programme; John Humphrys (b.1943), Sarah Montague, Lady Brooke (b.1966), Mishal Husain (b.1973), Justin Webb (b.1961) and Nick Robinson (b.1963). Shafran (b.1964) filmed in and around the *Today* studio over three days in July 2017, asking each presenter questions about their daily lives, interspersing these recollections with scenes of empty studios and workspaces. The audio element provides a paradoxical connection to the presenters' voices, which are normally associated with world affairs. Sometimes humorous and often tender, Shafran's work is celebrated for revealing poignant situations that at first appear incidental.

JENNY LIND AND MARIETTA ALBONI, COUNTESS PEPOLI
William Edward Kilburn, 1848
Hand-coloured, quarter-plate Daguerreotype, 115 x 89mm • NPG P956
Hand-coloured Daguerreotypes combined two demanding techniques – photography and miniature painting. Colouring was an extremely skilled task, often carried out by former miniaturists, who applied finely ground pigment to the plate using a dry brush. To highlight gold or silver jewellery worn by the sitter, real gold would often be used or the plate scratched away to reveal the silver underneath the emulsion. This hand-coloured Daguerreotype by William Kilburn (1818–91) of singers Jenny Lind (1820–87; left), known as 'the Swedish nightingale', and Marietta Alboni, Countess Pepoli (1823–94; right), is a remarkable example of outstanding artistic skill and meticulous craft.

SOLDIER
Antoine Claudet, 1842–4
Quarter-plate Daguerreotype, 107 x 82mm • NPG x199971
Named after its French inventor, Louis Daguerre, the Daguerreotype was the first photographic process to be announced to the public, in 1839. Each Daguerreotype is a unique, direct positive image on a highly polished, silvered copper plate. Early examples, like this one, were left–right reversed. Trained by Daguerre himself, Antoine Claudet (1797–1867) was among the first to practice Daguerreotype portraiture in England. In 1841 he established a portrait studio in London, on the roof of the Adelaide Gallery, behind St Martin-in-the-Fields Church, across the road from the National Portrait Gallery's current premises. This is where this portrait of an unknown soldier – who is most likely a Colour Sergeant of the Coldstream Guards – was made. He must have been a man of means, since to have a Daguerreotype portrait made, especially at this large size, was expensive. Claudet positioned the sitter in front of a painted background, making this one of the earliest known photographs with a studio backdrop.

THE MISSES GRIERSON
David Octavius Hill and Robert Adamson, *c.*1845
Calotype, 194 x 141mm • NPG P6(168)
David Octavius Hill (1802–70) and Robert Adamson (1821–48) entered into partnership in 1843, to found one of Scotland's first photographic studios. During their brief but fruitful association they produced some of the most

influential photographs of the 1840s, cut short only by the untimely death of Adamson at the age of twenty-six. While they are perhaps best known for using the new technology of photography to portray notable Scottish figures, they were also drawn to the subject of children, exploring the precious and fleeting state of childhood. In this double portrait, the young daughters of the Reverend James Grierson are pictured close beside one another, joining hands and seemingly occupied by something happening outside of the photographic frame. The relaxed, naturalistic quality of this portrait is remarkable for this period, when long exposure times often resulted in sitters appearing tense and wooden. In reality, by leaning on one another the two girls made themselves more stable, reducing blur.

SPIRIDIONE GAMBARDELLA
Attributed to Sir Anthony Coningham Sterling, *c.*1852
Calotype, 86 x 72mm • NPG P171(13)
During the new medium's first decades, photographic emulsions were painfully slow, requiring exposures of several seconds, even under bright lighting conditions. This presented a particular challenge in portraiture, as it is difficult for sitters to remain still for such long periods of time. This photograph is all the more remarkable, then, as Sir Anthony Coningham Sterling (1805–71), or someone in his circle, seems to have captured the Italian painter Spiridione Gambardella (*c.*1815–86) unaware, as if discovered on the street, with an authentic facial expression. Although the pose was almost certainly staged, the natural appearance of the sitter is unprecedented in photographic history. This photograph was originally found in a portrait album of members of the family of the philosopher Thomas Carlyle, his wife Jane, and their friends. In the variant P171(14), Gambardella poses with his son, Dion (1849–86).

SIR RICHARD ENGLAND
Roger Fenton, 1855
Salt print, 184 x 154mm • NPG Ax24911
In 1855 Roger Fenton (1819–69) was commissioned by the Manchester publisher Thomas Agnew & Sons to document the Crimean War, which pitted British, French, Ottoman and Sardinian allies in a war against Russia, for control of the Black Sea region. Widely regarded as the first war photographer, Fenton travelled under royal patronage and with the assistance of the British government. He produced some 360 photographs, none of which shows actual combat scenes. This was due to the slow photographic process of the time, but also a desire to avoid confronting Victorian sensibilities. Fenton instead produced portraits of those participating in the war, such as Sir Richard England (1793–1883). Sir Richard was an unlikely subject in some regards, since he had been briefly dismissed from the army for taking too many casualties during campaigns in Afghanistan in the 1840s. However, a need for fresh leaders resulted in his being called to action in Crimea, where he served doggedly, and left only when doctors said he could not continue, at around the same time this picture was made. In order to increase illumination on the subject and reduce exposure times, Fenton positioned England in front of the flaps of a white tent, which served as a makeshift light reflector.

THE OLD GARDENER SIMPSON AND HIS WIFE
George Washington Wilson, 1854
Albumen print, 102 x 96mm
• NPG P22(14) (detail)
In 1854, George Washington Wilson (1823–93) was invited to photograph the royal estate at Balmoral, Scotland, where he produced portraits of the royal family and household. Unusually, Wilson photographed the families of foresters and gillies that worked there; people who would not have been deemed worthy of painted portraits, but could now be immortalised through photography. Portraits such as this offer a unique window into the life of the estate. The folded arms of the gardener, Simpson, and the clasped hands of his wife make the sitters look impatient; more probably, given the long exposure times necessary to make such a picture, they were intended to minimise blur. The layer of albumen (egg-white solution) that binds the photographic emulsion to the paper gives a smooth surface that adds to its highly detailed, jewel-like appearance.

ISAMBARD KINGDOM BRUNEL
Robert Howlett, 1857
Albumen print, 286 x 225mm
• NPG P112
Robert Howlett (1831–58) posed the legendary engineer Isambard Kingdom Brunel (1806–59) standing confidently in front of the launching chains of one of his most ambitious and frustrating projects, the grand ocean steamship *Great Eastern*. After numerous delays, the ship would not be launched until a year after this picture was made, and suffered a crippling explosion during its maiden voyage. Designed by Brunel himself, it was five times the size of its nearest rival,

and revolutionary in design and construction. This portrait was taken as part of a series of photographs commissioned to document the building of the vessel. (The most familiar photograph from the series is shown here with the variants P662 and P1979 – the latter a stereoscopic slide.) The decision to show Brunel standing against the chains, and not near the hull or on the deck of the ship itself, was inspired. The contrast in scale reinforces the seemingly superhuman power of Victorian engineering, but it also humanises Brunel, showing him dwarfed in front of one of his own creations.

EDITH, INA AND ALICE LIDDELL
Lewis Carroll (Charles Lutwidge Dodgson), 1858
Albumen print, 156 x 176mm
• P991(4) (detail)
Edith (1854–76), Ina (1849–1930) and Alice (1852–1934) Liddell were daughters of Henry Liddell, Dean of Christ Church, Oxford. Following their father's appointment in 1855, the family moved to Oxford, where they lived on the college grounds. During this time, the Liddells befriended Lewis Carroll (1832–98), a lecturer in mathematics at the college and a keen amateur photographer. Carroll specialised in portraiture, especially of children, and Alice quickly became one of his favourite sitters. She was later made famous by Carroll as the title character in *Alice's Adventures in Wonderland* (1865), while Edith and Ina provided inspiration for the characters of 'Eaglet' and 'Lory'.

UNKNOWN YOUNG WOMAN
Oscar Gustaf Rejlander, 1863–6
Albumen print, 205 x 149mm
• NPG P2011(26)
Oscar Rejlander (1813–75) made a name for himself in the 1850s as the creator of composite photographs, combining two or more negatives to create artificial compositions. For this reason he is often described as 'the father of Photoshop', as computer technologies have now made such pictures commonplace. However, in the late 1850s and 1860s Rejlander turned his attention to expressive portraiture, becoming one of the most naturalistic photographers of the time. He inspired the photographers Julia Margaret Cameron and Lewis Carroll, and provided so-called 'photographic studies' to painters, including the Pre-Raphaelites and their associates, such as John Everett Millais, G.F. Watts, and Dante Gabriel Rossetti. This picture of a pensive young woman is one of seventy-one photographs by Rejlander contained in an album purchased by the National Portrait Gallery in 2015. An inscription in the album records that it was lent to both Prince Albert and Pope Pius IX.

JAMES PINSON LABULO DAVIES AND SARAH FORBES BONETTA
Camille Silvy, 1862
Albumen print, 108 x 129mm
• NPG Ax61385 (detail)
Sarah Forbes Bonetta (1843–80; 'Mrs Davies') was born of Yoruba descent in West Africa, where she was captured at the age of five during the Okeadon War. She was thought to be of royal lineage and was presented to Queen Victoria, as if a gift from King Gezo of Dahomey (now Benin). Sarah was named after Captain Frederick E. Forbes of the Royal Navy, who brought her to England, aboard his ship HMS *Bonetta*. As Queen Victoria's protégée, Bonetta was brought up among the British upper class, and educated in both England and Sierra Leone. She became an accomplished pianist and linguist. In 1862 at St Nicholas's Church in Brighton she married the merchant and philanthropist James Pinson Labulo Davies (1828–1906). This photograph is one of several that were taken to mark their marriage. Davies was born in Sierra Leone to Nigerian parents and enlisted with the Royal Navy. He is credited with pioneering cocoa farming in West Africa. The couple returned to Africa soon after their wedding. Queen Victoria was godmother to their first child, Victoria, who later attended Cheltenham Ladies' College. The photographs are pasted into one of the daybooks that record the work of Camille Silvy (1834–1910), one of the most successful portrait photographers in London at the time.

CHARLES DICKENS
John & Charles Watkins, 1863
Albumen print, 203 x 163mm
• NPG x14339
Charles Dickens (1812–70) is widely regarded as the greatest novelist of the Victorian era. His writings vividly portray the class system of the period, addressing social deprivation and injustice. This photograph shows Dickens in a pensive mood, and was taken at a time when he had suffered two family bereavements, losing his second son, Walter, who died in India, and also his mother. A detail from this image was produced as a carte-de-visite, which could be bought cheaply by the public, satisfying an insatiable demand for Dickens's portrait.

G.F. WATTS
David Wilkie Wynfield, 1863
Albumen print, 210 x 160mm • NPG P86
One of the most celebrated painters of

the Victorian period, George Frederic Watts (1817–1904) is known for his allegorical and history works, in addition to his portraits – most notably his 'Hall of Fame' series, of which the National Portrait Gallery holds almost fifty canvases. This portrait of Watts by David Wilkie Wynfield (1837–87) is one of a series featuring leading artists and writers whom he represented wearing historical dress, in large, arresting close-ups. Victorian pioneer photographer Julia Margaret Cameron credited Wynfield as a major influence, and many qualities now associated with her work can be found in his portraits.

CHARLES DARWIN
Julia Margaret Cameron, 1868
Albumen print, 330 x 256mm • NPG P8
The naturalist, geologist and biologist Charles Darwin (1809–82) made a meticulous survey of life-forms and the conditions that governed their evolution in his book *On the Origin of Species by Means of Natural Selection* (1859). He also wrote important works on botany, zoology and geology. In the summer of 1868, Darwin and his family rented a cottage on the Isle of Wight from the Camerons and it was then that he sat for this portrait. Julia Margaret Cameron (1815–79) took up photography as an amateur in 1863 at the age of forty-eight, when her daughter and son-in-law gave her a sliding-box camera, and she became one of the leading photographers of the nineteenth century. She was a pioneer in her artistic vision, concerned from the beginning of her career with the relationship between art and photography.

OSCAR WILDE
Napoleon Sarony, 1882
Albumen panel card, 305 x 184mm
• P25 (detail)
Dublin-born dramatist, writer and wit Oscar Wilde (1854–1900) was renowned as an aesthete from an early age. His unconventional behaviour, witty and paradoxical remarks and dandified pose brought him notoriety. In 1882 Wilde embarked on a lecture tour of North America. Shortly after his arrival in New York, he posed for a series of extravagant portraits by Napoleon Sarony (1821–96), including this one. Later, Wilde's period of greatest creativity, including the publication of *The Picture of Dorian Gray* (1891) and a succession of stage comedies culminating in *The Importance of Being Earnest* (1895), was cut short by two years' imprisonment with hard labour as a result of his then-illegal love affair with Lord Alfred Douglas.

ADELAIDE PASSINGHAM
Eveleen Myers, early 1890s
Platinum print, 293 x 222mm
• NPG Ax36315
As a child, Eveleen Myers (1856–1937) had posed for the celebrated photographer Julia Margaret Cameron. Visits to Cameron's studio may have inspired Myers to take up photography in 1888. This evocative portrait of Adelaide Passingham (1867–1954), simply posed with her hair loose, is one of Myers's early successes, and appears to have been inspired by Cameron's style. Myers used the medium primarily to record her children, but also set up a studio in the family home, Leckhampton House in Cambridge, where she made portraits of eminent contemporaries.

AUBREY BEARDSLEY
Frederick Henry Evans, 1894
Platinum print, 149 x 105mm
• NPG P115 (detail)
This portrait of the illustrator Aubrey Beardsley (1872–98) was taken by his friend and patron Frederick Henry Evans (1852–1943) at the time when the young artist was gaining notoriety for his scandalous illustrations for the first English-language edition of Oscar Wilde's *Salomé*, published in 1894. Evans took up photography in the mid-1880s while running a bookshop in Cheapside, London. He is reported to have spent hours studying Beardsley, wondering how best to approach his subject. In this carefully lit composition, Beardsley peers out from under his combed fringe, highlighting his delicate bone structure. Evans commented at the time that Beardsley's profile, also shown here in a variant pose (P114), reminded him of a gargoyle – much to Beardsley's pleasure.

UNKNOWN MAN
Cavendish Morton, 1900s
Platinum print, 154 x 110mm
• NPG x128847
In 1903 the first musical performed by a cast of black actors, *In Dahomey*, was staged in London. With music by Will Marion Cook, lyrics by Paul Laurence Dunbar and book by Jesse A. Shipp (all three of whom were African-Americans), the show enjoyed huge success. The photographer Cavendish Morton (1874–1939) made several portraits of the cast members. In this photograph he focuses on the beauty of the sitter's profile and torso, and the use of light sensually delineates his features. Morton was born in New York to British parents and took up photography in the late 1890s, opening a studio in London at 60

Primrose Mansions, Battersea Park. He specialised in stage and society portraits and became a leading photographer of the Edwardian period.

VIRGINIA WOOLF
George Charles Beresford, 1902
Platinum print, 152 x 108mm
• NPG P221
George Charles Beresford (1864–1938) photographed twenty-year-old Virginia Stephen (1882–1941; later Woolf) just as she was beginning her literary career, writing reviews for *The Times Literary Supplement*. She would later become one of the major writers of English fiction, pioneering the 'stream-of-consciousness' novel, and, together with her sister, the painter Vanessa Bell, was a central figure of the Bloomsbury Group. Woolf was photographed at Beresford's commercial studio in Knightsbridge. The resulting image was printed using platinum paper, a technique that produces a rich range of nuanced tones, and beautifully delineates her delicate features. During this sitting several poses were produced, including P220 and P222, shown here.

HARLEY GRANVILLE-BARKER
Alvin Langdon Coburn, 1906
Gum platinum print, 221 x 241mm
• NPG P1031
The actor, director and playwright Harley Granville-Barker (1877–1946) had a major influence on drama in the early twentieth century. At London's Court Theatre (1904–7) – now the Royal Court Theatre – he introduced works by Galsworthy, Masefield and Ibsen and was closely associated with George Bernard Shaw. In Shaw's play *Man and Superman* (1905) Granville-Barker played opposite the actress Lillah McCarthy, whom he married the following year. Boston-born Alvin Langdon Coburn (1882–1966), who first visited England in 1899, was associated with the so-called Pictorial photographers, who used labour-intensive printing methods to evoke light, mood and atmosphere. Coburn photographed Granville-Barker at a time when Sigmund Freud's theories attempted to explore the subconscious mind – which may account for its orange cast, made by adding pigment to a photo-sensitive gum bichromate emulsion.

GORDON CRAIG
Edward Steichen, 1908
Gum platinum print, 231 x 162mm
• NPG P508
The son of actress Dame Ellen Terry, the actor, director and designer Edward Henry Gordon Craig (1872–1966) is perhaps best known for his Modernist writings on theatre. He advocated for the use of large, neutral screens in theatre sets, which he believed could serve as blank slates for the pure emotional expressions of actors. Here Craig himself poses like a screen – a solid, formidable presence. The print itself is unique, built up by hand by the photographer Edward Steichen (1879–1973) by coating an emulsion of photosensitive gum arabic solution over a print made of platinum salts.

LADY OTTOLINE MORRELL
Baron Adolph de Meyer, *c.*1907
Half-plate Autochrome • NPG P1099
Lady Ottoline Morrell (1873–1938) was a society hostess and a patron of the arts known for her flair for fashion and her vivid appreciation of colour. She was also a keen amateur photographer. The National Portrait Gallery holds twelve of her photographic albums, assembled and annotated by Morrell and her daughter, Julian. This Pictorialist-inspired photograph, which resembles an impressionist painting, was made using the then-new Autochrome colour process. Baron Adolph de Meyer (1868–1946) captured the sitter's dynamic personality through dramatic use of colour, lighting and composition. A pioneer in the new genre of fashion photography, De Meyer moved to New York in 1913 to work as a photographer for *Vogue* and *Vanity Fair*.

INDIRA, MAHARANI OF COOCH BEHAR
Bertram Park, *c.*1920
Gelatin silver print, 287 x 223mm
• NPG x199899
Bertram Park (1883–1972) set up studios at 43 Dover Street, London, in 1919 with fellow photographers Marcus Adams and Yvonne Gregory, whom Park had married in 1916. The elegance and modernity of the Maharani of Cooch Behar (1892–1968) are reflected through Park's clever use of light, to delineate the sitter's form and beauty. Throughout the 1920s and 1930s, the Maharani was one of the leading social figures in Anglo-Indian society and popularised the wearing of saris as a mode of dress in London. She opposed the Purdah system of female seclusion and often showed herself unveiled.

KATHARINE LEGAT
Olive Edis, mid-1910s
Whole-plate Autochrome • NPG x45517
Olive Edis (1876–1955) was a pioneer of Autochrome, the first commercially available full-colour photographic process, which was introduced in 1907. (She even designed her won Autochrome viewer.) Edis took portraits of eminent personalities, but achieved her most

impressive results when photographing her two sisters with artful arrangements of fabrics and flowers. In this profile of Edis's sister Katharine (1880–1963), the curl of hair and headpiece are perfectly focused, rather than the face as one would expect, with the photographer skilfully exploiting the vivid but muted colours that Autochrome produced. Edis joined the Royal Photographic Society in 1913 and was made a Fellow the following year.

GABRIELLE RAY
Bassano Ltd, 1910
Whole-plate glass negative
• NPG x101227
Gabrielle Ray (née Cook, 1883–1973) made her first stage appearances as a child, and became one of the most popular picture-postcard beauties of the day. In his book *The Glass of Fashion* (1954), the photographer Cecil Beaton described Ray's 'intriguing perversity' and 'excessive prettiness'. She posed successfully for the camera in many extravagant studio set-ups and costumes. During this sitting, several variant poses (including x101226, shown here) were produced. Alexander Bassano (1829–1913) established one of the most important photographic portrait studios of the Victorian era, photographing royalty, aristocracy and leading names from politics and the arts. The National Portrait Gallery maintains a collection of over 40,000 negatives by the Bassano studio, dating from the 1870s to the 1970s.

SURVEILLANCE PHOTOGRAPHS OF MILITANT SUFFRAGETTES
Criminal Records Office, 1914
Gelatin silver print mounted on identification sheet, 174 x 210mm
• NPG x132847
These two groups of surveillance photographs of militant Suffragettes were issued to public galleries, including the National Portrait Gallery, in 1914. Most of the photographs show women serving sentences in Holloway and Manchester prisons, and were taken undercover in prison exercise yards. Of those featured, Gertrude Ansell (1861–1932; bottom row, second from the left), a professional typist, attacked Hubert Herkomer's portrait of the Duke of Wellington at the Royal Academy and was forcibly fed 236 times. The actress Kitty Marion (1871–1944; top row, third from the left) is the only subject represented with a professional portrait photograph. Imprisoned seven times, she wrote an autobiography that is a valuable account by a 'foot soldier' of the suffrage movement.

WILLIAM STRANG
Malcolm Arbuthnot (Malcolm Lewin Stockdale Parson), 1914
Platinum print, 157 x 126mm
• NPG x12826
Malcolm Arbuthnot (1877–1967) photographed the painter and printmaker William Strang (1859–1921) in his recently established New Bond Street studio. That same year, Arbuthnot signed the Vorticist manifesto, which set out the aims of an avant-garde movement that favoured geometric forms and abstraction. The linear backdrop energises the composition and references Strang's own draughtsmanship. When taking portraits, Arbuthnot favoured a long-focus lens and a long exposure time, which he felt enabled the sitter to settle into his or her true self. He also experimented with pigment processes, such as gum, bromoil and platinum printing, giving his images superb depth and richness.

SIR CHARLES ('CHARLIE') CHAPLIN
James Abbe, 1922
Gelatin silver print, 245 x 190mm
• NPG x138888
Sir Charles Chaplin (1889–1977) is seen here in *The Pilgrim* (1923), a film in which he played an escaped convict who steals a priest's clothes and is mistaken by the new minister of a Wild West town. In this portrait, the American photographer James Abbe (1883–1973) directed Chaplin in a studio session on the film set, pioneering a new genre of portraiture. Abbe recorded: 'Charlie had probably been in a new mood the night he got into his off-beat clerical "Pilgrim" garb and make-up; he left every pose to me. He responded so rapidly I used up the 24 8x10 films of my 24 film holders within 45 minutes.'

D.H. LAWRENCE
Edward Weston, 1924
Gelatin silver print, 243 x 193mm
• NPG P1028
The American photographer Edward Weston (1886–1958) photographed the writer David Herbert Lawrence (1885–1930) in Mexico at a time when both were living in states of voluntary exile. Lawrence had left Britain shortly after the First World War, during which time he had been harassed by the authorities for his political associations (his wife, Frieda Richthoven, was German) and candid writings about homosexuality. Lawrence travelled widely and made three extended trips to Mexico, where he met Weston, who was there with his mistress, the Italian photographer Tina Modotti. Weston shows Lawrence as he himself must have felt – wistful and beleaguered, yet defiant.

DAME GLADYS COOPER
Curtis Moffat, *c.*1924
Gelatin silver print, 285 x 244mm
• NPG P430
Dame Gladys Cooper (1888–1971) made her stage debut in 1905, before joining the Gaiety Theatre as a chorus girl. In 1916 she began to act at the Playhouse, the London theatre that she was later to manage. This portrait by New York photographer Curtis Moffat (1887–1949) was taken at the time when Cooper played the title role in *Peter Pan*; it shows a combination of glamour and informality. Like Bill Brandt and Lee Miller, also included in this book, Moffat had been an assistant to Man Ray. Moffat set up his own studio in London in 1925, where he produced portraits of notable figures of the day.

JAMES JOYCE
Berenice Abbott, 1926
Gelatin silver print, 238 x 194mm
• NPG P609
This sensitive portrait of the Irish writer James Joyce (1882–1941) is considered one of the defining images of the author, known for his experimental 'stream-of-consciousness' novels *Ulysses* (1922) and *Finnegan's Wake* (1939). Berenice Abbott (1898–1991) photographed Joyce on two occasions, the first in 1926 at his home in Paris, the second in 1928 at her studio. A former assistant to Man Ray, Abbott employed softly diffused lighting to suggest a complex, introverted character. Since the 1910s, Joyce had suffered from eye problems. He had, in all, eleven ophthalmic operations and at the time of this photograph was blind in his left eye.

TILLY LOSCH
Emil Otto ('E.O.') Hoppé, 1928
Gelatin silver print, 193 x 202mm
• NPG P1995
Tightly cropped, with the sitter facing directly into the camera and her head held level, this resolutely modern portrait of Tilly Losch (1907–75) presents the dancer as a powerful and formidable figure. It was made in 1928, the same year as the passing of the Representation of the People Act, which gave women equal rights to vote. The photographer E.O. Hoppé (1878–1972) had become famous in the 1910s and 1920s for his photographs celebrating the physical beauty of women, such as those published in his *Book of Fair Women*. Over the years, his approach to photographing women evolved, and by the time this picture was made he was himself a vocal advocate for women's suffrage.

LILLIAN GISH
Cecil Beaton, 1929
Gelatin silver print, 232 x 202mm
• NPG x40158
The silent-film star Lillian Gish (1893–1993) was born in Springfield, Ohio, and is best remembered for her long association with film director D.W. Griffith, as the star of several of his epics, including *Birth of a Nation* (1915), *Intolerance* (1916) and *Broken Blossoms* (1919). In 1929, having risen through London society, Cecil Beaton (1904–80) headed for New York, where he took a number of celebrity sittings. Playing with mirrors, Beaton here presents an almost cinematic portrait of the actress. In his *Book of Beauty* (1930), he wrote of Gish: 'She is a magnificent actress in spite of her frail delicacy … she creates gigantic effects with a minimum effort.'

ELSA SCHIAPARELLI
Man Ray (Emmanuel Radnitzky), *c.*1930
Gelatin silver print, 285 x 190mm
• NPG P2019
The avant-garde fashion designer Elsa Schiaparelli (1890–1973), shown here at around the time she opened her influential boutique in London in 1933, was one of Man Ray's models and artistic collaborators. Renowned for her form-fitting, wrap-around dresses, she appears wearing one of her own creations. During this period, Man Ray (1890–1976) was arguably at the height of his Surrealist powers. To make the gridded bars visible across the image, he exposed the picture multiple times under the enlarger, each time masking part of the image to vary the intensity of exposure.

ANNA MAY WONG
Dorothy Wilding, 1929
Gelatin silver print, 418 x 295mm
• NPG x26341
The actress Anna May Wong (1905–61) was born in Los Angeles to second-generation Chinese-American parents. She appeared in over sixty films and is best known for her starring roles alongside Marlene Dietrich in Joseph von Sternberg's *Shanghai Express* (1932) and in the classic British silent melodrama *Piccadilly*, released in 1929 – the year that leading photographer Dorothy Wilding (1893–1976) took this portrait. In her autobiography, *In Pursuit of Perfection* (1958), Wilding recalled: 'Anna May Wong … had the first long red fingernails I had ever seen. When I lifted her hands to "drape" them, they were so fragile that one felt one was holding the most delicate snowdrops. She was the softest and gentlest creature one can imagine.'

ALDOUS HUXLEY
Howard Coster, 1934
Gelatin silver print, 283 x 234mm
• NPG P714
Howard Coster (1885–1959) portrayed the writer Aldous Huxley (1894–1963) just two years after the publication of his most famous work, the dystopian novel *Brave New World* (1932). Stricken with a serious eye disease as a child, Huxley had impaired vision and wore thick corrective lenses. Here the photographer has used Huxley's glasses to partially conceal his eyes, suggesting a deep inner vision, while at the same time revealing the extent of his weakened sight, which improved in later life. The image also serves as a metaphor for the optical properties of the camera, which was a subject of great interest to Modern photographers such as Coster.

PRIMROSE SALT
Paul Tanqueray, 1933
Gelatin silver print, 248 x 198mm
• NPG x22344
From the mid-1920s Paul Tanqueray (1905–91) was one of London's leading studio portrait photographers, and his work appeared regularly in society and illustrated magazines. A former student of portrait photographer Hugh Cecil, Tanqueray set up his own studio in London at 139 Kensington High Street before moving to 8 Dover Street in 1930. 'Debutante of the Year' Primrose Salt (1915–2005) is shown with her fashionable Eton crop. Using a spotlight and light reflected from an umbrella, Tanqueray created an atmosphere of style and glamour, with a visual language directly influenced by Hollywood still-photography and cinema.

MARGOT ASQUITH, COUNTESS OF OXFORD AND ASQUITH
Lucia Moholy, 1935
Gelatin silver print, 165 x 147mm
• NPG x76368
An acerbic wit, widely criticised for her outspoken views, Margot Asquith (1864–1945) was the second wife of H.H. Asquith, British prime minister from 1908 to 1916. When he died in 1928, Margot fell into financial difficulty, and took to writing her memoirs as a source of income. Here, she is shown by the Czech émigré Lucia Moholy (1894–1989) in full profile, with her face obscured. Moholy is now recognised as a key figure in the Bauhaus art school, although at the time her works were largely overshadowed by her husband, László Moholy-Nagy. In 1933, anticipating the Second World War, the two emigrated separately to London.

T.S. ELIOT
Bill Brandt, 1945
Gelatin silver print, 216 x 184mm
• NPG P190
The American poet, critic, and publisher Thomas Stearns Eliot (1888–1965) settled in England before the First World War. While working for Lloyd's Bank, he published *Prufrock and Other Observations* (1917) and *Poems* (1919), hand-printed at the Hogarth Press by Leonard and Virginia Woolf. Eliot founded the literary magazine *The Criterion* in 1922, publishing his long poem *The Waste Land* in the first issue. In 1925, he joined the publishing house Faber & Faber and established its reputation for promoting new poetry. Later work included *Murder in the Cathedral* (1935) and *Four Quartets* (1935–42). Published in *Harper's Bazaar*, this portrait by Bill Brandt (1904–83) was made at the Faber offices in Bloomsbury. Born in Germany, Brandt assisted the Surrealist photographer Man Ray in Paris before settling in London in 1934. The bright light from the window, set against deep shadow that obscures much of Eliot's face, lends the portrait a mysterious air.

CHRISTOPHER ISHERWOOD AND W.H. AUDEN
Louise Dahl-Wolfe, 1938
Gelatin silver print, 250 x 206mm
• NPG x15195
Christopher Isherwood (1904–86) and Wystan Hugh Auden (1907–73) first met at preparatory school in Surrey. After a brief romantic relationship, the two became lifelong friends and literary collaborators. They travelled together to China to report on the Sino-Japanese war, and jointly produced the prose and verse book *Journey to War* (1939). They returned from China by way of the United States, and it was during this visit that they were photographed by the pioneering fashion photographer and *Harper's Bazaar* contributor Louise Dahl-Wolfe (1895–1989) in New York's Central Park. A year later, both writers moved to the city. Isherwood's novel *Goodbye to Berlin* (1937), with its famous opening line 'I am a camera,' was published just prior to their voyage.

HUMPHREY JENNINGS
Lee Miller, 1942
Gelatin silver print, 390 x 371mm
• NPG P156 (detail)
In this surreal portrait, the writer, painter and documentary filmmaker Humphrey Jennings (1907–50) appears near an implausible-looking cloud of cigarette smoke, which seems to be coming out of his mouth, even though no cigarette is seen. The cloud resembles a human

head, like a ghostly figure looking back at him. Lee Miller (1907–77) made this photograph for *Vogue* magazine in 1942, but her friendship with Jennings predated the Second World War, their having been associated with the British Surrealist group. By 1932, after Miller's artistic and romantic relationship with Man Ray had run its course, she returned to her native New York to establish her own studio, and later moved to London to live with the Surrealist artist, historian and poet Roland Penrose.

SIR WINSTON CHURCHILL, FRANKLIN ROOSEVELT AND JOSEPH STALIN AT THE YALTA CONFERENCE
Yevgeny Khaldei, 1945
Gelatin silver press print, 208 x 245mm
• NPG x199337 (detail)
The Ukranian photographer Yevgeny Khaldei (1917–97) produced press images for the Telegraph Agency of the Soviet Union that capture some of the most iconic moments of the Second World War. In February 1945 Sir Winston Churchill (1874–1965), Franklin Roosevelt (1882–1945) and Joseph Stalin (1878–1953), leaders of the UK, US and Soviet governments, respectively, met in the Livadia Palace on the outskirts of the Black Sea resort of Yalta in the Crimea to discuss the post-war reorganisation of Europe. Churchill advised against 'dismembering' Germany too quickly and opposed too high a demand being placed on the defeated country. But it was the subject of Poland that dominated the conference, and Churchill was later forced to defend his support for Stalin's demands that the Soviet Union annex part of the country. Many in Britain saw this as a betrayal of the role that Poland had played in supporting the Allies.

SIR ALFRED HITCHCOCK
Irving Penn, 1947
Gelatin silver print, 244 x 194mm
• NPG P593
Born in Leytonstone, London, Sir Alfred Hitchcock (1899–1980) directed what is commonly accepted as Britain's first sound feature film, *Blackmail* (1929), and from 1939 worked in Hollywood. Constantly exploiting technical innovations and prolifically inventive, he became known as the 'master of suspense' for films such as *Spellbound* (1945), *Notorious* (1946), *Rear Window* (1954), *Vertigo* (1958), *North by Northwest* (1959) and the horror classic, *Psycho* (1960). In this photograph, published in American *Vogue*, Hitchcock is sitting in profile on a mound of grey carpet. It is a definitive example of the visual language of the American photographer Irving Penn (1917–2009), whose use of low-key lighting and subtle choreography of pose and gesture hints at the interior life of his subjects.

AUDREY HEPBURN
Angus McBean, 1950
Gelatin silver print, 295 x 380mm
• NPG P1295
This photograph of the Belgian-born actress Audrey Hepburn (1929–93) was originally used as an advertisement for Crookes 'lacto-calamine skin-cream' in 1951. With its clever use of props and bizarre juxtapositions of scale, the portrait creates a fantastical tableau. Asked to find a 'new face', Angus McBean (1904–90) remembered Hepburn's distinctive beauty from the previous year, when he had photographed the stars of the London theatrical-revue *Sauce Tartare*. The advertising campaign was hugely successful, appearing in fashion magazines such as *Vogue* and *Tatler*. Hepburn made her Broadway debut in the title role of *Gigi* in the same year. This led to her being cast opposite Gregory Peck in the film *Roman Holiday* (1953), for which she won an Oscar.

BETSY DRAKE AND CARY GRANT
Sanford H. Roth, early 1950s
Gelatin silver print, 342 x 258mm
• NPG x199796
Betsy Drake (1923–2015) and Cary Grant (1904–86) first met by chance aboard the *Queen Mary* on a voyage from London to New York. She had just finished a London stage production that had captivated him. They were married on Christmas Day 1949, with film director Howard Hughes as best man. Grant, born Archibald Leach in Bristol, performed in British music halls before emigrating to New York in 1920 and becoming one of the most celebrated movie stars. This intimate and relaxed portrait by New York photographer Sanford H. Roth (1906–62) shows the couple at their home in Mulholland Drive, Los Angeles, at the time when they were both appearing in the film *Room for One More* (1952). Drake went on to become a writer. They divorced in 1962 and she eventually settled in London.

WENDA PARKINSON
Norman Parkinson, 1951
Gelatin silver print, 304 x 254mm
• NPG x30181
Norman Parkinson (1913–90) first met Wenda Rogerson (1923–87) when she appeared as a young actress at the Arts Theatre Club, supplementing her salary through modelling. She became his model and they married in 1947. In a

career that spanned seven decades, Parkinson was celebrated for his inventiveness as a fashion photographer. His long association with *Vogue* and his numerous assignments for *Harper's Bazaar*, *Town & Country* and other international magazines brought him worldwide recognition. His innovative images, many of which were made outdoors in carefully chosen locations, transformed the static approach to fashion photography. In this example, Wenda is dressed in a Hardy Amies suit. The composition, with the open umbrella and bare outline of the leafless tree shown against moving traffic at Hyde Park Corner, accentuates her silhouette.

MARILYN MONROE
Antony Beauchamp, 1951
Gelatin silver print, 162 x 182mm
• NPG x126696
Antony Beauchamp (1918–57) opened his London studio in 1939, photographing numerous actresses. (His mother also established herself as the society photographer Vivienne.) In 1949, Beauchamp married the actress Sarah Churchill and moved to Los Angeles. Here he was introduced to the American film actress and model Marilyn Monroe (1926–62) through her agent, Johnny Hyde. Over two weeks he photographed her and the results featured in numerous publications over the following five years.

DYLAN THOMAS
Rollie McKenna, 1953
Gelatin silver print, 333 x 262mm
• NPG P1684
Rollie McKenna (1918–2003) recalled that as she photographed the Welsh poet and writer Dylan Thomas (1914–53) during rehearsals for the first performance of his play for voices, *Under Milk Wood*, he urged the actors to 'Love the words. Love the words!' McKenna's portrait reveals an astounding energy, and established this pose as a defining one. She remembered that an hour before taking this photograph, Thomas had been extremely unwell, yet he gathered the strength to direct his cast for three hours. He wrote *Under Milk Wood* over several years, and frantically reworked it in the last months of his life. This photograph is part of a significant portfolio of work by McKenna, one of the most important photographers of American and British modern poets.

ALAN TURING
Elliott & Fry, 1951
Gelatin silver print, 161 x 117mm
• NPG x27078
One of Britain's most influential mathematicians and computer scientists, Alan Turing (1912–54) worked throughout the Second World War for the Government Code and Cypher School at Bletchley Park. Known to colleagues as 'Prof', Turing was central to the breaking of the German naval cypher, the Enigma. After the war, he joined the National Physical Laboratory where he led the work to develop a large-scale electronic digital computer. In March 1952 Turing was brought to trial for having a sexual relationship with a man. In order to avoid prison, he agreed to take oestrogen injections. His position as a government consultant was ended and his personal life came under scrutiny. On 8 June 1954 Turing was found dead. The inquest ruled suicide by cyanide. This photograph by the London studio Elliott & Fry (active 1863–1962) is one of very few images of Turing.

DAME MARGOT FONTEYN
Yousuf Karsh, 1957
Gelatin silver print, 498 x 400mm
• NPG P490(32)
Prima ballerina assoluta of the Royal Ballet, Dame Margot Fonteyn (1919–91) joined the Vic-Wells Ballet in 1934 and made her debut as a snowflake in Tchaikovsky's *The Nutcracker*. She became lifelong muse of the choreographer Frederick Ashton, who created many roles for her, including the title roles in *Daphnis and Chloë* (1951), *Sylvia* (1952) and *Ondine* (1958). Her celebrated dance partnerships included most famously, Rudolf Nureyev, with whom she performed all over the world. Fonteyn is shown here as Cinderella in Ashton's ballet. Although she is shown in traditional three-quarters profile and with the direct, artificial lighting favoured by Yousuf Karsh (1908–2002), the Armenian-born photographer has posed Fonteyn smiling, with arms raised, as if enacting a moment from the ballet. Consequently, the lines between Fonteyn's own personality and her role as a dancer are blurred.

DAME BARBARA HEPWORTH
Ida Kar, 1961
Gelatin silver print, 250 x 253mm
• NPG x88502
Dame Barbara Hepworth (1903–75) studied at Leeds School of Art and at the Royal College of Art, and joined the avant-garde Seven and Five Society in 1931. Ben Nicholson became her second husband in 1938, and with him she moved to St Ives in Cornwall. She achieved international recognition in the post-war period. Ida Kar (1908–74), of Armenian heritage, became known for her portraits of artists and writers. She made her home in London with her husband, the owner

of Gallery One, Victor Musgrave. Her portfolio of St Ives artists was published in the 26 July 1961 edition of *Tatler & Bystander* magazine. Hepworth is seen here at work on the armature of a sculpture in her studio, a former cinema and dance hall.

SIR MICHAEL CAINE
David Bailey, 1965
Gelatin silver print, 409 x 407mm
• NPG P951
Born Maurice Micklewhite in London, Sir Michael Caine (b.1933) came to prominence in the film *Zulu* (1964). He starred in many hit films of the 1960s and 1970s, with trademark glasses and cockney accent. His most memorable films include *Alfie* (1966) and *The Italian Job* (1969). Caine has made more than a hundred films, and was nominated for an Oscar for *Educating Rita* (1983). He is photographed here in the year he first played cockney spy Harry Palmer in *The Ipcress File*. The portrait is a variant of a shot that David Bailey (b.1937) included in his *Box of Pin-Ups* (1965), a portfolio of thirty-six prints, published by Weidenfeld and Nicolson, which sold for 63 shillings (£3.15). The 'pin-ups' included the fashionable elite of the 1960s, photographed by Bailey against a plain white background.

JOE ORTON
Lewis Morley, 1965
Gelatin silver print, 508 x 410mm
• NPG P512(16)
Lewis Morley (1925–2013) chronicled the new idols of 1960s society in a style that captured the buoyant spirit of the times. In 1965 he was commissioned to photograph the playwright Joe Orton (1933–67) to publicise the US opening of the play *Entertaining Mr Sloane*. He was told that Orton wished to be photographed like a body-builder and so was startled when confronted by his slim frame. Realising that photographs of the playwright in his underwear would be deemed risqué, Morley nonetheless agreed to photograph Orton as he wished. The resulting portrait reveals Orton's nonconformist and mischievous nature. He was a pioneer of black farce, his works characterised by a stylish and macabre outrageousness, and he often collaborated with his partner Kenneth Halliwell. Their tempestuous relationship ended in tragedy when, in August 1967, Halliwell murdered Orton and took his own life.

CELIA HAMMOND
Sandra Lousada, 1962
Inkjet print, printed later, 404 x 302mm
• NPG x135470
One of the top fashion models of the 1960s, Celia Hammond (b.1941) worked with most of the leading photographers of the era, including Norman Parkinson and Terence Donovan. She had trained alongside Jean Shrimpton at Lucie Clayton's modelling school. From the early 1970s, Hammond gave up her career in modelling to devote herself to animal welfare. A variant pose from this sitting was published on the front cover of the 20 March 1962 edition of *Queen* magazine. As well as being a successful theatre and portrait photographer, London-born Sandra Lousada (b.1938) has worked in fashion and advertising.

THE WHO
ROGER DALTREY, KEITH MOON, JOHN ENTWISTLE AND PETE TOWNSHEND
Tony Frank, 1965
Colour coupler print, printed later, 550 x 756mm • NPG P1380
Formed in 1964, The Who are considered one of the most influential rock bands of the twentieth century. Their original line-up consisted of Roger Daltrey (b.1944; vocals), Keith Moon, (1946–78; drums), John Entwistle (1944–2002; bass) and Pete Townshend (b.1945; guitar). The band members were photographed by Tony Frank (b.1945) in London, standing on the tracks at Wembley Park station. Frank is a French photographer who worked in the 1960s for the magazine *Salut les Copains*.

TWIGGY
Ronald Traeger, 1967
Cibachrome print, printed later (enlarged from the original contact sheet), 430 x 355mm • NPG x125452
Launched by a famous cropped haircut, shaped by Leonard and coloured by Daniel Galvin, Twiggy (b.1949) was arguably the world's first supermodel. Born Lesley Hornby, she was given the pet names 'Sticks' and 'Twigs' because of her thin legs. Named 'The Face of 1966' in an article by the *Daily Express* journalist Deirdre McSharry, she was the embodiment of the 1960s look and influenced a generation of teenagers. Her acting career developed when she appeared in Ken Russell's film version of Sandy Wilson's stage musical *The Boy Friend* (1971), and she made her Broadway debut in *My One and Only* (1983–5), based on music by George and Ira Gershwin. American photographer Ronald Traeger (1936–68) photographed her on a number of occasions. The contact sheet (x125453) shows his method of working and is inscribed by him to show Twiggy's favoured shots.

THE BEATLES
SIR PAUL MCCARTNEY,
SIR RINGO STARR, GEORGE
HARRISON AND JOHN LENNON

Linda McCartney, 1967
Platinum print, printed later,
352 x 552mm • NPG P577

The most famous Britons of the 1960s, The Beatles – Sir Paul McCartney (b.1942), Sir Ringo Starr (b.1940), George Harrison (1943–2001) and John Lennon (1940–80) – sold 150 million albums during the decade. On 19 May 1967 selected journalists and broadcasters were invited to the Belgravia home of their manager Brian Epstein, to meet the band and hear the group's forthcoming album *Sgt. Pepper's Lonely Hearts Club Band*. American-born Linda Eastman (1941–98), a photographer for music-industry magazines, had come to London to photograph British bands for the book *Rock and Other Four Letter Words* (1968). She recalled: 'I went to the press launch where Sgt. Pepper was played for the first time to the media, to take my first photographs of The Beatles.' She later married McCartney and settled in London.

LUCIAN FREUD

Harry Diamond, 1969
Gelatin silver print, 293 x 191mm
• NPG x135769

Soho habitué and photographer Harry Diamond (1924–2009) photographed his friend, the painter Lucian Freud (1922–2011), on numerous occasions. Freud also painted Diamond several times; Diamond disliked the first of these, *Interior in Paddington* (1951), for making his legs appear too short. Diamond's direct and spontaneous approach to photography was applied universally to his subjects, which ranged from artist and musician friends in Soho, London, to East End locals. Diamond also photographed the streets of London, building a remarkable body of documentary work. His archive, comprising approximately 20,000 negatives as well as vintage prints made between 1970 and 2000, was bequeathed to the National Portrait Gallery in 2012. It joins the Lucian Freud Archive, also held at the Gallery.

THE SEX PISTOLS
STEVE JONES, GLEN MATLOCK,
JOHNNY ROTTEN (JOHN LYDON)
AND PAUL COOK

Peter Vernon, 1976
Gelatin silver print from original negative, printed later, 310 x 455mm
• NPG x88356

The members of the anarchic punk-rock group The Sex Pistols – Steve Jones (b.1955), Glen Matlock (b.1956), Johnny Rotten (John Lydon, b.1956) and Paul Cook (b.1956) – were brought together by boutique-owner and entrepreneur Malcolm McLaren in 1975. Matlock was replaced in 1977 by Sid Vicious (John Ritchie), who died of a heroin overdose in New York two years later. The band courted notoriety with their excessive behaviour. This spontaneous expression of punk was captured by EMI's official photographer, Peter Vernon (b.1946), at the entrance to the firm's car park after The Sex Pistols signed their short-lived contract. It appeared on the band's bootleg album *The Filth and the Fury* after its use in the *Daily Mirror* under the same headline, following their infamous appearance with presenter Bill Grundy on Thames Television's regional news programme *Today* in December 1976.

GRAHAM NASH

Self-portrait, 1974
Gelatin silver print, 328 x 485mm
• NPG x200033

The singer-songwriter and musician Graham Nash (b.1942) grew up in Salford and co-founded The Hollies in the early 1960s with his school friend Allan Clark. Nash encouraged the band to write their own songs, was instrumental in forging their successful harmonies and took his first solo lead with them on the hit 'On a Carousel'. Nash met David Crosby and Stephen Stills in 1966 on a Hollies US tour and later that decade left the band to form Crosby, Stills & Nash, which later became a quartet with Neil Young. After moving to California, Nash's political engagement was reflected in his songs. He took this self-portrait in 1974, assisted by his then girlfriend Calli Cerami, at the Plaza Hotel, New York, at the end of the first Crosby, Stills, Nash & Young stadium tour. His most recent album, *The Path Tonight*, was released in April 2016. Nash became an influential photography collector in the early 1970s, and in 1976 hired Graham Howe as his curator, touring his collection over several years. In the late 1980s Nash became a pioneer of digital printing, researching and making early digital fine-art prints using an altered Iris printer, which he further adapted and distributed under Nash Editions from 1991.

GLENDA JACKSON

Mayotte Magnus, 1977
Gelatin silver print, 406 x 308mm
• NPG x18618

Glenda Jackson (b.1936) made her stage debut in 1957. During her film career she won Oscars for performances in *Women in Love* (1969) and *A Touch of Class* (1973). Jackson was the Labour Member of

Parliament for Hampstead and Highgate from 1992 to 2010 and for Hampstead and Kilburn from 2010 before standing down in 2015. On taking up photography, Mayotte Magnus (b.1934) won an Ilford photographic prize in 1972, and exhibited her portraits of eminent women at the National Portrait Gallery in 1977. Her numerous projects included collaborations with her late husband Jorge Lewinski. Magnus captured inner and physical strength in her portrait of Jackson, who was preparing for her role as the poet Stevie Smith. Magnus described the actress as a 'sad clown'.

DAVID HOCKNEY
Bernard Lee ('Bern') Schwartz, 1977
Dye-transfer print, 470 x 378mm
• NPG P1183
Bradford-born David Hockney (b.1937) studied at the Royal College of Art and became a leading figure in Pop Art. His first retrospective was held at the Whitechapel Art Gallery, London, in 1970. Bern Schwartz (1914–78), an American businessman, took up photography in the early 1970s as a second career. In just a few years, he made memorable studies of many well-known personalities of the time including artists, politicians and royalty. The Bern Schwartz Foundation donated 140 original dye-transfer prints to the National Portrait Gallery in 2007.

DAVID BOWIE
Antony Armstrong Jones, 1st Earl of Snowdon, 1978
Gelatin silver print, 362 x 297mm
• NPG P1855
Lord Snowdon (1930–2017), who was once married to Princess Margaret, sister of Queen Elizabeth II, photographed many celebrities and royalty of his day. The National Portrait Gallery holds a large collection of his work. This portrait of David Bowie (1947–2016), with its sensitive handling of light, shade, pose and framing, celebrates the musician's androgynous elegance. A man of many guises, Bowie's breakthrough came with his song *Space Oddity* (1969). Gaining prominence throughout the 1970s, his ever-evolving musical style and shifting personas were always conceptually informed. Bowie's albums include *The Rise and Fall of Ziggy Stardust and the Spiders from Mars* (1972), *Diamond Dogs* (1974) and *Let's Dance* (1983). As an actor, he starred in films that include *The Man Who Fell to Earth* (1976) and *Labyrinth* (1986), among others.

KATE BUSH
Thomas Patrick John Anson, 5th Earl of Lichfield, 1980
Inkjet print, 649 x 487mm
• NPG x126911
Singer-songwriter Kate Bush (b.1958) was the first female British singer to top the charts with a self-composed song, *Wuthering Heights* (1978). She signed to her record company at the age of sixteen, having already composed 200 songs. Her four-octave voice and use of mime in performance made her a compelling and unique star. As a cousin of Her Majesty the Queen, Patrick Lichfield (1939–2005) was known for his intimate portraits of the Royal Family. He was also an established society and fashion photographer for *Vogue* magazine, and a leading participant in, and chronicler of, the Swinging Sixties. Bush was included in Lichfield's 1981 book of portraits, *The World's Most Beautiful Women*.

JOE STRUMMER
William Eggleston, *c.*1980
Inkjet print, 508 x 406mm
• NPG P2074
In 1976 Joe Strummer (1952–2002) co-founded legendary punk band *The Clash*, and would be their lyricist, lead vocalist and rhythm guitarist until their break-up in 1986. In the 1990s, Strummer collaborated with a succession of bands. In December 2002, at the age of fifty, he died suddenly from an undiagnosed congenital heart defect. William Eggleston (b.1939) has photographed his family and friends, but also musicians and artists. A pioneer of colour photography in the late 1960s and early 1970s, the American's first solo exhibition of colour prints was held at the Museum of Modern Art, New York in 1976. Forty years later, *William Eggleston: Portraits* at the National Portrait Gallery, London, was the first major exhibition to focus on his portrait photography.

MICHAEL CLARK
Chris Garnham, 1984
Gelatin silver print, 294 x 290mm
• NPG x26055
Chris Garnham (1958–89) trained as an illustrator at the Royal College of Art before working for trend-setting magazines such as *The Face* and *Blitz*. The latter voted him Photographer of the Year in 1984, but his life and career were abruptly ended in the *Marchioness* riverboat accident of 1989. Garnham's background in illustration gave his work a distinctive and imaginative style, as did his use of multiple exposures. The trailblazing dancer Michael Clark (b.1962) was a bright star of the Royal Ballet School, but left to pursue a more provocative style of dance. At the age of twenty-two, in the year this portrait was taken, Clark

set up his own eponymous dance company, choreographing scandalous punk performances to avant-garde music. Clark has collaborated with some of the most progressive talents of his generation, including fashion designers BodyMap, the artists Sarah Lucas and Leigh Bowery, and musicians Mark E. Smith, Wire, Jarvis Cocker, Scritti Politti and Relaxed Muscle.

HANIF KUREISHI
Jillian Edelstein, 1989
Gelatin silver print, 256 x 259mm
• NPG x34146
Playwright, novelist and screenwriter Hanif Kureishi (b.1954) was born in Bromley, Kent, to an English mother and a Pakistani father. His screenplays and novels broke new ground in their focus on sub-cultures within British society, employing his distinct literary voice and satirical humour to highlight controversial issues surrounding race, class and sexuality in 1980s Britain. South African-born Jillian Edelstein (b.1957) photographed Kureishi the year before his novel *The Buddha of Suburbia* (1990) won the Whitbread Prize for Best First Novel. Edelstein seeks collaboration in her portraits: 'It is a two-way process and I am dependent on the other person. It is a bit like a dance, albeit a brief one.'

FRANCIS BACON
Guy Bourdin, 1986
Colour coupler print, printed later, 307 x 335mm • NPG x199965
Dublin-born Francis Bacon (1909–92) left Ireland at the age of sixteen, settling permanently in England in 1928. The work *Three Studies for Figures at the Base of a Crucifixion* (1944, Tate) established him as an artist of international importance. Bacon used diverse source imagery and became known for his bold, abstracted figurative paintings with their tormented and powerful view of the human condition. Parisian-born Guy Bourdin (1928–91) was one of the most radical and influential fashion photographers of the twentieth century. His fusion of surreal and erotic imagery graced the pages of international magazines such as French *Vogue* during the 1970s and 1980s. Bourdin made this portrait of Bacon at the Marlborough Gallery in 1986. In the background the artist's work *Triptych – Study of a Self-Portrait* (1985–6) can be glimpsed. Through the movement of the sitter, Bourdin recreates the swirling forms of Bacon's painting.

MORRISSEY
Nick Knight, 1985
Gelatin silver print, 462 x 531mm
• NPG x26092
Manchester-born Morrissey (Steven Patrick Morrissey; b.1959) was the lead singer of the band The Smiths, until embarking on a solo career in 1987. Nick Knight (b.1958) photographed him in 1985 when he was touring with the band and recording *The Queen is Dead*, which reached number two in the UK album charts. Knight's pared-down portrait captures a smouldering intensity and was shown in the National Portrait Gallery's exhibition *Twenty for Today* (1985), which celebrated the use of photographic portraiture in 1980s fashion magazines. Knight's status as a visionary photographer endures. He founded the fashion website SHOWstudio in 2000 and described being a photographer as 'a way of finding out about people – finding out about life – and experiencing what they experience'.

TILDA SWINTON
The Douglas Brothers, 1992
Platinum print, 500 x 400mm
• NPG P2006
Tilda Swinton (b.1961) was photographed for *Sight & Sound* magazine on the release of the film *Orlando* (1992), in which she played Virginia Woolf's gender-swapping title character. The Douglas Brothers recalled how the actress, with her commanding screen presence and striking features, transformed before their camera: 'Tilda was sharp, funny, mesmerising. The moment she got in front of the camera she became some kind of deity.' Andrew Douglas (b.1952) assisted the photographer Lord Snowdon before collaborating with his younger brother Stuart Douglas (b.1962) in 1986. Using large-format plate cameras and long exposure times, the brothers also returned to time-consuming and labour-intensive printing methods, which allow for greater artistic creativity. Platinum printing gives Swinton's portrait a velvety, tactile softness and brings out rich nuances of tone.

ALEXANDER MCQUEEN AND ISABELLA BLOW
David LaChapelle, 1996
Colour coupler print, 734 x 1012mm
• NPG P1403
David LaChapelle (b.1963) began his career at Andy Warhol's *Interview* magazine. His striking photographs of celebrated figures in fashion, music and politics have been exhibited at museums and galleries internationally. This double portrait of Alexander McQueen (1969–2010) and Isabella Blow (1958–2007) was published in the March 1997 'Swinging London' edition of *Vanity Fair*. McQueen was a fashion designer famed for his conceptually daring

approach. Blow, a fashion stylist, was a great champion of McQueen, buying his graduate collection 'Jack the Ripper Stalks His Victims' in 1992. For this photograph, taken at Hedingham Castle, Essex, the pair dressed in clothes designed by McQueen, and Blow's hat is by milliner Philip Treacy. LaChapelle subverts gender norms and notions of chivalry in this image, which also acts as a theatrical record of the sitters' playful friendship.

DIANA, PRINCESS OF WALES
Mario Testino, 1997
Digital gelatin silver print, printed later, 1243 x 1001mm • NPG P1016
Perhaps the most photographed royal of the twentieth century, Diana, Princess of Wales (1961–97) generated global interest and was constantly scrutinised by paparazzi photographers eager to generate tabloid sensation, particularly after her divorce from Prince Charles in 1996. The following year, Diana sat for the Peruvian fashion photographer Mario Testino (b.1954), who created some of the most iconic portraits of the Princess. Styled without royal paraphernalia, the images suggested a relaxed and modern woman exuding polished glamour. The images, published in *Vanity Fair* magazine, were the last official photographs taken of Diana before her untimely death later that year.

STUART HALL
Dawoud Bey, 1998
Colour Polaroid prints (diptych), 762 x 559mm each • NPG P730
Born in Kingston, Jamaica, Stuart McPhail Hall (1932–2014) was a cultural theorist, campaigner for racial justice, scholar and founding editor of the *New Left Review*. He won a Rhodes scholarship to Oxford University, arriving in 1951. He became Director of the Centre for Contemporary Cultural Studies at Birmingham University in 1972 and Professor of Sociology at the Open University in 1979. He was Chair of Autograph ABP (a charity that works internationally in photography and film, cultural identity, race, representation and human rights) and Iniva (the International Institute of Visual Arts). In 1998, the National Portrait Gallery, in partnership with Autograph ABP, commissioned the American photographer Dawoud Bey (b.1953) to create a portrait of Hall for its Collection. The diptych consists of unique photographs created with a 20 x 24-inch Polaroid camera, one of only five ever made.

J.K. ROWLING
Neil Wilder, 1999
Colour coupler print, 391 x 391mm • NPG x125493
The creator of the phenomenally successful Harry Potter books, Joanne Kathleen Rowling (b.1965) studied French and Classics at Exeter University and began writing while working for Amnesty International in London. Rowling has said that the characters and plot of the first novel, *Harry Potter and the Philosopher's Stone* (1997), came to her 'fully formed' during a train journey in 1990. The series has been translated into sixty-one languages, sold over a quarter of a billion copies worldwide and been made into major feature films. Born and brought up in Cape Town, South Africa, Neil Wilder (b.1959) has taken portraits of international celebrities for leading magazine publications. He photographed Rowling in Edinburgh, where she wrote the early Potter novels in a café overlooking the city's castle.

QUEEN ELIZABETH II
Hiroshi Sugimoto, 1999
Gelatin silver print on aluminium, 1492 x 1194mm • NPG P1002
This strangely disconcerting portrait of Queen Elizabeth II (b.1926) appears both lifelike and artificial. It forms part of a series of photographs of wax effigies taken by Japanese artist Hiroshi Sugimoto (b.1948) in public attractions such as Madame Tussaud's in London. In the style of an old-master portrait, the wax figure is posed in three-quarter-length view and dramatically lit against a black background. A long exposure of up to nine minutes captures minute details of the figure's clothing and expression. Printed larger than life, Sugimoto's portrait has a deeply uncanny quality. What appears to be a photograph of a living human being is revealed to be a photograph of a stiff and artificial recreation, a wax figure whose likeness was carefully modelled from other photographic reproductions of the sitter: a portrait three times removed from the Queen herself.

PETER SAVILLE
Wolfgang Tillmans, 2002
Colour coupler print, 610 x 508mm • NPG P1010
Peter Saville (b.1955) has been a pivotal figure in design and style culture. He designed record sleeves for Factory Records in the late 1970s and is best known for his album-cover artwork for Joy Division and New Order. He has also produced iconic images for bands such as Roxy Music and Suede, ground-breaking fashion campaigns for Yohji Yamamoto and Stella McCartney, and has collaborated in several art projects. This photograph by German-born Wolfgang Tillmans (b.1968) shows the designer at ease and

in control of his surroundings – almost like a snapshot, moments that are revealing only in their spontaneity.

STELLA MCCARTNEY
Mary McCartney, 1998
Colour coupler print, 496 x 394mm
• NPG x126205
British fashion designer Stella McCartney (b.1971) worked with Christian Lacroix and Betty Jackson before studying fashion at St Martin's School of Art, London, where she graduated in 1995 with a star-studded catwalk show in which her friends Kate Moss, Yasmin Le Bon and Naomi Campbell modelled her clothes. McCartney's clothes are known for their sharp, simple tailoring with a feminine edge. In 1997, she succeeded Karl Lagerfeld as the creative director of Parisian fashion house Chloé, and in 2001 she launched her own eponymous label. She is seen here in a photograph taken by her sister, Mary McCartney (b.1969) – both are daughters of former Beatle Sir Paul McCartney and photographer and animal-rights activist Linda McCartney. Mary followed in her mother's footsteps by taking up photography, and has created instinctual and candid portraits of many eminent subjects.

LILY ALLEN
Nadav Kander, 2008
Inkjet print, 558 x 465mm
• NPG x132588
Singer-songwriter Lily Allen (b.1985) was born in Hammersmith, London, to actor Keith Allen and film producer Alison Owen. Her first album, *Alright Still* (2006), was produced by Mark Ronson, and she has since collaborated with Kaiser Chiefs, Basement Jaxx, Dizzee Rascal, and Robbie Williams. After releasing her second album, *It's Not Me, It's You* (2009), Allen won the Brit award for Best British Solo Female in 2010. Born in Israel, Nadav Kander (b.1961) lived and worked in South Africa before establishing his London studio in 1986. Photographed against a minimal backdrop, Allen is bathed in atmospheric and painterly light. Celebrated for his portraiture and landscape work, Kander was awarded an Honorary Fellowship by the Royal Photographic Society in 2015.

BONNIE GREER
Maud Sulter, 2002
Colour Polaroid print, 804 x 560mm
• NPG P965
Maud Sulter (1960–2008) was an artist of Ghanaian and Scottish heritage, who lived and worked in Britain. She photographed the American-born social commentator, writer and academic Bonnie Greer (b.1948) during the making of a BBC Four television programme that highlighted the role and identity of black subjects in historic and contemporary art history. The inspiration for this portrait was Marie-Guilhelmine Benoist's painting *Portrait d'une Negresse* (1800), which Greer had seen by chance while browsing in a London bookshop. In Benoit's painting, an anonymous black slave woman is dressed in lavish costume. In Sulter's large-format Polaroid portrait, Greer styled herself as a contemporary reworking of the painting to make a statement on representations of black women in western art.

BENEDICT CUMBERBATCH
Spencer Murphy, 2010
Colour coupler print, 434 x 356mm
• NPG x134408
British actor Benedict Cumberbatch (b.1976) studied drama at Manchester University and the London Academy of Music and Drama. He came to prominence playing Sherlock Holmes in the BBC series *Sherlock* (2010) and has appeared in the films *Tinker Tailor Soldier Spy* (2011), *War Horse* (2011), *Star Trek: Into the Darkness* (2013), *The Hobbit: The Desolation of Smaug* (2013) and the Oscar-winning *12 Years a Slave* (2013). Cumberbatch received Golden Globe and Oscar nominations for his starring role as Alan Turing in the biopic *The Imitation Game* (2014). He was photographed at iconic Soho restaurant Kettner's, London, for the *Guardian Weekend* magazine by British photographer Spencer Murphy (b.1978). In 2013 Murphy was the winner of the National Portrait Gallery's Taylor Wessing Photographic Portrait Prize.

AMY WINEHOUSE
Charles Moriarty, 2003
Colour coupler print, 406 x 608mm
• NPG x199205
Amy Winehouse (1983–2011) trained at the Sylvia Young Theatre School, London, and sang as a vocalist with the National Youth Jazz Orchestra. She made three internationally acclaimed albums and won five Grammys, three Ivor Novello Awards and a Brit Award for Best Female Artist. In this portrait, Charles Moriarty (b.1981) captures his friend applying lipstick in a New York hotel shortly before the release of her first album, *Frank* (2003). The intimate, relaxed and youthful image provides a striking contrast to later tabloid imagery of the troubled singer. Winehouse's battle with addiction was widely covered in the media and she died at the age of twenty-seven.

LIKE A PAINTING (LILY COLE)
Miles Aldridge, 2005
Digital colour coupler print,
506 x 380mm • NPG x131994
Lily Cole (b.1987) was spotted by a model scout in Soho at the age of fourteen and signed to Storm model agency. At sixteen, Cole was booked for her first British *Vogue* cover and was named Model of the Year at the 2004 British Fashion Awards. Since then, she has read history of art at King's College, Cambridge, and branched out into acting and charity work. Miles Aldridge (b.1964), son of graphic designer Alan Aldridge, began by working as a fashion photographer for British *Vogue*. His portrait of Cole, influenced by the fifteenth-century portrait of Ginevra d'Este by Pisanello, was published in the February 2005 edition of Italian *Vogue*.

SIR TIM BERNERS-LEE
Adam Broomberg and
Oliver Chanarin, 2005
Colour coupler print, 508 x 406mm
• NPG P1103
Sir Tim Berners-Lee (b.1955) graduated from Queen's College, Oxford, in 1976. There he built his first computer with a soldering iron, a processor and an old television. He worked in telecommunications before inventing the World Wide Web in 1989, and joined the Laboratory for Computer Science at the Massachusetts Institute of Technology in 1994. This portrait forms part of a series of key figures in the world of telecommunications commissioned by the National Portrait Gallery through the Deloitte Acquisition Fund. Utilising crafted lighting, redolent of classical painting, the portrait depicts an internal moment of reflection. London-based duo Adam Broomberg (b.1970) and Oliver Chanarin (b.1971) have worked together for over twenty years, developing an acclaimed conceptual practice.

KATE MOSS
Corinne Day, 2006
Gelatin silver print, 1510 x 1305mm
• NPG P1274
Talent-spotted at the age of fourteen, Kate Moss (b.1974) first appeared on the cover of *The Face* magazine in 1990, photographed by Corinne Day (1965–2010). Moss has subsequently appeared on over 300 magazine covers and continues to be one of the most highly sought-after models in the fashion industry. Self-taught photographer and former model Day was commissioned by the National Portrait Gallery to photograph her long-term friend. Moss talked candidly during the shoot, which took place over one day, and the resulting portrait shows Moss relaxed before the camera.

SIR MO FARAH
Kate Peters, 2012
Colour coupler print, 508 x 407mm
• NPG P1833
Born in Somalia, distance runner Sir Mo Farah (b.1983) came, at the age of eight, to England, where his athletic talent was first identified by his school physical-education teacher. At the London 2012 and Rio 2016 Olympic Games, Farah won gold medals for the 5,000 metres and 10,000 metres races. He is the most decorated athlete in British history and was awarded a knighthood in the New Year's Honours for 2017. In this photograph, by the British photographer Kate Peters (b.1980), Farah's gaze seems distracted – the viewer might imagine he is focusing his mind for a race.

ADELE
Julian Broad, 2008
Colour coupler print, 457 x 342mm
• NPG x139549
Adele (b.1988) is one of the best-selling music artists of all time. This portrait, commissioned by *Vogue* in 2008, shows her in the year of her debut album *19*, which gained her critical and commercial success. She released *25* (2015) after a three-year break, and the following year *Time* magazine named her one of the world's most influential people. Julian Broad (b.1964) assisted Ken Griffiths, Norman Parkinson and Lord Snowdon before gaining commissions for *Arena* and *The Face* magazines. His portrait and fashion commissions have since appeared in many publications, including *Vanity Fair*, for which he is a contributing photographer.

HANNAH WHELAN, JENNIFER PINCHES, BETH TWEDDLE AND REBECCA TUNNEY
Anderson & Low, 2011
Inkjet print, 812 x 1066mm
• NPG P1805 (detail)
Long-term collaborators Jonathan Anderson and Edwin Low were commissioned by the National Portrait Gallery to create portraits of leading British athletes to celebrate the London 2012 Olympics. This meticulously arranged formal tableau features members of the British women's gymnastics team: Beth Tweddle (b.1985; second from the right), Britain's first World Champion in women's gymnastics and bronze medallist at the 2012 Games, Rebecca Tunney (b.1996; right), who at the age of fifteen was Britain's youngest Olympic athlete, and their teammates Hannah Whelan (b.1992; left) and Jennifer Pinches (b.1994; second from the left).

SIR DAVID ATTENBOROUGH
Sam Barker, 2015
Inkjet print, 456 x 386mm
• NPG x199654
The distinguished broadcasting career of Sir David Attenborough (b.1926) began in 1952 when he joined the BBC. He launched his first Natural History programme, *Zoo Quest*, in 1954, and in 1957 formed the BBC's Travel and Exploration unit. As Controller of BBC Two from 1965, Attenborough oversaw the introduction of colour television in Britain two years later. He is celebrated for writing and presenting the 'Life' series and in recent years has adopted a more environmentalist stance. This photograph, commissioned by the *Sunday Times* for Attenborough's ninetieth year, concentrates our gaze to the 'great mind'. Sam Barker (b.1971), the youngest of fifteen children by poet George Barker, has worked as a photographer in both editorial and advertising since 1997.

CATE BLANCHETT
Rineke Dijkstra, 2008
Colour coupler print, 1235 x 995mm • NPG P2073
Cate Blanchett (b.1969) is an Australian actress and theatre director. She has made important contributions to British cinema, notably in her breakthrough role as Elizabeth I. Her portrayal of Katharine Hepburn in Martin Scorsese's 2004 film *The Aviator* brought her critical praise, including an Oscar for Best Supporting Actress. In 2013, she starred in Woody Allen's film *Blue Jasmine*, winning the Oscar for Best Actress. In this portrait, Dutch-born photographer Rineke Dijkstra (b.1959) manages to convey a vulnerability, challenging the boundaries of celebrity portraiture. The minimal contextual details in this photograph encourage us to focus on the exchange between photographer and subject and the relationship between viewer and sitter.

QUEEN ELIZABETH II AND THE DUKE OF EDINBURGH, WINDSOR CASTLE, 2011
Thomas Struth, 2011
Colour coupler print, 1633 x 2062mm
• NPG P1665
This portrait of Queen Elizabeth II (b.1926) and Prince Philip, Duke of Edinburgh (b.1921) was commissioned by the National Portrait Gallery to mark the Queen's Diamond Jubilee in 2012. The couple are posed in the Green Drawing Room at Windsor Castle shortly before Prince Philip's ninetieth birthday, during what was the sixty-fourth year of their marriage. The couple met during the Second World War, when Prince Philip was a naval officer. On their marriage, the Prince renounced his own royal title to become a Windsor. Photographed by the German photographer Thomas Struth (b.1954), the portrait is a sensitive portrayal of the royal couple away from their official and ceremonial roles, but the splendid setting reminds the viewer of their status. Reflecting royal protocol, the image subtly places the Queen in a more prominent position than Prince Philip, and recalls Cecil Beaton's coronation portrait in which Prince Philip stands in close attendance to the Queen.

DAME VIVIENNE WESTWOOD
Juergen Teller, 2014
Colour coupler print, 1219 x 812mm
• NPG P1980
In the 1970s, Dame Vivienne Westwood (b.1941) co-founded, on London's King's Road, the boutique Let It Rock, later renamed SEX, which defined British Punk. Twice named Designer of the Year, she is also a campaigner for human rights, environmental issues and climate change. German-born Juergen Teller (b.1964) has shot Westwood's fashion campaigns since 2007. This informal and intimate portrait shows Westwood in the garden of her London home.

DAVID HAREWOOD
Simon Frederick, 2016
Inkjet print, 380 x 260mm
• NPG P2048
THANDIE NEWTON
Simon Frederick, 2016
Inkjet print, 380 x 260mm
• NPG P2063
The *Black is the New Black* portfolio of photographer Simon Frederick includes thirty-seven black British sitters chosen for their achievements across a variety of fields, including politics, business, culture, religion and science. These first and second generation black Britons include David Harewood (b.1965), celebrated for his role in the television series *Homeland* and actress Thandie Newton (b.1972), who is of Zimbabwean and English descent and has spoken of the racism she experienced growing up in Cornwall and the lack of film roles for people of colour. Frederick's portraits – with their close cropping, sensitive compositions and skilful lighting – allow the viewer to connect intimately to the subjects.

INVOCATION
Adam Fuss, 2013
Cibachrome photogram, 1143 x 889mm
• NPG x200013
In this photogram, Adam Fuss (b.1961) returns to the early-nineteenth-century 'sunprint' photogenic drawings of

William Henry Fox Talbot and evokes camera-less photographs made by modernist photographers such as Man Ray and László Moholy-Nagy in the 1920s. Fuss suspended a baby in water over a sheet of photographic paper, and exposed the scene to a flash of artificial light, which recorded the outline of the baby's body on the paper. The child's silhouette is rendered life-size and the gradations of tone give the figure a sculptural quality. The portrait evocatively manifests light and shadow, and speaks of the familiar and the universal.

GLOSSARY

albumen print
Popular from the 1850s to 1890s; a thin sheet of paper was coated with a layer of egg-white (albumen) containing salt and sensitised with a silver nitrate solution, then printed in contact with a negative, using daylight. The finished print had a smooth surface and a fine sheen. Frequently toned with a gold chloride solution, which gave a rich, purplish-brown colour to the image and improved permanence.

Autochrome
The first commercially available full-colour photographic process, patented in 1904 by the Lumière brothers in France. Colour was obtained by coating a glass plate with a mosaic of potato-starch granules dyed red, blue and green. During exposure, only light from corresponding parts of the spectrum travelled through the granules to reach the light-sensitive emulsion below. Autochromes were translucent and could be shown in special viewers, held up to the light, or projected.

Cibachrome
Also known as a dye destruction print or by the rival trade names Ilfachrome and Fujichrome, a colour print made from a transparency enlarged directly on to reversal paper. The paper is unique in that dyes are incorporated into the emulsion on the paper instead of being formed chemically, giving exceptional colour brilliance. Considered more permanent than the more common colour coupler print (see below).

colour coupler print
The most common form of full-colour photograph in the late twentieth century. Usually made from a negative, colour coupler paper contains at least three emulsion layers, each sensitised to one of the three primary colours of light. Dyes are added after initial development to form the colours in the emulsion layers. A chromogenic print contains no silver in the final image. Frequently referred to by the Kodak brand name Type-C.

digital colour coupler print
A conventional colour coupler print made from digital files, using lasers to expose the photographic paper. These are sometimes called Lamda or Lightjet prints.

dye-transfer print
A type of print that has its origins in the 1870s, in which three carefully superimposed layers of dye are transferred by hand to a gelatine-coated base. The dye-transfer process is time-consuming but permits considerable control of results and produces a relatively permanent print not containing silver. A close cousin of the Technicolor process in cinema.

Daguerreotype
Named after its French inventor, Louis Daguerre, the Daguerreotype was the first photographic process announced to the public, in 1839. Each Daguerreotype is a unique, direct positive image on a highly polished, silvered copper plate. The plate is sensitised with iodine fumes and the image developed over heated mercury vapour. Daguerreotypes are usually mounted behind protective glass in a decorative case.

gelatin silver print
The most common form of black and white photographic paper in the twentieth and early twenty-first centuries, introduced into general use in the 1880s. Prints are made with silver halides (silver bromide, silver chloride) suspended in a layer of gelatin on fibre-based paper. They are developed using the three-bath chemistry of developer, stop and fixer, and can be chemically toned to alter the finished look of the print.

digital gelatin silver print
A gelatin silver print made from a digital file. The paper is exposed by lasers but developed using conventional chemistry.

glass negative
In many photographic processes a negative is considered a master image from which other prints are produced. Negatives have been produced on paper, glass and later chemical-coated plastic. A negative image is a tonal inversion of a positive image, in which light areas appear dark and vice versa. A negative colour image is additionally colour reversed, with red areas appearing cyan, greens appearing magenta and blues appearing yellow.

gum platinum print
A handmade photographic print consisting of two emulsions printed in perfect registration, one on top of the other. In a gum platinum, the underlayer is a platinum print (see below), while the upper layer is made using a water-soluble solution of gum bichromate mixed with gum and pigment.

inkjet print
Popular names include Iris, Giclée, and digital pigment prints. A printing method in which droplets of ink are sprayed by a computer printer on to paper to create an image.

platinum print
A platinum print is made with paper containing light-sensitive iron salts and a platinum compound, rather than the conventional silver salts, exposed to light in contact with a negative. Often mixed with the cheaper metal palladium. The process was invented in 1873 by William Willis and made commercially available in 1879. Platinum prints are valued for their permanence and tonal sensitivity, but a dramatic rise in the price of platinum after the First World War led to the decline of the process.

Polaroid
The first instantaneous one-step photographic process, developed by the American inventor E.H. Land in 1947. Initially, black-and-white film was used, with Polacolour introduced in 1962. There are two types: the integral system, in which the photograph develops directly on to the print; and the peel-apart system, in which the print is separated from a negative backing after exposure. Many of the areas in which Polaroid was used, such as studio or scientific photography, now use digital photography.

salt print
The earliest process for making positive photographic prints, invented by William Henry Fox Talbot in 1840. The print was made on high-quality writing paper that had been immersed in a solution of common salt and then floated in a bath of silver nitrate. A finished salt print is matt in finish, reddish brown in colour, and has no surface gloss. It can be toned with a gold chloride for a richer, purplish tone and greater permanence. Salt prints were superseded by albumen prints in the 1850s.

PICTURE CREDITS

Unless otherwise stated, all illustrations are © National Portrait Gallery, London. The publisher would like to thank the following for permission to reproduce works for which they hold the copyright. Every effort has been made to contact the holders of copyright material, and any omissions will be corrected in future editions if the publisher is notified in writing.

p.2 © Estate of Marcus Adams; p.5 © Yevonde Portrait Archive; p.12 © Nigel Shafran. Commissioned by the Trustees of the National Portrait Gallery, 2017; p.45 © The Universal Order; p.46 © The Estate of Edward Steichen/ARS, NY and DACS, London 2018; p.48 © Estate of Bertram Park; p.54 © Estate of Malcolm Arbuthnot. Given by Marion Harry Spielmann, 1939; p.57 © James Abbe Archive 2018. Given by Terence Pepper, 2014; p.58 © 1981 Center for Creative Photography, Arizona Board of Regents; p.59 © Estate of Curtis Moffat; p.60 © Berenice Abbott/Masters/Getty Images; p.61 © 2018 Curatorial Assistance, Inc./E.O. Hoppé Estate Collection; p.63 © Cecil Beaton Studio Archive, Sotheby's London. Accepted in lieu of tax by H.M. Government and allocated to the Gallery, 1991; p.64 © Man Ray Trust/ADAGP, Paris and DACS, London 2018. Purchased with support from Chuck Close in honour of Sandy Nairne, 2016; p.65 © William Hustler and Georgina Hustler/National Portrait Gallery, London. Given by the photographer's sister, Susan Morton, 1976; p.67 © Estate of Paul Tanqueray. Given by Paul Tanqueray, 1975; p.69 © DACS 2018. Given by the Bauhaus Archive, 1995; p.70 © Bill Brandt Archive; p.71 © 1989 Center for Creative Photography, Arizona Board of Regents. Given by the Benjamin Britten Estate, 1981; p.73 © Lee Miller Archives, England 2018. All rights reserved. leemiller.co.uk; p.77 Alfred Hitchcock, New York, 1947. Photograph by Irving Penn for *Vogue*, February 15, 1948 © Condé Nast; p.78 © reserved; collection National Portrait Gallery, London; p.79 © reserved; collection National Portrait Gallery, London. Given by Tracy Granger, 2016; p.80 © Norman Parkinson Ltd./courtesy Norman Parkinson Archive. Given by Norman Parkinson, 1981 in conjunction with the National Portrait Gallery exhibition *Norman Parkinson: 50 Years of Portraits and Fashion*; p.81 © reserved; collection National Portrait Gallery, London; p.82 © Rosalie

Thorne McKenna Foundation; courtesy Center for Creative Photography, University of Arizona Foundation. Given by the Rosalie Thorne McKenna Foundation, 2011; p.85 Photograph by Yousuf Karsh, Camera Press London. Given by Yousuf Karsh, 1991; p.89 © David Bailey; p.90 © Lewis Morley Archive. Given by Lewis Morley, 1992; p.92 © photograph shot for *Queen* magazine 1962 by Sandra Lousada; p.93 © tonyfrank/National Portrait Gallery, London; pp.94, 95 © Estate of Ronald Traeger; pp.96–7 © 1967 Paul McCartney/ Photographer: Linda McCartney. Given by Linda McCartney, 1994; pp.100–1 Courtesy of Universal Music Group; p.102 © Graham Nash. Given by Graham Nash, 2017; p.103 © Mayotte Lewinska; p.106 © Armstrong Jones/Reproduced with permission of Trunk Archive. Given by Lord Snowdon, 2013; p.107 © Lichfield. Given by Patrick Lichfield, 2003; p.108 © Eggleston Artistic Trust. Given by the Eggleston Artistic Trust, 2017; p.110 © Estate of Chris Garnham/ National Portrait Gallery, London; p.111 © Jillian Edelstein; p.112 © The Guy Bourdin Estate 2018/Courtesy of Louise Alexander Gallery; p.115 © Nick Knight, Morrissey, 1985; p.116 © The Douglas Brothers. Given by The Douglas Brothers, 2015; pp.118–9 © David LaChapelle. Purchased with help from Daphne Guinness and The Marrakech Gallery Foundation, 2010; p.120 © Mario Testino, Diana, Princess of Wales, London, *Vanity Fair*, 1997. Given by Mario Testino, 2003; p.122 © Dawoud Bey. Commissioned by the Trustees of the National Portrait Gallery, 1998; p.123 © Neil Wilder; p.124 © Hiroshi Sugimoto; p.127 © Wolfgang Tillmans. Purchased through the Deloitte Acquisition Fund, 2003; p.128 © Mary McCartney; p.129 © Nadav Kander; courtesy Flowers Galleries. Given by Nadav Kander, 2009; p.130 © Maud Sulter; p.131 © Spencer Murphy; pp.132–3 © Charles Moriarty. Given by Charles Moriarty; p.134 © Miles Aldridge. Given by Miles Aldridge, 2008; p.137 © Estate of Corinne Day/Commissioned by the Trustees of the National Portrait Gallery, London, 2007/trunkarchive.com; p.138 © Kate Peters; p.139 © Julian Broad/National Portrait Gallery, London; pp.140–1 © Anderson & Low All Rights reserved. Commissioned by the Trustees of the National Portrait Gallery jointly with BT for *Road to 2012*, 2011; p.142 © Sam Barker; p.143 © Rineke Dijkstra/Courtesy of Marion Goodman Gallery. Purchased with funds given by Jane and Michael Wilson, Renee and Robert Drake, and Ellen Shapiro, 2017; pp.144–5 © Thomas Struth, 2011. Commissioned by the Trustees of the National Portrait Gallery, 2011; pp.148, 149 © Simon Frederick. Given by Simon Frederick with support from AOL, 2017; p.151 © Adam Fuss, courtesy of Fraenkel Gallery, San Francisco/Photography by Prudence Cuming Associates. Given by Adam Fuss, 2017

Additional commissioning and acquisition information for images © National Portrait Gallery, London:

p.8 Given by the sitter's son, Sir Mayson Beeton, 1932; p.9 Commissioned by the Trustees of the National Portrait Gallery, 1924; p.10 Transferred from National Portrait Gallery Reference Collection, 1976; p.17 Given by an anonymous donor, 1973; p.23 Given by Mr and Mrs A.J.W. Vaughan, 1972; pp.24–5 Purchased jointly with the National Science and Media Museum, Bradford, with help from the Art Fund and the National Heritage Memorial Fund, 2002; p.27 Purchased with help from the Art Fund, Jane and Michael Wilson, and Stephen Barry, 2015; p.31 Given by M. Hutchinson, 1965; pp.38, 39 Given by Robert R. Steele, 1939; p.41 Given by the photographer's son, Cavendish Morton, 1991; p.47 Purchased with help from the Friends of the National Libraries and the Dame Helen Gardner Bequest, 2005; p.49 Given by Rooks Rider Solicitors, 1987; pp.50, 51 Given by John Culme, 1996; pp.52–3 Given by the Criminal Record Office, 1914; p.55 Given by Marion Harry Spielmann, 1939; p.66 Given by the Howard Coster Estate, 1959; p.83 Given by the sitter's mother, Ethel Turing, 1956; p.98 Harry Diamond bequest, 2012; pp.104–5 Given by Bernard Lee Schwartz Foundation, 2007; p.135 Commissioned by the Trustees of the National Portrait Gallery through Deloitte Acquisition Fund, 2006; p.147 © National Portrait Gallery, London/Photo: Juergen Teller. Commissioned by the Trustees of the National Portrait Gallery; made possible by J.P. Morgan through the Fund for New Commissions, 2014

Published in Great Britain by National Portrait Gallery Publications, St Martin's Place, London WC2H 0HE

For a complete catalogue of current publications, please write to the National Portrait Gallery at the address above, or visit our website at www.npg.org.uk/publications

ISBN 978 1 85514 741 6

A catalogue record for this book is available from the British Library.

10 9 8 7 6 5 4 3 2 1

Printed in Italy

Managing Editor: Christopher Tinker
Proofreader: Kara Green
Production Manager: Ruth Müller-Wirth
Publishing Assistant: Tijana Todorinovic
Designer: Peter Dawson, www.gradedesign.com

Caption texts written jointly by Georgia Atienza, Clare Freestone, Sabina Jaskot-Gill, Gerlind-Anicia Lorch, Georgina Mind and Phillip Prodger. Edited by Phillip Prodger.

All photographs are vintage, unless otherwise specified.

Dimensions expressed height x width (mm)

ACKNOWLEDGEMENTS
The National Portrait Gallery Collection has grown through the generosity of many institutions, families and individuals who have donated important works. Equally important has been the support over many decades of the Art Fund (formerly known as the National Art Collections Fund), and in more recent years of the National Heritage Memorial Fund and the Heritage Lottery Fund. The Gallery's own Portrait Fund has become increasingly significant, and the National Portrait Gallery is very grateful to all those who have supported the Fund as well as the public campaigns to acquire particular portraits.

FSC
www.fsc.org
MIX
Paper from responsible sources
FSC® C015829